Studies in Rhetorics and Feminisms

Series Editors, Cheryl Glenn and Shirley Wilson Logan

Women Physicians and Professional Ethos in Nineteenth-Century America

CAROLYN SKINNER

Southern Illinois University Press
Carbondale

An earlier version of chapter 4 appeared in *Rhetoric Review*
26.2 (2007): 240–59 as "'The Purity of Truth': Nineteenth-Century American Women Physicians Write about Delicate
Topics."

17 16 15 14   4 3 2 1

Library of Congress Cataloging-in-Publication Data
Skinner, Carolyn, 1977–
Women physicians and professional ethos in nineteenth-century America / Carolyn Skinner.
    pages   cm. — (Studies in rhetorics and feminisms)
Includes bibliographical references and index.
ISBN-13: 978-0-8093-3300-4 (pbk.)
ISBN-10: 0-8093-3300-7 (paperback)
ISBN-13: 978-0-8093-3301-1 (ebook)
1. Women physicians—United States—History—19th century.
2. Women in medicine—United States—History—19th century.
3. Women physicians—Employment—Social aspects. I. Title.
R692.S587 2014
610.82—dc23   2013021634

Printed on recycled paper. ♻

The paper used in this publication meets the minimum requirements of American National Standard for Information
Sciences—Permanence of Paper for Printed Library Materials,
ANSI Z39.48-1992. ∞

For Beth, a twenty-first-century woman physician

Contents

Illustrations

Acknowledgments

I am grateful for the support of many colleagues and friends who helped me in a variety of intellectual, emotional, and material ways. I am fortunate to count among my mentors Carol Mattingly and Nan Johnson, both of whom read drafts and talked me through the revision, restructuring, and rethinking necessary to bring this project into its current form. My writing group, Liz Weiser and Cassie Parente, helped me see things I couldn't see in my own writing and made suggestions that constantly impressed me with their generosity and commitment. Lindal Buchanan also read for me and offered advice and a sympathetic ear.

I am also thankful for the support and advice of others who contributed along the way. At the University of Louisville, Nancy Theriot, Beth Boehm, and Debra Journet all offered support and thoughtful feedback. At Ohio State, Brenda Brueggemann, Susan Delagrange, and Jim Fredal read drafts and provided useful suggestions. I counted on Kimberly Harrison and Wendy Hayden to answer questions and offer sound advice. Anne-Marie Pedersen, always a careful reader, kept me on my writerly toes. Colleagues at OSU–Mansfield—Cynthia Callahan, Susan Delagrange, Norman Jones, and Barbara McGovern—listened as I talked my way through sticking points and encouraged me throughout the process.

I also appreciate the support extended by Rod and Rosie Tolliver, who allowed me to stay in their home while I visited archives. Theodora Kopestonsky helped me think through various conceptions of ethos, and Bethany Skinner helped me interpret nineteenth-century medical thought, explaining contemporary obstetrics and gynecology to me so that I could make sense of historical medical research.

The interlibrary loan staff at the University of Louisville and OSU came through for me time and time again, locating rare, old books for me. Matt

Herbison, archivist at the Drexel University College of Medicine, assisted me in accessing texts and images from the Woman's Medical College of Pennsylvania archives. Rebecca Jewett, assistant curator in the Rare Books and Manuscripts Library at OSU also helped me locate an image. The staff at OSU's College of Arts and Sciences Digital Media Services assisted me in collecting several images in electronic form. I benefited from an OSU-Mansfield Campus Seed Grant, which afforded me time to revise this project, and Campus research funds that defrayed publication costs. I am also grateful for financial assistance from OSU's College of Arts and Humanities.

Cheryl Glenn and Shirley Wilson Logan, editors of the Studies in Rhetorics and Feminisms series, provided tough but ultimately very helpful revision suggestions, pushing this project farther along than I had imagined it could go. Kristine Priddy, Wayne Larsen, Barb Martin, and copy editor John Wilson at Southern Illinois University Press were always available to answer questions and provide valuable assistance.

Finally, I am immensely grateful to my family, who encouraged me throughout the years I've been writing and revising: my parents, Thomas and Glenda Skinner, my sister Bethany, my brother Allen, and my grandparents, Glenn and Alice Williams, all of whom listened when I needed to talk and left me alone when I needed to work. My husband, Dan, deserves more thanks than I can express for his support, patience, advice, careful reading, and so much more.

Women Physicians and Professional Ethos in Nineteenth-Century America

Introduction:
The Ethos of the Feminine Professional

Medical literature and medical feeling, it is all too obvious,
need the refining and ennobling influences that the purity,
and peculiar endowments of the true woman are calculated
to give. You bring into the profession your womanly tact
and insight, your quick sympathies, your watchful care, and
your high ideal of the purity and delicacy befitting the sacred
office you have assumed. As women, with the experiences of
your womanhood, and looking at the subject from a fresh
standpoint, you cannot fail to unfold new resources in the
art of healing, and, if you are true to yourselves, the gifts you
bring must *enrich* as well as refine the profession you enter.
—Ann Preston, "Valedictory Address to the
Graduating Class of the Woman's Medical
College of Pennsylvania" (1870)

On March 12, 1870, Ann Preston, dean and professor of physiology and
hygiene at the Woman's Medical College of Pennsylvania, advised the
graduating class on the role of women in medicine. Like many proponents
of the nineteenth-century American woman-doctor movement, Preston
maintained that women would bring an important feminine perspective to
medical research and practice. In doing so, she presented the class of 1870
with a model for behaving, speaking, and writing as feminine professionals;
in other words, she suggested an ethos for women physicians that embraced
femininity as an advantage, not a liability, to the individual practitioner, her
patients, and the profession. Although many opponents of women physicians
found femininity incompatible with the physical and intellectual work of
medicine, thousands of women in nineteenth-century America thrived in

their careers. Many converted their new professional roles into a standpoint from which to speak authoritatively to their patients, to their communities, and to their medical colleagues.

Women Physicians and Professional Ethos in Nineteenth-Century America examines the public speech and writing of women who practiced medicine as the field began its transformation into the authoritative, professional collection of expert practitioners and institutions that we know today. Women's presence in medicine during this important development means that, as Susan Wells has observed in *Out of the Dead House: Nineteenth-Century Women Physicians and the Writing of Medicine*, "Women doctors intervened in medical discourse at the very formation of the modern scientific profession" (12). It also means that women sought admission to a field that increasingly insisted on traits that were, according to nineteenth-century gender ideology, inaccessible to women: authority, specialized expertise, and independence. The profession sought to associate these characteristics with medicine's professional identity in order to secure an elevated social status for its members. Yet a woman physician who displayed only these characteristics would have been derided as "manly'" and "unsexed" and so find herself without patients or collegial support. Indeed, much of the debate over whether or not women should be physicians hinged on the character of the woman physician: was it possible for a woman to possess the traits of a successful physician? If so, would she still be recognizably feminine enough to associate with? For nineteenth-century women, communicating as physicians required the development of multiple and complex versions of ethos (pluralized as *ethē*) that would appeal to both public and professional audiences. Although women's behavior is less tightly constructed today than it was in the nineteenth century, modern professional women still often find themselves juggling competing expectations for speaking as women and as professionals, balancing the authority and assertiveness expected of the professional with the self-effacement many women are socialized to perform. In the rhetoric of nineteenth-century women physicians, we see an early phase of this common dilemma for professional women.

Nineteenth-century American women physicians spoke and wrote in a range of genres appropriate to their status as physicians. Because my interest is in women physicians' strategic uses of ethos in their efforts to influence popular and medical discourse, I have selected texts that addressed relatively large audiences, including articles in popular and professional periodicals, books written for a nonprofessional readership, and speeches at women's rights conventions rather than texts intended for smaller audiences, such as medical school theses, patient histories, or letters. In order to achieve a broad perspective on the rhetorical activity of the thousands of women who had practiced medicine by 1900, I sought texts not only by well-known pioneers in the profession but also by women who have received less attention from contemporary scholars. The prominent women physicians provided leadership to other women in the field, so their approaches to building and using ethos are important; however, women occupied a range of positions in the profession, and a narrow focus on only the most famous in the field would skew our perception of the discursive practices of professional women. Therefore, in addition to texts by well-known physicians, I examine texts by women who did not consider themselves to be leaders to discover how they communicated with the public and the profession. Performing these "everyday" rhetorical acts was necessary if women were to achieve more than a token presence in the field.

Although most of the women whose speech and writing is discussed here were practitioners of "regular" medicine (called "allopathy" by those who practiced alternative medicine, whom the "regulars" in turn called "irregular"), several were members of alternative sects, such as homeopathy, eclecticism, and hydropathy. A few might have been called "healers" or "abortionists" by their contemporaries, but I use "women physicians" to refer to all of them, following Mary Roth Walsh, who argues that historians have required greater proof of women's professional medical standing than they have of men's: "The fact that Elizabeth Blackwell is usually credited with being America's first woman doctor reflects a historical double standard. Blackwell's status results from having been the first woman to have received a medical degree, a standard which, if applied to her male colleagues, would have sharply reduced the number of male doctors in the country. Historians have scrutinized the credentials of female physicians more carefully than those of male physicians, many of whom practiced with no medical degree whatsoever" (1). In addition to the rationale offered by Walsh, this book's focus on the construction of medical professionalism as a resource for women's ethē makes attending to the rhetoric of a broad range of "physicians" appropriate, because it allows for an examination of the ways that differently situated women imagined and capitalized on their relationship to "the profession."

I have also made an effort to be as geographically comprehensive as possible, though many of the women discussed here lived near (and often worked at) the institutions offering medical education to women in Philadelphia, New York, and Boston; the Midwest is also relatively well represented, as schools in states such as Ohio and Michigan provided early sites for women's medical education. I was unable to locate many texts by women physicians addressing large audiences in the western United States, perhaps because of their distance from the eastern centers of publishing and the large hospitals and medical schools that provided much of the material and motivation for medical writing. Although most of the women practicing medicine in the nineteenth century were white, African American and American Indian women physicians contribute important elements to our understanding of how professional women crafted and employed ethos.

Although I rely extensively on histories of medicine, and particularly histories of women in medicine, to understand the context surrounding nineteenth-century women physicians' rhetorical activity, this book itself is not a history of women in medicine in the usual sense. Instead, it is a study of women physicians' rhetorical strategies, especially their strategies for constructing persuasive characters—their ethē—at a time when *woman* and *physician* were believed to be incompatible roles. Because I am interested in the persuasive tools developed by practicing women physicians, I do not trace in detail the long struggles women faced in gaining admission to medical colleges and professional organizations; the opening of women's medical schools around midcentury (and the communities of support they created) and the closure of many of them near the turn of the century (and the subsequent loss of communities of women as professional peers and mentors); the restricted opportunities women had for clinical instruction following graduation and some women's pursuit of clinical training in Europe; or the variety of paths women physicians' careers took into private practice, hospital work, public health, missionary fields, and institutional sites such as colleges, asylums, and insurance companies.[1] These and other historical factors influenced the rhetorical situations in which women physicians spoke and wrote; as such, they are considered as part of the context to which women physicians responded as they crafted their ethē and the other rhetorical strategies that made them persuasive participants in the public and professional discourses of their time.

This project makes two substantial contributions to women's rhetorical historiography. First, it illuminates the role of medical professionalism as a rhetorical resource for historical women, offering persuasive tools, subjects for discourse, and access to genres previously unavailable to them. For example, women physicians actively and persistently used their medical knowledge to challenge conventional representations of women, seeking to alter the social, political, occupational, and rhetorical opportunities available to them. Second, the examination of women physicians' rhetoric presented here intervenes in conventional theorizations of ethos by exploring how marginalized speakers and writers have developed persuasive ethē despite the belief that they were not supposed to be effective or authoritative communicators.

In acknowledging their practices as part of our understanding of how ethos is crafted and how it functions to persuade, we not only learn about the rhetorical practices of the marginalized, but we also gain a more nuanced understanding of how ethos operates for all speakers and writers.

I begin with texts participating in the debate over women's pursuit of medical careers: chapter 1, "Debating the Character of the Woman Physician," analyzes how the character of the woman physician was constructed by supporters and opponents of women in medicine. In doing so, it takes up spatial conceptions of ethos and suggests that when rhetors lack access to the "space"—the social position—that one audience values, they may turn to another audience who is more appreciative of the ideals that they can demonstrate. Chapter 2, "Prescribing for Society: Women Physicians' Reform Rhetoric," charts women physicians' use of professional authority, expertise, and experience in their reform rhetoric addressed to public audiences. In advocating woman suffrage, temperance, and improved living conditions for African Americans and American Indians, women physicians used their professional ethos to construct a relationship with their audience in which the public was bound to follow their professional advice.

In chapter 3, "Educating the Public: Women Physicians' Popular Health Advice," health information and advice texts composed by women physicians such as Anna M. Galbraith, Alice B. Stockham, Anna M. Longshore-Potts, Rachel B. Gleason, and Rebecca Crumpler demonstrate the ways that women physicians capitalized on the "expert" ethos associated with health advice literature to argue for improved attitudes toward the female body. Before they could do so, however, women physicians had to teach their audiences how to understand writers who were both "feminine" and "professional." Related to health information and advice books were texts composed to educate readers about human sexuality and reproduction. Chapter 4, "Teaching Women to Talk about Sex" focuses on how physicians such as Emma F. Angell Drake and Mary Wood-Allen not only taught women and children about sex but also demonstrated that nonprofessional women could speak about human sexuality and related subjects with propriety. By adopting some aspects of women physicians' ethos, nonprofessional women could educate their own children and even advocate publicly for behaviors and values that would ensure the nation's moral and physical health.

Chapters 5 and 6 turn to nineteenth-century American women physicians' writing composed for professional audiences. "Developing Collective Ethos in Medical Editorial Writing" examines editorials published in the *Woman's Medical Journal* in which women physicians articulated a collective ethos for themselves, teaching each other professional values while recognizing the limitations of their status as novelties. "Revising the Physician's Ethos: Women Physicians' Medical Research" focuses on strategies for improving one's ethos indirectly. A counterpart to direct ethos strategies (the efforts of an individual to present herself positively that are typically recognized as ethos), indirect ethos strategies work not primarily to shape audience perceptions of the speaker but instead influence attitudes toward others like her, indirectly enhancing her own ethos. For example, women physicians' acceptance as medical researchers was hindered by doubts about women's physical health and intellectual capacity. To counter the profession's negative assumptions about women, physicians such as Margaret A. Cleaves, Grace Peckham, and Electa B. Whipple wrote research articles in which ethos functioned both directly, as the writers conveyed their adherence to medical values, and indirectly, as the writers sought to construct all physicians as scientists (thereby creating a professional identity in which women were experts) and all women as naturally healthy. Altering perceptions of physicians and women would have indirectly benefited the ethē of women who pursued medical research.

Finally, the conclusion draws together the facets of ethos revealed by nineteenth-century American women physicians' speech and writing in order to begin to articulate a feminist model of ethos that reflects the persuasive strategies employed by marginalized rhetors. Speakers and writers who have historically been excluded from the centers of rhetorical activity must often "first invent a way to speak in the context of being silenced and rendered invisible as persons" (Ritchie and Ronald xvii). Consequently, their strategies for developing persuasive ethē are often more complex and diverse than those used by speakers and writers with greater access to traditional social and institutional positions of power. Marginalized rhetors often cannot present a persuasive rhetorical character simply by demonstrating their adherence to their audience's values, because that very value structure may cast the speaker as inherently unworthy to speak. In order to speak convincingly, such rhetors must first persuade audience members to reprioritize their values in a way that creates a more hospitable context for the speaker. Furthermore, for members of marginalized groups, it is often the case that ethos not only manifests as an individualized appeal but also involves collective efforts to alter audience perceptions of the groups to which they belong. Acknowledging the negotiated nature of ethos as it is revealed in women physicians' speech and writing contributes to the feminist project of identifying the rhetorical practices of all people, especially those who, because of their position outside the center of cultural and rhetorical authority, must overcome obstacles to their ethē before they can begin to persuade.

1

Debating the Character of the Woman Physician

Human kind might be divided into three groups—men, women, and women physicians.
                —Dr. William Osler, quoted in Dr. Lilian Welsh,
                Reminiscences of Thirty Years in Baltimore (1925)

In 1860, Harriot Hunt, one of the earliest and most prominent participants in the nineteenth-century woman-doctor movement, marked twenty-five years of medical practice with a silver anniversary celebration. One reporter drew attention to the novelty of Hunt's role as a woman professional by noting that the celebration "was called the Silver Wedding of Miss Harriot K. Hunt and Harriot K. Hunt, M.D.," suggesting that Miss Hunt, the woman, and Dr. Hunt, the physician, were like two different people united in marriage ("Our Boston Letter"). Another report of the event stated that fifteen hundred guests attended the ceremony, representing three generations of Hunt's patients (Safford Blake). Amid "a profusion of flowers," Hunt, who wore a double wreath in her hair, received a gold ring "to consecrate the marriage to her profession" (Cheney 52–53). At her anniversary, Hunt was reported to have said, "I have been so happy in my work; every moment occupied; how I long to whisper it in the ear of every listless woman, 'do something, if you would be happy'" (qtd. in Safford Blake). Yet even as Hunt urged women toward active lives, her anniversary celebration framed her own career in conventional terms, making her devotion to her career comprehensible to others by likening it to the devotion of a wife who has been married for twenty-five years. In presenting her career as a marriage, Hunt connected herself to a traditional feminine role, resisting the doubts raised about her femininity throughout her career by critics such as the author of an 1858

New York Times article who described Hunt as "one of the dozen women in the United States who pine because Nature did not make them men" ("Abolishing Women").

In the context of such criticism, Hunt's anniversary celebration might be viewed as a rhetorical act intended to "domesticate" her professional career, just as many other nineteenth-century women activists had domesticated their public roles. Women reformers' effort to cast public speech and reform work as extensions of women's maternal and moral roles (Johnson 16; O'Neill 353) was one means of resolving the mismatch between the femininity of women speakers and the traits—conventionally associated with masculinity—of speakers who asserted their opinions in public. Maintaining that public speech and activism were extensions of women's domestic interests protected the ethos of the woman speaker by allowing her to insist that she was still feminine and that she did not seek to alter the fundamental characteristics of women. Nineteenth-century women physicians, however, could not rely exclusively on this strategy for developing an acceptable ethos. Although many did emphasize the feminine aspects of medical practice, women physicians sought full membership in a profession that valued "masculine" virtues such as autonomy, authority, and strength of will (with scientific expertise and a scientific mindset added by the end of the century), and therefore women physicians needed to develop strategies in addition to the domestication of medical practice in order to claim a professional ethos.

Nineteenth-century women physicians faced a challenge common to many speakers and writers who, because of their gender, race, class, or educational background, have lacked access to the virtues valued by their audiences: how does a rhetor whose social position inescapably locates her outside a privileged group nevertheless develop an ethos that wins her insider status? To rely exclusively on highlighting the feminine aspects of medical practice would never make women full members of the medical profession; yet demonstrating only the "masculine" traits of a physician would make them unrecognizable in the context of nineteenth-century gender roles. As physician William Osler's categorization in the 1890s of humanity into "men, women and women physicians" (qtd. in Welsh 44) indicates, for some commentators the woman physician could not be located in nineteenth-century gender ideology: she was neither woman nor man.

Although women's presence in the medical field was never universally accepted in the nineteenth century, women physicians did succeed in making a place for themselves in medicine: estimates of the number of American women in medicine by 1900 range from three thousand (Bonner 158) to seven thousand (Morantz-Sanchez, *Sympathy* 92), including 160 African

American women (Sterling 450). In this chapter, I examine the ethos positions constructed by and for women physicians across the various and changing contexts produced by medicine's evolving professional identity and position in nineteenth-century American society. These contexts generated complex combinations of opposition and support as well as rhetorical constraints and opportunities for women pursuing medical careers. Women physicians' arguments for the propriety of medical careers for women not only defended their reputations as both feminine and professional but also established the foundations for the ethos strategies women physicians used in other venues. Because the woman-doctor debate was carried on as women were already practicing medicine and speaking and writing from their positions as medical professionals, women physicians' arguments on behalf of their right to practice medicine often laid the groundwork for the ethos choices made in texts written for purposes ostensibly unrelated to the woman-doctor debate.

Professionalism offers an informative window into ethos because its influence depends heavily on characteristics attributed to the professional; in other words, the power of the professional lies largely in his or her ethos as a professional. Along with his or her education and professional affiliations, the professional's performance of expertise, authority, and status in rhetorical interactions with colleagues, patients/clients, and the public mark that person as professional. Additionally, the nineteenth-century woman-doctor debate is an appropriate site for a study of ethos, because much of the debate hinged on questions of the woman physician's character. Studying ethos in this context, however, is not straightforward, because the characteristics of both the ideal physician and the ideal woman were in flux, especially in the second half of the nineteenth century, the time in which women began practicing medicine in significant numbers.

The wide range of genres, rhetors, and arguments involved in the woman-doctor debate make it an opportunity to pursue the "studies of *ethos* in written discourse that extend outward to include multiple texts as well as the historical and political context for those texts, the ways they are read and responded to, [and] the ways they get interpreted, adjusted, or appropriated" called for by Nedra Reynolds (334). Such an approach complicates discussions of ethos, because looking across texts means looking across differing rhetorical situations, constraints, and opportunities. Changes among these variables complicate efforts to define the features of the ethos of a person or a group as precisely as one can when analyzing a specific text. Even though they may not yield conclusive descriptions of rhetorical practices, broader studies of ethos are worthwhile, because paying conscientious and systematic attention to the broad rather than primarily the immediate context in which a rhetor develops a persuasive ethos foregrounds different rhetorical strategies than those highlighted by the traditional model of the autonomous speaker responding to a specific audience's values.

This chapter focuses on nineteenth-century American women physicians' responses to the contextual features affecting their efforts to construct acceptable ethē as feminine professionals. After outlining opponents' characterizations of women physicians that impeded the development of a positive ethos, I argue that women physicians took advantage of their location between femininity and medical professionalism to select and combine the most persuasive values of each social position. Because the nineteenth-century woman-doctor debate took place across public and medical discourse, even if women physicians could not persuade men physicians to grant them full membership in the profession, they could still convince the public that they possessed an important set of virtues. In fact, women physicians' ethos based in simultaneous "insider" and "outsider" status allowed them to critique the existing profession and to maintain that women would correct some of medicine's faults and were therefore necessary for the public's, and particularly women's, welfare.

Nineteenth-Century Women Physicians' Ethos Problem

In the *Rhetoric*, Aristotle defines three means of persuasion: ethos, pathos, and logos. Ethos is the means of persuasion that "depends on the personal character of the speaker" (1356a). He names three things that give audience members confidence in a speaker's character: "good sense, good moral character, and goodwill." Explaining the persuasive nature of a positive ethos, Aristotle states that "It follows that any one who is thought to have all three of these good qualities will inspire trust in his audience" (1378a). It might be argued that a nineteenth-century American audience would doubt the good sense of a woman pursuing a career for which she was, as a woman, unsuited; the moral character of a woman who would voluntarily choose a career that required her to study human anatomy and to travel the streets alone at night; and the goodwill of a woman willing to abandon her domestic and familial duties in order to achieve professional success. However, attending to the three aspects that constitute Aristotelian ethos does not lead to a precise description of women physicians' ethos problem. Beneath any claim about women physicians' lack of good sense, good moral character, and goodwill lay a deeper, prior claim that interfered with their ability to construct positive ethē: women who studied and practiced medicine were doing things women were not supposed to do. Although an Aristotelian definition of *ethos* begins to identify the rhetorical problem women physicians faced, its origin in a culture in which the right to speak was confined to a select group of men limits its usefulness in explaining the rhetorical activity of speakers and writers who sought to move beyond the boundaries of their conventional roles.

More recent descriptions of ethos take into account the social and material constraints on rhetors and so offer better tools for understanding the rhetorical choices of a range of speakers. Risa Applegarth offers one such description of ethos: "As simultaneously a spatial and a social concept, *ethos* is a situated practice, neither fully and freely chosen nor yet thoroughly determined, but shaped through the interaction between individual rhetors and the social and material environments within which they speak" (49). In other words, while some components of ethos are under the rhetor's control as he or she selects virtues to display from the surrounding culture, other components are imposed upon him or her by that culture. This definition allows rhetoricians to account for not only the strategic choices a woman physician made in presenting herself to her audience but also the character features that the audience attributed to her, such as nineteenth-century women's supposed physical and psychological frailty, which was believed to make medical study and practice impossible for them.

The assumption that women did not possess the character traits of the physician posed a significant obstacle to their success as physicians and as rhetors, because it located them outside the recognizable nineteenth-century social positions that they needed to access in order to speak as medical professionals. This difficulty is clarified by conceptions of ethos that explain the appeal in spatial and social terms, as S. Michael Halloran does in tracing the etymology of the term: "In contrast to modern notions of the person or self, *ethos* emphasizes the conventional rather than the idiosyncratic, the public rather than the private. The most concrete meaning given for the term in the Greek lexicon is 'a habitual gathering place,' and I suspect that it is upon this image of people gathering together in a public place, sharing experiences and ideas, that its meaning as character rests. To have *ethos* is to manifest the virtues most valued by the culture to and for which one speaks" (60). Understanding Aristotelian ethos as an appeal generated in public settings and through public communicative exchanges highlights its insufficiency for explaining the role of ethos in women's rhetoric: because women have historically been excluded from the public sphere, a public setting for the development of the values to be conveyed through ethos means that women have often not been permitted to participate in shaping those values. Instead, virtuous women have often been defined in opposition to the characteristics associated with a positive male ethos. For example, if a good man is involved in public life, courageous, and assertive, a good woman would be defined according to the antonyms of those values: private, delicate, and self-effacing. Consequently, women who display characteristics associated with masculinity have often been judged negatively.

However, demonstrating feminine qualities has not always been a means of achieving a positive ethos either, because women and members of other marginalized groups have often been associated with negative characteristics such as a lack of intelligence and of morality. As Coretta Pittman has demonstrated through examining the cases of three African American women, some rhetors are positioned in society in ways that preclude them from demonstrating the positive characteristics valued by their community. In other words, sexist, racist, and classist beliefs limit some speakers' and writers' ability to claim virtue; regardless of the characters they construct through their rhetoric, popular assumptions make it difficult for them to be perceived as moral and intelligent. In a self-reinforcing cycle, those barred from participating in the public sphere are believed to lack the qualities of a good citizen; unable to claim persuasive ethē, marginalized individuals have only limited opportunities to shape communal values and to alter assumptions about their own virtue.

The nineteenth-century women who sought to practice medicine, and by extension to speak and write as physicians, constitute one group who had limited opportunities to assemble in the "habitual gathering place" represented by medicine's institutions and discourse. Consequently, women's contributions to the "sharing [of] experiences and ideas" that made up medicine's identity and epistemology were rare or were accomplished indirectly. Nineteenth-century women physicians faced a relatively common problem among marginalized groups: if one has been excluded from the process of developing "the virtues most valued" by her audience and has in fact been assigned characteristics incompatible with the audience's values, how does she convert her outsider status into a position inside the discourse community she wishes to join? In the case of women physicians, one part of the answer to that question emerges from the complex state of medical professionalism in the nineteenth-century United States. Medical professionalism, science, masculinity, and femininity were concepts with differing and competing meanings and social functions at various moments in the nineteenth century. It was in the context of (and sometimes against) these evolving concepts that women physicians positioned themselves in their efforts to establish effective ethē. Even as women were joining the profession, medicine's sense of itself, its purposes, and its values were changing, opening up spaces in which women could claim that medicine and femininity were compatible. When women made their first forays into medicine, for instance, they could argue that their "natural" role as nurturers suited them for a career requiring caregiving and sympathy. The site of most medical care at the time—the home—also made medical work appear to be relatively compatible with conventional femininity.

Near the end of the century, however, the medical profession began to identify with modern science, relying on new devices for measuring bodily functions, laboratory methods for studying disease, and a mindset that privileged precision and rationality over a holistic approach to caring for patients. At the same time, the physician's work increasingly took place in the hospital and its operating room, further distancing medical practice from women's traditional locations. Indeed, as medicine developed a sense of itself as scientific, science was also becoming associated with masculinity, tightening the linkage between medicine and masculinity. Yet, as historian Arleen Marcia Tuchman explains, drawing on notions of gender as "performed," the unsettled perceptions of science and gender in the nineteenth century created opportunities for some women to claim science for themselves: "The huge amount of ink spilled in the nineteenth century to proclaim women's inability to engage in scientific activity testifies to the instability of these categories and the anxiety thus generated about how to fix in place the boundaries of a moving target. But if the instability caused anxiety for some, it opened up possibilities for others, allowing individuals . . . to 'perform' alternative positions" ("Situating Gender" 39). Women physicians characterized their roles as feminine medical professionals in a variety of ways: some insisted that the primary role of the physician, whether female or male, was as a caregiver, not a scientific researcher; some promoted definitions of science and professionalism that accommodated the kind of medicine they wanted to practice; and some adamantly claimed that science was as accessible to women as it was to men, using the moment of cultural uncertainty to resist the gendering of science as masculine. In taking these stances, women were often not alone; men also endorsed a range of medical professional identities. For women, however, definitions of "physician" and the compatibility of that role with femininity were crucial to women's success in the medical field.

The woman-doctor debate began in earnest in the late 1840s, when Harriot Hunt, already a practicing physician,[1] applied to and was rejected by Harvard Medical College (1847 and 1850), and when Elizabeth Blackwell became the first woman to earn a medical degree in the United States when she graduated from Geneva Medical College (1849). Blackwell's graduation at the top of her class made headlines in the United States and Europe (Blackwell, *Pioneer* 131). Although women had always practiced medicine as midwives and herbalists, the arrival of the formally educated and certified woman physician challenged medicine's professional identity in ways that earlier women who cared for the sick and injured never had. Men did not universally oppose women physicians, however. As early as 1867, physician Ann Preston, dean of the Woman's Medical College of Pennsylvania, referred to the masculine profession's recognition of women physicians' authority on matters of women's health: "Physicians, too,—the father, husband, and brother,—have asked our counsel in the cases of those dearest to them; and they have asked it because we were women, and as such, they believed we might elicit the cause of suffering and apply the means of relief, as they had not been successful in doing" (393).[2] In homeopathy, where women contributed to the field's knowledge by testing drugs' effects on women, women physicians were valued because it was believed that they would further homeopathy's therapeutic effectiveness (figure 1.1).[3]

Despite such marks in women physicians' favor, many men physicians were resistant and even hostile to women in the field. A correspondent to the *Boston Medical and Surgical Journal* expressed his concern for regular medicine's reputation when he protested after reading news of Blackwell's graduation in 1849: "Would either of the other learned professions have received and graduated a female? Would any amount of study or learning have gained her admittance to the bar or the desk? Certainly not. Then why desecrate the profession of medicine, and publicly disparage it?" (D. K. 59). As this comment makes apparent, to some regular physicians, admitting women to the profession seemed a risky innovation in a context in which medicine's authority was doubted by many in the American public. Medicine was not a highly respected profession for much of the century, and this correspondent's comparison of medicine to more prestigious professions such as the ministry and the law reveals his anxiety about the status of physicians.

Furthermore, around the middle of the century, "regular" medicine competed with several "irregular" sects, and none had a clear advantage in producing successful outcomes. Among the numerous medical sects that arose in the nineteenth-century United States, Thomsonians, homeopaths, and hydropaths were the most popular (Numbers 43); all three of these developed as a reaction against the often harsh and ineffective treatments that had been employed by regular physicians. Thomsonianism, developed and promoted by Samuel Thomson in the early 1800s and popular from the 1820s through the 1840s, was a do-it-yourself approach that relied on botanical treatments to restore the body's natural heat (Numbers 44–46). Homeopathy, the creation of German physician Samuel Hahnemann, operated on the principle that disease could be cured by giving a patient a drug that produced in healthy

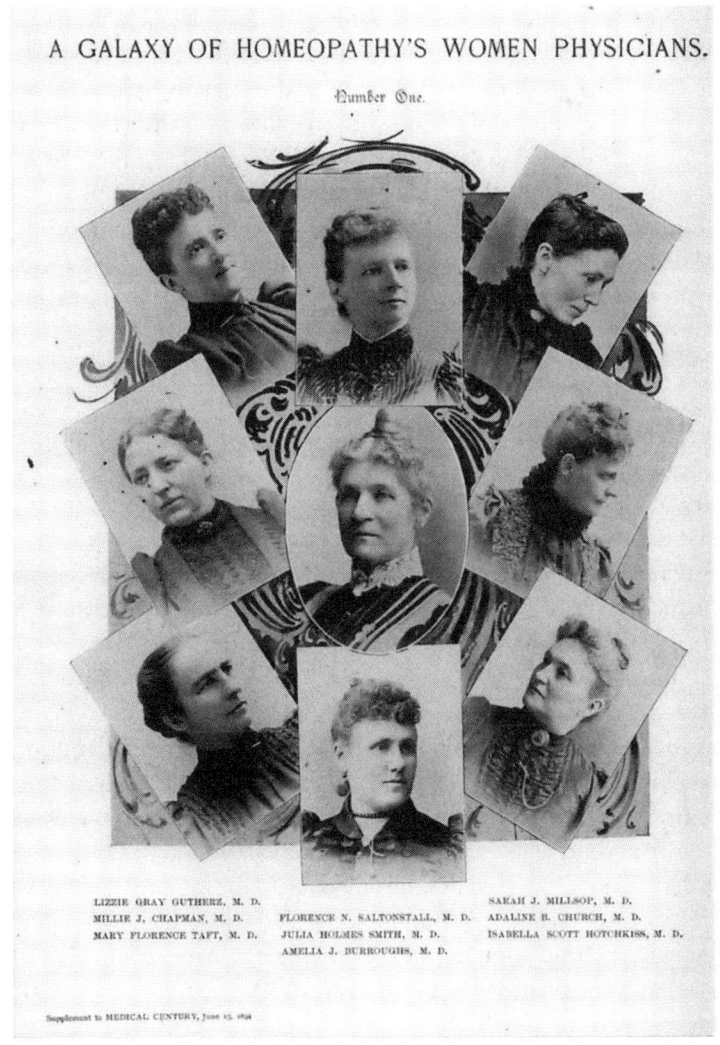

Figure 1.1. "A Galaxy of Homeopathy's Women Physicians," *Medical Century,* June 1894.

people symptoms similar to those from which the patient suffered and the principle that drugs were most effective in very small doses (Numbers 46). Homeopaths were formally educated and often combined homeopathic treatments with "regular" (what they called "allopathic") treatments. Homeopathy was a prominent therapeutic approach from the 1840s through the end of the century; it was popular among the affluent, and it was believed especially appropriate for children, which led women to patronize and promote it eagerly (Numbers 46). Also called "water cure physicians," hydropaths, who enjoyed a "craze" from the mid-1840s up to the 1860s (Numbers 49), treated patients by applying cold water internally and externally—through showers, baths, and the wrapping of the body in wet sheets—in an effort to remove the impurities believed to cause disease. All three of these approaches were popular among women: Thomsonianism spared women the embarrassment of examinations by men physicians, homeopathy offered women and children the milder treatments believed appropriate for their more delicate bodies, and hydropathy admitted women among its practitioners very early in the woman-doctor movement.

From a modern standpoint, these alternative medical approaches may seem unscientific, but as historian Anne Taylor Kirschmann explains in her account of women in homeopathy, "Throughout history, proponents of various medical systems claimed their methods of cure rested solidly on scientific principles, with the definition of science and its meaning to patients and physicians in specific places changing over time" (8). In the mid-nineteenth-century United States, according to historian Regina Morantz-Sanchez, sectarian competition and the concomitant relaxing of licensing laws made women's entrance into medicine possible: "This temporary fluidity allowed women who wished to achieve professional status to do so before definitions of professionalism crystallized once more" (*Sympathy* 31–32). In the context of competing medical sects, some regular physicians argued that admitting women would undermine the authority and prestige of practitioners of their therapeutic approach, but because no sect enjoyed dominance and because many medical schools were proprietary establishments dependent on tuition (even from women) for survival, opponents had limited institutional and legal options for excluding women. Unable to forbid women entirely from studying and practicing medicine, opponents instead argued that women *should* not pursue medical careers, often basing their resistance on the physical, temperamental, and intellectual characteristics attributed to women.

The woman-doctor debate could therefore be viewed as a struggle over women physicians' ethos locations: "Do women belong in the profession?" was another way of asking "Do women possess the characteristics associated with physicians?" The concept of "ethos locations" allows scholars to focus on issues especially relevant to women's ethos development, such as insider and outsider status, public and domestic spheres, and mind and body as the supposed determiners of behavior. In the context of nineteenth-century America, demonstrating certain (masculine) character features in speech and writing located one as a professional insider, as a participant in the public sphere, and as one whose decision-making occurred in the mind, while other (feminine) ethos locations positioned one as properly situated outside the professions and inside the domestic sphere, where behaviors dictated by the body or the nerves would do little damage to others. In thinking of ethos as a spatial concept, however, it is important to keep in mind that the boundaries around the "habitual gathering place[s]" (Halloran 60) in which ethos is developed vary in their degrees of permeability. In one sense, the unsettled nature of the medical profession in the nineteenth-century United States created openings in the boundaries around the space of its ethos through which women could enter. At the same time, however, the field's anxiety about its status sometimes produced even thicker walls intended to exclude those who might undermine medicine's efforts to improve its standing among the professions. Much of the opposition to women physicians composed by men in the field operated by imposing traits upon women (and women physicians in particular) and then asserting that those traits were antithetical to the characteristics of reputable physicians. In effect, in attempting to prevent women from practicing medicine, physician-opponents also denied women access to the ethē of respectable medical professionals, particularly the ethos of a physician who was simultaneously properly feminine and respectably professional.

The impossibility of the respectable feminine professional was suggested by opponents who expressed the fear that if even a few women entered a masculine space like medicine, the result would be a complete gender-role reversal. For example, in an address before a New York medical society, subsequently published in the *Boston Medical and Surgical Journal* in 1850, a physician identified as N. Williams asked, "If they are to turn doctors, lawyers, clergymen, &c., why may not we turn our attention to sewing, knitting, tending babies, and other household employment? Surely when they occupy our places, we must of necessity take possession of theirs; and when they become to all intents and purposes *men*, will we become, to the same extent, *women*" (69). The absurdity of the image of professional men sewing and caring for children to a nineteenth-century audience highlighted the challenge women physicians posed to medicine's masculine professional identity.

In addition to suggesting that women physicians would prompt a gender-role reversal, opponents also cited their perceptions of women's biology and temperament as evidence that women did not belong in the profession. These were particularly potent arguments because they came from physicians, whose professional expertise and experience authorized their claims about women's physical and temperamental "nature." In the same article in which he posed the threat of a gender-role reversal, Williams also compared the qualities expected of a physician with those associated with women: "To the female sex, then, may be ascribed the *nervous* or *excitable* temperament. To the male sex, the lymphatic, bilious and sanguine are more common. . . . I scarcely, then, need to add, that in a profession where the *utmost nerve* and *self-possession* are often required, the male sex is the most favorably constituted" (Williams 73). Physician-opponents, especially early in the woman-doctor movement, relied on their medical expertise to argue that a woman's biology excluded her from a position as a physician. Only the masculine body and mind, it was asserted, were suited for medical work. The counterpart to the belief that only men were fit for medical labor was the argument that women were especially suited for domestic work. For example, in 1859, one editorialist admitted that "woman has intellectual capacity for other pursuits than household duties. . . . Woman has mental capacity without doubt, but by certain immutable laws of her being, she is better adapted to fulfill one line of duties than another, and when nature adapts her lord to the fulfillment of the duties peculiar to the nursery, she may find something in the practice of medicine, and in other pursuits now by common consent regarded as 'masculine,' on which to employ her talents" ("Woman Doctors" 276). In this variation on the biological argument, women were positioned as "naturally" intended to fill domestic roles. In maintaining that women possessed characteristics compatible with household duties and incompatible with the work of the physician, opponents of women physicians not only provided reasons to exclude women from medicine but also denied them access to the virtues they would need to craft positive ethē as feminine professionals.

When physicians claimed that women's biological and temperamental "nature" was incompatible with physicians' work, they contributed medical arguments to an ongoing discussion about women's "place" and the work they were capable of. This issue was discussed widely in American popular periodicals beginning at midcentury and continuing for several decades, spurred on by advances in women's education, new property laws in some states that allowed married women to keep the money they earned, the opening of civil service and other jobs to women during the Civil War (and the expectation that women would give up their positions as veterans returned home), the loss of financial support resulting from the death of huge numbers of men in the war, and the large numbers of women who took jobs in textile and other factories. Biology, particularly women's reproductive physiology and their supposed tendency toward "nervous" ailments, was frequently deployed in efforts to restrict women's occupational opportunities.

Such arguments were particularly relevant in medicine, where those with the greatest expertise in human physiology continued to defend their professional "turf" from incursions by women after the close of the Civil War. For example, in its 1867 resolution prohibiting its members from consulting with women physicians, the Philadelphia County Medical Society invoked women's reproductive functions as an impediment to medical practice: "The physiological peculiarities of a woman, even in single life, and the disorders consequent on them cannot fail frequently to interfere with the regular discharge of her duties as physician in constant attendance on the sick." Moreover, the society argued, because of her sensitive nervous system, a woman would imperil her health by practicing medicine: "Her delicate organization and the predominance of her nervous system render her peculiarly susceptible to suffer from, if not liable to sink under, the fatigue and the moral shocks which she must encounter in her professional rounds" ("Female Medical Practitioners" 73). The Philadelphia County Medical Society's assessment of women's tenuous health posed significant obstacles to developing a positive ethos for women physicians: rather than being strong enough to care for patients, the woman the Philadelphia County Medical Society described was in need of attentive medical care herself.

As I noted above, accompanying many of the claims about women's "natural" abilities was the assertion that women's "natural" place was at home. Opponents frequently raised the specter of neglected husbands and children and of families who could not depend on the wife and mother to be home when she was needed because her work had called her out. In its rationale for refusing to support women physicians, the Philadelphia County Medical Society asked, "What would be the state of the household, what the present condition and prospects for the future of the children, when deprived to a considerable extent of their natural guardian, who would be engaged all day, and not secure against calls in the night, in the service of the sick? Nor when she is at home, can the mother, worried and fretted and anxious about her patients, give healthy milk to her infant, nor be in a fit frame of mind to interchange endearments with the other little ones, to receive their confidences and to offer advice" ("Female Medical Practitioners" 73). Suggesting that women physicians could not be good mothers cut right to the heart of their femininity, making them unrecognizable according to nineteenth-century American gender ideology. Such women would find it difficult to be respected as practitioners or listened to as rhetors.

In addition to questioning women physicians' femininity by casting doubt on their commitment to motherhood, some opponents argued that medical study and practice put women in positions that threatened their feminine virtue. A letter to the editor of the *Medical and Surgical Reporter* in 1867 expressed this fear:

> One would think that the *ordeal* through which a woman has to
> pass, who studies *all* the branches of medical science *along with
> men*, witnesses *all* operations in the presence of large numbers of
> *men*, studies her anatomy over the stinking, decaying, mutilated
> cadaver, in company with men, would be enough to make any
> right-minded woman recoil with a shudder at the mere mention
> of such a career for *her?* If the communities whose "moral sense"
> commends this "revolution," knew the details of this horrible
> curriculum *for a woman*, there is not a decent family in the land
> into which the admission of a woman who had passed through it,
> would not be, at least, *prejudiced*. Many would close their doors
> against her. (Sherry 20)

Lacking both professional authority and feminine virtue, the woman physician would have no "space" in which to construct a positive ethos.

An alternative to casting doubt on the femininity of women physicians
by questioning their virtue was claiming that medical study and practice
"unsexed" women. As the anonymous author of *Men and Women Medical
Students, and the Woman Movement* (1869) explained, "There is probably
no profession, in the preparation for, or in the practice of which a greater
tendency exists to make '*manly women*,' than in that of medicine, unless
we except *the military*" (5–6). The claim that women physicians would be
monstrous, unsexed beings also appears in the exposé of immoral women
of all classes, *The Women of New York, or the Underworld of the Great City*,
published in 1869 under the pseudonym of George Ellington. In the chapter
"Female Physicians," Ellington played on the widespread belief that women
who pursued medical degrees had been disappointed in love and so were
man-haters: "How must a woman delight to cut up the body of a powerful
and well-formed man! . . . Ah! Many a woman who studies medicine does so
just for the opportunity of cutting up such a glorious specimen of humanity"
(559). In addition to dissection, activities such as observing and handling
unclothed human bodies, living or dead, and learning about sexually transmitted diseases alongside men would, it was argued, destroy the innocence
and delicacy crucial to femininity. In arguments like these, women physicians
were described in horrific terms that presented them as a subversive force,
countering their efforts to demonstrate their usefulness to society.

Rather than characterizing women physicians as "unsexed," some opponents described them in highly sexualized terms, undercutting their feminine modesty and their professionalism. For example, a humorist writing
in 1880 under the name "Aiken Heart, M.D." recounted the story of a male
traveler who takes ill and is treated by a woman physician. The narrator

described the woman physician's physical form in terms fitting a romantic (if also humorous) heroine:

> But there SHE stood, a picture; rosy cheeks,
> > A clear blue eye whose depths were almost killing,
> Her lips were rubies, pouting when she speaks,
> > With pearls of teeth without a speck of—filling. (8)

It is not the medicine she prescribes that cures the narrator; instead, her examination of his body sends "a thrill, / Of life and health . . . bounding thro' [his] veins" (10). Although this story did not directly argue against women's medical practice, it did undercut their ability to be taken seriously as professionals.

While some commentators, such as "Aiken Heart," characterized women physicians as romantic heroines, others described them as unnatural, even dreadful. For example, in an address titled "Shall Woman Practice Medicine?" delivered to the Medical Society of North Carolina in 1885, L. Julien Picöt constructed this horrific picture of the woman physician, reminiscent of Ellington's: "How does she appear in the dissecting room, clad with oil-cloth aprons and armlets, knife in hand, cutting the dead man's flesh under the ghastly glare of gaslight? To every refined mind it is an appalling sight. . . . She has wit enough to grasp all the diseases incident to frail mortality. She should have, at least, for she 'first brought death into the world and all its woes.' She has courage enough, for nothing more delights an unsexed woman than blood and agony" (15). Echoing earlier opposition to women physicians, Picöt asserted that Providence had assigned men and women to separate spheres: "Woman is equally unfitted to handle the axe, the hammer and maul of the strong and hardy laborer as she is to wield the warrior's sword or manipulate the surgeon's knife" (17). Later he expressed his sense of disgust at women who sought occupations outside the home: "Mountains may be tunnelled and continents cut into one; inventions may apply all science, and art may fill the earth with its triumphs, yet the metamorphosis of women into men is a monstrosity that nature abhors. God intended women for wives and mothers. She doctors can never meet the full required duties" (18). Echoing the belief, expressed thirty-five years earlier, that women's pursuit of medical careers was equivalent to women becoming men, Picöt argued that women were not capable of practicing medicine, denying them access to the work of the profession as well as to the physician's ethos.

Picöt, like many of those who spoke against women physicians, addressed his remarks to a professional audience; however, physicians also used popular media to express their resistance to women in the field. One such authoritative and public argument against women's suitability for medical practice appeared in an article written in 1891 for the *Ladies' Home Journal* by George F. Shrady, the longtime editor of the *Medical Record,* a professional journal. Shrady maintained that the "exceptional few" women who had succeeded as physicians did so "not because they were women, but in spite of their being women." Exuding the confidence of his professional authority, he explained the internal conflicts facing a woman pursuing a medical career: "She is handicapped in many ways, simply because she is a woman. In the majority of cases she is physically unable to endure the hardships and privations of medical practice. She is incapable, also, by her natural sympathies, sensitive disposition and feminine prejudices, of fitting herself easily and profitably to her work. Her instincts are not in accord with her surroundings and its requirements. She is forced to cultivate the sterner qualities of her nature at the expense of her better womanly feelings—something always hard to do with one who may not be accustomed to the discipline of emergencies" (4). Shrady also questioned the woman physician's priorities: "What recompense would there be even in the discovery of a new bacillus or the writing of a prize thesis, when husband and children may be suffering neglect at home?" (4). In pointing to elements of women's temperament that he believed made them unsuited for medical practice and in arguing that professional labor was not compatible with a woman's duties, Shrady echoed earlier comments that limited women's access to character traits associated with trustworthy professionals.

By the time Shrady published this article in 1891, a substantial number of women were practicing medicine, women had established their own medical schools, and Shrady himself had published medical case reports by women in the *Medical Record.* Women had succeeded in a range of professional and occupational arenas: many colleges, particularly land-grant institutions, accepted women as students; thousands of women were practicing medicine; and well over one hundred women had earned certification as ministers. In the 1890s, many college graduates put their education to work in settlement houses and in political and social reform, constituting a group that Mary P. Ryan characterizes as "perhaps the most notable and politically powerful of their sex that American history has yet seen" (*Mysteries* 166). Although some men physicians continued to resist women's participation in the field, despite ample evidence of women's professional success, women physicians in the 1890s faced much less enmity than their predecessors had. Indeed, Shrady did not write with the hostile tone of earlier critics; his commentary on women in medicine reads more like a professional opinion warning women against choosing medical careers than an aggressive objection to women physicians. According to historian Ellen S. More, by 1889, the presence of women delegates at the annual meetings of the American Medical

Association was "rare but no longer controversial" (39). Furthermore, by the 1890s, Steven J. Peitzman observes, the study and practice of medicine by women "was less contentious an issue: few men in the medical profession could plausibly argue a radical position that women must not, or could not, become physicians, even though most no doubt still felt little comfort with the idea" (594). Men's toleration of women in the field did not, however, mean that any significant revision of professional identity to accommodate women had taken place; the typical physician was still assumed to be male, and the ideal physician still exhibited traits widely understood as masculine.

Even as the physician continued to be associated with masculinity, the shifting nature of masculinity and professionalism produced a range of positions in which nineteenth-century medical professionals could locate and describe themselves as physicians. For some, especially those associated with modern medical schools and hospitals, the emerging model of medical research and practice offered a position in the exciting new world of scientific epistemology, the opportunity to contribute to rapidly advancing medical knowledge, and the authority many in the public were beginning to attribute to science. For others, the older, holistic model, in which healthcare was practiced in the home by physicians with extensive knowledge of the patient's family and habits, offered a position of respect in a community and the rewards of caring for other human beings. Women located themselves across this continuum of professional identities, led by their interests, their beliefs about the future of medicine, and their rhetorical needs.

The woman-doctor debate was, at its heart, a debate over social roles: What did it mean to be a woman? What did it mean to be a physician? Could those two roles be combined? If they could, what kind of person would result? Would she still be recognizable as a woman, and would she fill the social and familial roles associated with femininity? Indeed, in her 1882 defense of women physicians, Mary Putnam Jacobi[4] characterized the opposition to women in medicine as more a matter of "taste" than the result of any true doubts about women's abilities: "They ask not, 'Is she capable?' but, 'Is this fearfully capable person nice?' Will she upset our ideal of womanhood, and maidenhood, and the social relations of the sexes? Can a woman physician be lovable; can she marry; can she have children; will she take care of them? If she cannot, what is she?" ("Shall Women" 54). Such questions pointed to the difficulty nineteenth-century women physicians faced in constructing a positive ethos for themselves as feminine professionals.

Many of the arguments written against women physicians were composed by male physicians addressing an audience of their professional colleagues. As such, these texts are good examples of relatively straightforward uses of ethos, in which the speaker must "manifest the virtues most valued by the culture to and for which one speaks" (Halloran 60). In the case of nineteenth-century American medicine, those virtues included authoritative masculinity and medicine's prerogative to determine the "natural" biological and temperamental traits of men and women. The opponents of women physicians not only displayed these values, but they also sought to reinforce them by excluding women from the rhetorical and social space occupied by physicians on one hand and by respectable women on the other. The social locations imposed upon women physicians by their opponents positioned them outside of the roles of "woman," "physician," and the combined role of the "feminine professional." If "to have *ethos* is to manifest the virtues most valued by the culture to and for which one speaks" (Halloran 60), then nineteenth-century women physicians did not have ethos, at least according to opponents' characterizations. In addition to efforts to exclude women from positive ethos spaces, many male physicians also sought to exclude women from the physical spaces of medical education and professional interaction. As the next section demonstrates, in some cases, these efforts produced a public backlash against the masculine profession that created an opening for the feminine professional.

"Masculine" Medical Spaces and the Ethos of the Woman Physician

Women's entrance into the sites of medical education and practice—lecture halls, clinical demonstrations, hospitals, and operating theaters—was often met with hostility from male students and professors. The harassment endured by the students at the Woman's Medical College of Pennsylvania when they first attended the Pennsylvania Hospital's surgical clinics in November 1869 is one infamous example. According to one newspaper report, in the course of the lectures, "various rude manifestations were made—missiles of paper, tin-foil, tobacco-quids, etc., were thrown upon the ladies, while some of these *men*(?) defiled the dresses of the ladies near them by spitting tobacco-juice upon them" ("Another Account" 3). When the students left the lecture hall at the end of the surgical demonstrations, they allegedly faced further hostility: "On Saturday afternoon, as about thirty ladies were leaving the hospital, upwards of four hundred of the male students formed a double line, through which the ladies were compelled to pass [,] taunted with hisses and sneers, and vulgar epithets and abuse. After running this gauntlet they were followed into the street by some of the more brutal brutes, who did not cease their insults till they were frightened by the approach of a policeman" ("The Outrage").

Although achieving access to persuasive ethos spaces was challenging for women physicians and medical students, achieving access to the physical spaces of medical study and practice was also an arduous accomplishment.

Historian Steven J. Peitzman suggests that the value nineteenth-century men placed on all-male spaces in which they could "smoke, drink, and swear, indulgences that could not be exercised in the presence of decent women" and their enjoyment of the company of other men may partially explain men's hostile responses to women's entrance into medical lecture halls and operating theaters (580). Indeed, some of the defenders of the male medical students involved in the 1869 incident in Philadelphia insisted that the men were behaving as they always did during lectures, claiming that stomping and shouting were part of students' ordinary conduct.

The popular press covered the events in Philadelphia eagerly, reporting accounts of the behavior of the men and women involved and printing editorials and letters defending both sides. Much of the coverage commented on whether or not the men had behaved in a "manly" fashion and the women with "feminine" decorum. For example, in "Another Account," a reprint in Philadelphia's *Press* of an article originally published in the *Evening Bulletin* of the same city, the appropriate behavior of the women is confirmed while the masculinity of the men is questioned: "It is but just to the ladies to say they maintained a quiet, modest demeanor, and seemed to realize their dignity as women, and their position as scientific students. It is quite evident from their general appearance that none of them had ever been accustomed to the association of such unmannerly men(?) before." An article in the *New York Herald* likewise claimed that the male students had behaved in an unmanly fashion: "They exhibited in their deportment the baser instincts of a contemptible jealousy, shallow ignorance, and unmanly cowardice, instead of the politeness and refinement of true manhood in their calling" (qtd. in "Barbaric Rowdyism"). A writer for New York's *Citizen and Round Table*, who was less sympathetic to the women's cause, called them "Wild Women" and suggested that their motives for attending the lectures were not strictly academic: "The hospital was invaded by twenty-five Wild Women, determined to witness the carving and cutting of the masculine form divine" (qtd. in "The Happy Hunting Ground"). Critics of both the men and the women used charges of behaving out of line with each group's respective gender to shame those they believed had acted disgracefully.

Many commentators, however, maintained that women's presence in medical institutions would improve the profession. A representative of the Woman's Medical College asserted, "The conduct of the students at the Pennsylvania Hospital last Saturday shows conclusively that some humanizing element has been wanting in their medical teaching, and is a striking evidence of the necessity for woman's influence in the profession" (qtd. in "The Esculapian Caldron"). A writer for the *Philadelphia Sunday Transcript* imagined a similar role for women in medicine: "In the pursuit of science all are equal, and the only objection to females can be, that they interfere with the time-honored custom of the male students to make sport of the miseries of suffering humanity, and jeer at the misfortunes of their fellows. If the females can effect a reform in this direction they deserve the thanks of every right thinking person in the community" ("The Modest"). For some in mid-nineteenth-century America, the decorum and sympathy attributed to femininity were traits physicians would do well to incorporate into their professional identity.

In fact, public and professional concerns about the quality of medical education might have made women's entrance into medical schools seem advantageous, because proper women physicians were nothing like the ignorant, uncouth young men who often attended medical school. In her biography of Elizabeth Blackwell, Julia Boyd describes Blackwell's peers at Geneva Medical College as "mostly local boys destined to become doctors only because they were thought too stupid to study law" (68). Twenty years after Blackwell attended medical school, the Philadelphia papers commented on the disorderly behavior of medical students just before the Civil War, events that were still part of the city's collective memory: "There was a time when 'the students' used to exercise their loaded canes and their knives and even pistols, at the expense of public order, and, not unfrequently [*sic*], at the cost of life" ("Medical Rowdyism"). In contrast, as women physicians and their supporters observed, medical settings that included women featured well-behaved, serious students. Prior to the harassment women faced at the lectures at the Pennsylvania Hospital, women had attended the Saturday clinics at the Philadelphia Hospital at Blockley. According to one commentator, the results of that experiment were favorable for all involved: following women's attendance at Blockley's winter clinics, "in all probability the universities never graduated better models of decorous manhood than they did last spring" ("The Esculapian Caldron"). Although medicine's efforts to shore up its reputation by improving the quality of medical students sometimes manifested in resistance to women students, in other situations the very same doubts about the quality of medical students and practitioners served to justify women's presence in the field. Rather than imposing characteristics that made the feminine medical professional undesirable, some commentators (usually nonphysicians) used the unsettled nature of medicine to attribute positive ethos features to women. Notably, they argued that women's propriety and decorum might improve the behavior of the masculine members of the profession.

Aside from women's salutary effects on their male classmates, supporters of women physicians also maintained that the nature of medical study made it accessible to both genders. Some of those who condemned the male students' behavior in Philadelphia asserted that the male students' reaction to women's presence, ostensibly resulting from their belief that it was immodest for women to study the human body alongside of men, actually arose from their misunderstanding of the nature of medical science. In criticizing the male students, an editorial in the *Press* described science as a noble, gender-neutral pursuit:

> Theoretically speaking, there is nothing immodest in science, and scientists who insist that there is are inappreciative, to say the least. If all medical students could be endowed with a proper conception of the work they have in hand they would quickly part with all restricting observances, would lose their personality in the great search for truth, would be transported to that ideal sphere where mind holds communion with the Infinite, and where no unclean thought is allowed to enter. They would drink in the ultimate aim and scope of scientific revelation, and be so absorbed in their philanthropic mission as to pass beyond the trammels of custom, rank, sex, and occasion. Thought would commune with thought, mind with mind, soul with soul. What have petticoats and pants, . . . modesty and masculinity, to do with all this? ("The Esculapian Caldron")

This passage suggests another opening for women created by medicine's evolving identity: the universality of science, an epistemology with which medicine increasingly identified in the later decades of the century. In describing science as universally accessible, the author of "The Esculapian Caldron" made an ethos as a medical student accessible to women, not by changing the characteristics attributed to women, but by altering the values of the profession in ways that ostensibly made gender irrelevant. According to this model of medical study, women would not study or practice medicine as women but as genderless minds engaged in a noble pursuit. The positive implications of this view of women's genderless study of science inverted negative accusations of women physicians' being "unsexed" by their decision to pursue medical careers.[5]

Thirteen years later, physician Mary Putnam Jacobi took arguments about the nobility of medical study one step further. In an essay in the *North American Review* in 1882, she turned men physicians' resistance to women at medical lectures, clinical demonstrations, and dissections into an implicit critique of their own attitudes toward medical study: "It seems scarcely credible that any physician who loves and honors his calling as it deserves, should dare to pronounce it too coarse or too hardening a pursuit for women" ("Shall Women" 62). Insisting that medical study and practice were noble activities was a savvy argument: it simultaneously appealed to the profession's desire for prestige and defended the reputations of women physicians and medical students. The multiple and evolving nature of "physician" across the nineteenth century presented women physicians and their supporters with a range of opportunities to develop positive, if sometimes contradictory, ethos locations for women physicians that responded to the changing attitudes of the public and of physicians themselves toward the medical profession. At various times, supporters described women as "domesticating" male medical students through their feminine influence, as participating in the genderless pursuit of science, and as being respectful of a noble profession.

Each of these ethos spaces would authorize nineteenth-century women physicians' speech and writing, at least for some audiences. Gaining access to the physical spaces of medical education was only one of the challenges faced by women who wished to speak and write from positions as medical professionals, however; they also needed to be accepted by the public. The comments of the editors cited above suggest that some members of the public approved of women in medicine, at least in principle. To succeed vocationally and rhetorically as physicians, however, women needed supporters who were willing not only to accept the idea of the feminine medical professional but also to put themselves under a woman's care and to attend to her speech and writing. To win over this audience, women physicians needed to construct ethos spaces for themselves as respectable feminine professionals who reflected the values desired by public audiences.

Constructing Positive Ethos Spaces for Women Physicians

Nineteenth-century women seeking access to medicine exemplify a relatively common rhetorical problem: how does a rhetor who is excluded from the "space" that makes a positive ethos possible ultimately gain access to that space? Nedra Reynolds offers a starting point for answering that question when she locates two sites of ethos formation based on feminist theories that emphasize decentering authority: the margins and the "betweens." Claiming marginality as a location from which to speak authorizes the knowledge and credibility of those historically located outside of the centers of power. The social nature of ethos suggests "between" as another location in which ethos is generated, "as writers struggle to identify their own positions at the intersections of various communities and attempt to establish authority for themselves and their claims." Focusing on ethos as functioning in the "betweens" allows for a more complex model of ethos formation: "By emphasizing where and how texts and their writers are *located*—their intersections with others and the places they diverge, how they occupy positions and move in the betweens—we can retain the spatial metaphors of *ethos* without limiting it to arenas of spoken discourse and without assuming that those gathering places are harmonious or conflict-free" (333).

The "betweens" also suggest strategies by which people who have been excluded from positions of authority and privilege might manage to access those positions. Because all rhetors belong to several discourse communities simultaneously, they can speak to a range of audiences, constructing ethos as appropriate to each community. This location *between* communities and *between* various sets of virtues constitutes an opportunity to intervene in powerful discourses and even to acquire an otherwise inaccessible ethos. The nineteenth-century woman-doctor movement exemplifies how being between communities can be used to expand one's rhetorical options. Because the woman-doctor debate occurred in a context in which women were already practicing physicians, the women physicians who participated in it could already claim, however tentatively and controversially, the social position of "physician." Despite women's educational achievements, many men physicians sought to block their access to the character values that the profession found persuasive. To overcome this obstacle, women physicians turned to another community to which they belonged: middle-class American society. Because men physicians also belonged to this community, addressing the middle-class public did not mean turning away from the profession-as-audience; instead, it meant emphasizing a somewhat different set of values. Although convincing the profession would require evidence of character traits above and beyond those demanded by the public, appealing to the values of the public—which included potential patients—allowed women physicians to begin the process of persuading both audiences.

One way that women physicians tapped into the values of nineteenth-century middle-class society was through reference to the modesty and delicacy attributed to women. The most effective argument for women physicians in the nineteenth century was the impropriety of gynecological examinations by men and of men's presence at childbirth. Elizabeth Blackwell attributed her earliest interest in medicine to a friend who "died of a painful disease, the delicate nature of which made the methods of treatment a constant suffering to her." This friend told Blackwell in the mid-1840s that "if I could have been treated by a lady doctor, my worst sufferings would have been spared me" (*Pioneer* 74). Elsewhere in her autobiography, Blackwell elaborated on the benefits women physicians might offer their female patients. She explained that once she had finally been admitted to medical school, she found much to arouse her sympathies and to reinforce her desire to help women. She included in her autobiography (1895) a journal entry, dated 11 January 1849, that demonstrated to her readers her compassion: "I called to see the pretty blind girl operated on this morning; she was all alone in the hotel, her friends far away. Poor child! she has no protector, within or without. . . . Such are the women I long to surround with my stronger arm. Alas! how almost hopeless does the task seem! But God is omnipotent" (*Pioneer* 124). Blackwell imagined herself in the conventionally masculine protector's role, and she articulated a desire to use her professional knowledge and authority to assist vulnerable women. This was an assumption of the masculine role that, because it had such clearly nurturing aims, would be difficult to deny women. Were it not for the image of Blackwell's "stronger arm," there would be little to distinguish her professional ability to protect this patient from maternal motivations to care for a child. In Blackwell's story, women's medical work was a natural extension of maternal impulses. This was an occupational and a rhetorical position unavailable to male physicians; it could be occupied only by the woman physician situated between professional expertise and feminine concern.

Another means by which women physicians reassured their public audience was through casting medical work as compatible with women's responsibility for domestic harmony. For example, Ann Preston, who would later become the dean of the Woman's Medical College of Pennsylvania,[6] gave the institution's valedictory address for the 1857–58 academic year. In this speech, which reached a public audience through the publication of excerpts in *Godey's Lady's Book*, Preston capitalized on the fact that mid-nineteenth-century health care took place in patients' homes to cast medical work as a sacred domestic duty: "Ladies, it is for the very purpose of making home enjoyments more complete that you have been delegated today to bear health and hope to the abodes you enter. You go into them when pain and sickness prostrate the body, often when fear and anguish prey upon the spirit. You meet your patients where dissimulation is laid aside, and the character is bare before you. Those who are thus admitted into the very sanctuaries of society, and intrusted with the most sacred confidences, should indeed be strong, and wise, and pure, and good" (qtd. in "Valedictory Address" 465–66). Note that it is the patient's character that is "bare" before the woman physician, not the body, and that she is entrusted with "confidences," not the authority to penetrate the body surgically or medicinally. In describing the woman physician as a practitioner who treats the spirit and not just its mortal home, Preston emphasized her virtue, a quality the public was likely willing to attribute to women.[7] A description of medical work as compatible with femininity was appropriate to midcentury medical practice, which often occurred in domestic spaces. According to historian Ellen S. More, "For the typical [mid-Victorian] practitioner, male or female, personal and professional life intersected in the household" (14). Moreover, in alluding to domesticity and in particular to women's role as moral and religious guides within the home, Preston demonstrated her identification with a model of femininity that had arisen by the 1840s with the publication of texts such as Catharine Beecher's *A Treatise on Domestic Economy* (1841) and continued to influence expectations for femininity for decades. In the forty years following Preston's address, women physicians were more likely to insist on medical and surgical skill as requisite abilities for women physicians, but they also continued to demand virtue. In this way, women physicians could rely on the persuasive advantages of the morality expected of women in the nineteenth century while adding to those advantages the persuasiveness of the expertise associated with professionalism.

The domestic setting and moral overtones of much medical practice in the mid-nineteenth century made establishing a professional and rhetorical position "between" the attributes of the physician and those of the middle-class woman relatively accessible for women physicians. In fact, More argues that women physicians "not only endured but positively thrived on the creative tension between their professional and their feminine roles" (12). The value women physicians found in positioning themselves at the intersections of medical professionalism and femininity is evident in *Medicine as a Profession for Women*, written by Elizabeth Blackwell and her sister Emily, who was also a physician. In this address, delivered in December 1859, the Blackwells described the woman physician's location between medicine and femininity as her most useful feature: "At present, when women need medical aid or advice, they have at once to go out of their own world, as it were; the whole atmosphere of professional life is so entirely foreign to that in which they live that there is a gap between them and the physician whom they consult, which can only be filled up by making the profession no longer an exclusively masculine one" (15). Whereas "the medical profession is at present too far removed from the life of women," women physicians could provide a "connecting link between the science of the medical profession and the every-day life of women" (9). For the Blackwells, it was precisely women physicians' location between the medical profession and women's lives that made them necessary to society.

Even if women physicians themselves behaved immodestly by attending dissections and clinical lectures, they claimed to uphold the modesty of their female patients and to provide them with health care that they were reluctant to seek from men. Women physicians thus cultivated the sense that they were useful to women and guardians of feminine delicacy. Stories of women who suffered in silence because they could not bring themselves to discuss their symptoms with male physicians also helped promote the cause. Physician Georgiana Glenn made such an argument before the Northwest Ohio Medical Association in 1875: "While we are no advocate of the false delicacy that is often manifested by women in necessary examinations by physicians, yet it is nevertheless true that there are women so constituted, either by nature or education, that it is impossible for them to acquaint their physician with the symptoms in their case necessary to make a correct diagnosis; furthermore, it will not be denied that woman can comprehend more readily the feelings of woman" (244). Proponents of the woman-doctor movement crafted the character of the woman physician in ways that took advantage of nineteenth-century beliefs about women's physical modesty and their unique experiences as members of the feminine "sphere."

Glenn went on to explain her belief that it was "important . . . that the mother should have access to a medical adviser whom she can approach unrestrainedly and without reserve. One to whom she can open all her maternal heart: to one who can fully sympathize, as *only woman can*, with all her imaginary woes or real sufferings!" (244). In emphasizing women physicians' ability to empathize with their female patients, Glenn capitalized on the separate spheres ideology, arguing that women patients needed women physicians. Constructing the woman physician as especially attuned to women's problems and needs would also become a significant source of authority for her: because men and women were believed by many in the nineteenth century to be utterly different in terms of biology, experience, spirit, and intellect, no man could claim to understand women fully. Women physicians filled this void, constructing an ethos "in between" their roles as physicians and as middle-class women, combining their professional authority with the experiential authority earned by living as a woman among women. For a society frequently distraught by questions about women's health and social purpose, a writer or speaker who could speak simultaneously as a medical professional and as one who truly understood women could claim a significant amount of attention and influence.

In defense of their career choices late in the century, women physicians also drew on the growing respect of both the general public and the profession for the scientific measurement of phenomena. For example, to convince the public and the profession that women possessed the physical and nervous strength to succeed as physicians, women physicians turned to surveys of their colleagues—an empirical, scientific approach—to present an image of women physicians who were not broken down by their study and practice, but rather strengthened. One example of a survey of this type was reported in 1881 by Emily F. Pope, Emma L. Call, and C. Augusta Pope, staff physicians at the New England Hospital for Women and Children, who had surveyed over four hundred women physicians with sponsorship from the American Social Science Association (Morantz-Sanchez, *Sympathy* 55). In their report, Pope, Call, and Pope concluded that medical careers did not place undue strain on the female physique: "When we see the large proportion of women who have borne the strain of from five to thirty years' practice, not only without breaking down, but with actual improvement of their physical condition, it seems as if some unnecessary anxiety had been wasted on this point. We do not think it would be easy to find a better record of health among an equal number of women, taken at random from all over the country" (7).[8] Relying on empirical evidence to counter opponents' claims that women were too frail to practice medicine simultaneously positioned women as healthy enough for medical work and as participants in the profession's move toward science and its premium on values such as objectivity and measurability.

Other women physicians went further, claiming that women's work as physicians not only improved their physical health but also complemented the performance of feminine duties. For example, another survey from 1881 demonstrated that women's professional work was supportive of maternity. Rachel L. Bodley, dean of the Woman's Medical College of Pennsylvania, gave a commencement address reporting on a survey of alumnae in which she noted that 45 out of 52 women physicians believed that their medical work had had a positive influence on their domestic roles as wives and mothers (9). Bodley reassured her audience that women physicians were still good mothers and could continue to claim the respect and authority associated with motherhood. At the same time, she defended them against some of their opponents' attacks and attributed several broad benefits to the professional lifestyle: "If it be true as our statistics have shown, that an earnest purpose in life transforms invalids into healthy women, if it extracts the sting from morbid grief, if it renders that unholy thing, a marriage of convenience, inexcusable, and leaves every woman free to enter the estate of matrimony from the purest motives only, then how desirable is the possession of such a purpose!" (16). Bodley used her survey evidence to prove that, rather than undermining women's physical strength and social positions, professional careers actually solved many of the problems that had resulted in widespread anxiety about the health and role of women in the nineteenth-century United States.

In reporting the results of surveys of women physicians, Pope, Call, Pope, and Bodley drew on the appreciation of science growing among members of the nineteenth-century public and the medical profession. In doing so, these women claimed the rhetorical space of speakers who held institutional positions within medicine (staff physicians and the dean of a medical college, respectively) and who had empirical evidence to support their claims that women could succeed as physicians. In 1881, the editor of the *Medical and Surgical Reporter* acknowledged the persuasive potential of a scientific approach to the issue of women in medicine when he introduced excerpts from Bodley's address:

> There is nothing like the logic of facts. To it all theories must be brought and tested. It is vain to attempt to escape its verdict.
>
> The question [of] whether women are calculated to be successful in the profession has been debated vigorously. Now is the time when we can ask, *Have they been* successful? The record is before us and open for inspection. ("Women as Physicians" 354).

The idea that women physicians ought to be judged on the basis of their record was also expressed by Pope, Call, and Pope, who concluded their report by asking that accounts of women's success or failure in medicine be based on a fair chance for women physicians: "As to the doubts which are expressed in regard to the mental fitness of women to practice medicine, all we ask is: give them as good a chance to gain knowledge as the men-students have, and then let them stand or fall by the results" (12). In presenting to the public and the profession empirical data regarding women physicians' careers, Pope, Call, and Pope and Bodley reflected the value both audiences placed on scientific evidence and fair play.

Because of the "intertwined" nature of ethos, logos, and pathos (N. Reynolds 327), the rhetorical stance (scientific researcher) adopted by Pope, Call, and Pope and Bodley allowed for logical arguments (based on quantitative evidence) and appeals to emotion (a sense of justice) that speakers positioned in other ethos locations might not have been able to make. Furthermore, in adopting a scientific or "objective" stance, Pope, Call, and Pope and Bodley defended against opponents' emotional arguments (fear of "manly" women and of the social changes women physicians represented) by shifting the debate from sentimental to scientific grounds. Their stance thus resisted emotions that hindered the positive representation of women physicians. This combination of appeals was persuasive: the editor of the

Medical and Surgical Reporter concluded that "As far as it goes, [Bodley's evidence] is a strong vindication of the propriety of those women studying medicine who have tastes and talents in that direction" ("Women as Physicians" 356).

Despite the fame of a few well-known women physicians and despite the profession's increasing acceptance of women among its ranks, even women who acquired their medical education later in the century faced the criticism that their careers had compromised their femininity. Women's efforts to overcome this criticism are described in a short story titled "A Maiden Effort" published in *Daughters of Æsculapius* (1897), a collection of short fiction, biography, and autobiography composed by students and alumnae of the Woman's Medical College of Pennsylvania (figure 1.2). This story, by then-medical student Julia Grice,[9] features three fictional students who discuss the popular opposition to women physicians and their strategies for overcoming it. While the problem they discuss was a real dilemma of representation for women physicians, the women in this narrative poke fun at themselves and at those who worry that their professional endeavors will undermine their femininity. For example, one of the characters describes her efforts to convince her friends and family that she has maintained her femininity:

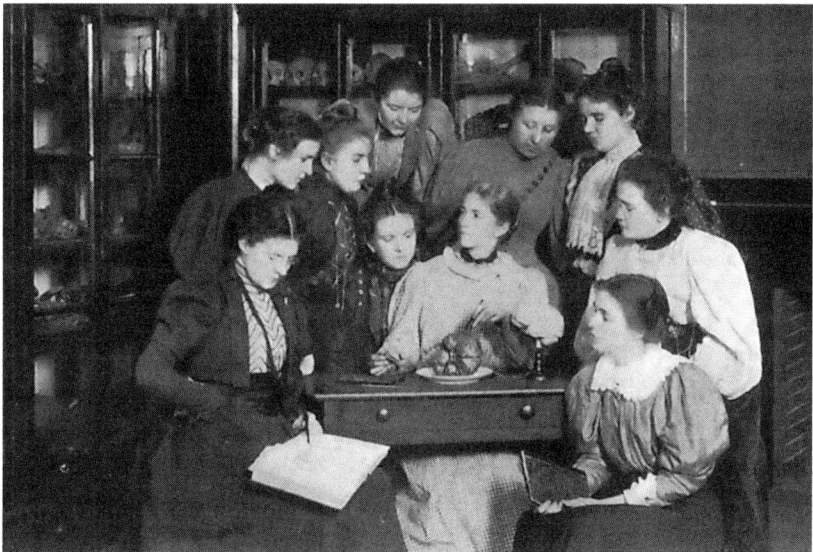

Figure 1.2. "A Brain Demonstration," frontispiece, *Daughters of Æsculapius*, 1897. Courtesy Rare Books and Manuscripts Library at the Ohio State University.

> It is strange how much prejudice still remains concerning the deteriorating effect of our work upon our womanliness. I am afraid that the personal effort to overcome some of the prejudice in my own family has added greatly to my vanity, for I have never dwelt so much upon the advantages of personal attractiveness as I have this winter. And I never owned such giddy head-gear as the Leghorn I hid under red roses the day I announced to the astonished world my intention of studying medicine, just to show that the concomitant idea was not bloomers or a billycock hat. (48–49)

In this passage, the fictional woman medical student evinces an awareness of the effect of her appearance on her ethos that Carol Mattingly identifies across nineteenth-century women rhetors. Mattingly notes that "clothing and appearance constituted a major component in the ethos women presented, an element taken for granted by men." Furthermore, "Women speakers' visual appearance, marking gender (feminine) and intersecting with location (public and improper for women), might instantly preclude a credible ethos and negate efforts to employ logical and pathetic appeals" (5). In the scene described above, the student's hat marks her gender (feminine), which intersects with the location in which she aspires to position herself (professional and improper for women). Maintaining a feminine ethos through feminine attire was one of the strategies this fictional woman, and possibly the woman who composed the narrative, used in persuading her family and friends of her desire to study medicine and in reassuring them that such a desire did not compromise her femininity.

The medical student then goes on to speak of her interactions with a young man who had difficulty accepting her career choice:

> But I've never been able to overcome the effect of one miserable incident that happened in connection with Sidney Brooke. He had evinced so much sympathy for my former schemes that I took its continuance for granted in this work. . . . But medicine! At first he occasionally came up to see me rather tentatively, and I talked so much about the femininity of our girls that he finally got the idea that we did little else at college than embroider pink roses and sing glees! But one afternoon he called for me at college, as bad luck would have it, just as the hall was full of girls in bloomers. They were on their way to the gym. class, but he couldn't know that. Then I appeared with a handful of scalpels which belonged to different girls, and which I was taking to have sharpened. I shall never forget that man's face. It had a don't-try-to-explain expression that nearly made me laugh; and I am sure I heard him mutter, "What some men have escaped! I never realized before what medicine had done for us!" We talked of every other subject

as we walked home—Mme. Melba and the Venezuela question—
and I have not seen him since. (49–50)

Although the medical student relating these events seems to be making fun
of Sidney Brooke, she also seems to regret the loss of his friendship. This
anecdote and the lengths to which this fictional student went to reassure
her friends and family that her decision to study medicine had not destroyed
her femininity indicate the writer's awareness of how crucial overt markers
of femininity were for women physicians.

The student's appearance with scalpels in hand, following as it did Brooke's
encounter with the bloomer-clad young women, linked medicine with man-
nishness in his mind. The scalpels, indicative of surgery (and therefore physical intimacy and penetration of the physical form), held by the handful,
suggested the horrific images of callous women conjured by some opponents
of women in medicine. Interestingly, the medical student has simple explanations for everything Brooke sees—the bloomers are for gym class and the
scalpels belong to other students—suggesting to readers that any unusual
behavior they may have witnessed or heard attributed to women physicians
also had reasonable, reassuring explanations. These explanations, however,
demonstrate how necessary it was for women physicians to maintain an
appropriately feminine self-presentation: What could the student have said
if bloomers were the everyday wear of medical women? What would it have
meant to readers for one young lady to own a handful of scalpels? For women
physicians, medicine could not appear to have undermined their femininity in the least; their goal, then, was to use rhetoric, including narrative, to
create an image of a feminine professional, one who gracefully balanced her
intellectual accomplishments with her feminine charms.

Just as the earliest women physicians justified their career choices on the
grounds that female patients needed women physicians, women later in the
century also pointed to the benefits they could offer their female patients.
For example, in the short story "*Mater Dolorosa—Mater Felix*: A Sketch from
Hospital Life," a woman physician single-handedly changes the course of her
patient's life. This narrative was written by Anna M. Fullerton[10] for *Daughters
of Æsculapius*. In the story, a woman physician helps her patient with what she
calls "the old, sad tale of an orphaned girl, defenseless, destitute, hungering
for love and the sweetness of home-life, trusting, in the utter abandonment of
girlish devotion, the promises of her lover, and finding herself at last betrayed
and forsaken" (54–55). After reminding her patient's lover of his responsibilities as a man and as a father, she convinces him to marry her patient. Years
later, the mother, now married, returns to the doctor and exclaims, "I could
not forget how my happiness came through you. I owe it all to you, dear

doctor, all to you!" (65). This narrative cast women physicians as sympathetic toward vulnerable women and uniquely positioned by virtue of their expertise and their standing as professionals to assist them. It also suggested the effects women physicians might have on society: if there were more women with the authority to enforce men's moral duties toward women, women would benefit financially and socially, and illegitimacy might occur less frequently.[11]

Taken together, the accounts (in fiction and nonfiction) *of* women physicians written *by* women physicians demonstrate that although they could capitalize on their position between medicine and proper femininity in order to construct an ethos that reflected nineteenth-century society's concern for vulnerable women, women physicians also had to reassure their public audiences that they had not sacrificed their own femininity for their careers. In other words, women physicians' role as a bridge between medicine's expertise and women's concerns was not enough to ensure their acceptance; they also needed to prove that they had not "unsexed" themselves. One proof of women physicians' continued femininity was offered by prominent Brooklyn surgeon and medical researcher Mary Dixon Jones,[12] who in 1898 maintained that "There is nothing that ever was, or ever can be in the medical profession, sufficiently bright or dazzling to make women forget their little ones. Women are women, whether they be physicians, day laborers, students, or queens in their palaces; they all alike love their homes and love to care for their children" (Rev. of *Woman's Medical* 172). Ironically, nineteenth-century women physicians often insisted, as did their opponents, on the immutable nature of femininity. Unlike their opponents, however, women physicians believed that femininity was not an obstacle to success in medicine. Instead, they maintained that their professional work strengthened them physically and made them better able to care for their families and their patients.

The Persuasive Character of the Woman Physician

In the nineteenth-century woman-doctor debate, rational arguments for and against women physicians intertwined with constructions of the character of the woman physician. In order to gain access to the profession, women physicians contested opponents' claims that women lacked the physical and temperamental strength to be physicians and that they would upset the social order by moving into a "masculine" domain through constructing a competing version of the character of the woman physician. For those audiences who found the values embodied by the ideal woman physician persuasive, women physicians possessed authority and expertise that combined the most influential characteristics of *woman* and *physician*. As physician Charles F.

Folsom explained in 1891, "The community needs . . . a woman's educational view of morality, rectifying and raising standards; and therein, perhaps, is one opportunity of many for the woman physician of the future to help. By bringing the work of the best women into the practice of medicine the medical profession must be benefited and the world may be improved." Folsom's certainty about the benefits women physicians offered their communities was far from universal, however. There were some in the nineteenth-century American public and in the medical profession who never accepted the positive characteristics women physicians sought to associate with their new professional role. Although supporters found the merging of *woman* and *physician* appealing, others found the combination unsettling.

The constraints women physicians faced in crafting an effective ethos and the persuasive opportunities they developed through strategic ethos construction demonstrate the need for a comprehensive feminist model of ethos. Almost every scholar of historical women's rhetorical activity has noted that one of the primary obstacles to women's participation in the rhetorical sphere has been the ethos problem posed by the incompatibility between the characteristics associated with speakers and those associated with women. The points of incompatibility were multiplied when women claimed to speak and write as professionals. As the following chapters demonstrate, women physicians' efforts to persuade through ethos were much more complex than character appeals made by rhetors who enjoy "insider" status and who are from groups historically permitted to engage in rhetorical activity.

Therefore, the rhetoric of nineteenth-century women physicians can be used as a case study to aid in the articulation of the strategies whereby historical women have crafted, resisted, and made use of ethos. The feminist model of ethos (which neither essentially nor exclusively pertains to women's rhetoric) that begins to emerge from this study acknowledges the following features of ethos:

- It is constrained by the social beliefs about and the material resources available to certain classes of rhetors (Pittman; Applegarth).
- It is often not crafted in response to a coherent and identifiable set of audience values but instead is composed in a dynamic context that includes multiple competing ideas about the "best" virtues, which can make it difficult to select and represent the audience's most esteemed values; consequently, ethos formation frequently involves value negotiations and often reciprocity between rhetor and audience identity constructs.

- It is intertwined with other discursive features, such as genre (Applegarth).
- It influences not only an individual rhetor's immediate communicative situation but also the broader context and the persuasive options available to other potential speakers and writers.
- It can be collectively developed and deployed (Micciche 175); consequently, a rhetor can develop her ethos indirectly, by shaping her audience's perception of the groups to which she belongs.

A comprehensive feminist model of ethos will help us better identify the rhetorical practices of women and others whose exclusion from the conventional rhetorical sphere has required them to invent persuasive strategies not accounted for in the theory and instructional methods developed to meet the needs of those with easier access to positions from which to speak and write.

2

Prescribing for Society: Women Physicians' Reform Rhetoric

> As a Physician, the author believes that her duties are not *all* in the sick-room, for, after an experience of over fifteen years, she finds herself loudly called to diagnose the great body politic, more thoroughly than ever before, and her prognosis is, that *doubling* the dose at the Ballot-box will produce convalescence.
> —Mary Edwards Walker, *Hit* (1871)

In *Hit* (1871), a book addressing all the major reform issues of the day, Mary Edwards Walker[1] strategically reminded her readers of her professional status. She used medical terminology, including *diagnose, prognosis, dose,* and *convalescence* in her call for women's votes (122). In positioning herself as a physician authorized to comment on the state of the nation and ordering a course of action, Walker moved beyond the role of personal medical consultant that physicians typically performed; she even moved beyond the role of the public health adviser. Instead, Walker converted her position as a professional into an ethos that authorized her advocacy of women's rights. In this chapter, I argue that Walker and other nineteenth-century women physicians relied primarily on their professional status, rather than on conventional feminine rhetorical resources such as morality and maternity, to authorize their intervention in a variety of situations that fell within the wide sphere of nineteenth-century medical influence. John S. Haller and Robin M. Haller note that "as the medical profession became more and more aware of the link between mental state and physical well-being, and recognized the significance of psychosomatic illness, the doctor, through his diagnostic and healing skills, soon found himself with the additional responsibility of acting as the arbiter of fashion, the watchman of morals, and the judge of personal needs" (x). Because health was understood to be affected by factors as diverse as building codes, educational practices, occupational opportunities, diet, marriage, and the environment, women physicians' professional expertise and experience served as important components of their ethē when they advocated social reforms.

Many nineteenth-century women physicians participated in the suffrage movement and other efforts to increase rights and opportunities for women.[2] In fact, the woman-doctor movement was intricately woven into the broader women's rights movement. The two movements even shared a common starting point: Elizabeth Blackwell's matriculation at Geneva Medical College (November 1847), Harriot Hunt's first request to attend medical lectures at Harvard (December 1847), and the Seneca Falls women's rights convention (July 1848) all occurred within nine months of each other. In fact, the Declaration of Sentiments, the product of the Seneca Falls convention, included among its resolutions a demand for women's admission to the professions and other occupations: "Resolved, That the speedy success of our cause depends upon the zealous and untiring efforts of both men and women, for the overthrow of the monopoly of the pulpit, and for the securing to woman an equal participation with men in the various trades, professions, and commerce" (Seneca Falls Convention 142).

Women prominent in the woman-doctor movement were often also leaders in the women's rights movement. For example, homeopath Clemence Lozier, who founded the New York Medical College and Hospital for Women in 1863, also served as president of the National Woman Suffrage Organization from 1877 to 1878. Marie Zakrzewska, who founded the New England Hospital for Women and Children in 1862, was active in the Massachusetts Woman Suffrage Association, the New England Woman Suffrage Association, and the Association for the Advancement of Women (Tuchman, *Science* 170).[3] Both supporters and detractors recognized the woman-doctor movement as an arm of the women's rights movement. For example, in 1894 woman physician and suffrage advocate Mary Putnam Jacobi wrote of the links between the activism of sisters-in-law Elizabeth Blackwell and Lucy Stone: "the work of these two women, the one in medicine, the other for equal suffrage, constituted the two necessary halves of one idea" ("Common Sense" 49).[4]

In addition to their work on behalf of women's rights, many women physicians also participated in the other reforms that middle-class nineteenth-century women supported, particularly those related to health, including the temperance, dress reform, social purity, and urban reform movements. In doing so, however, women physicians drew on different rhetorical resources than nonprofessional women did, particularly their expertise and experience as physicians. In order to understand women physicians' ethos strategies and the role of professionalism as a rhetorical resource on which they drew, it may be helpful to bear in mind the contexts in which their ethē were deployed, particularly the features of nineteenth-century rhetoric, women's reform strategies, and women's roles in the public sphere.

In the nineteenth-century United States, the moral and religious grounds on which women had historically based their ethē were being surpassed by respect for professional expertise and authority. Gregory Clark and S. Michael Halloran describe the evolution of rhetorical values over the course of the nineteenth century, stating that "the traditional principle of collective moral authority" was challenged by individual moral authority and, eventually, by "the authority of the expert": "It was this new public morality of expertise that defined the professional culture we see characterizing the United States by the end of that century" (3). This shift in rhetorical authority reflected the rapid changes occurring in American society: "as the political and economic realities of the American community changed during the nineteenth century, its public discourse, in theory as well as in practice, changed as well" (3). Specifically, and importantly for women who had relied on their supposed moral superiority to authorize their reform work, the basis for reform changed after the Civil War, with the decline of morally and religiously driven reforms "and the beginning of the ascension of a new faith and commitment to science and scientific reform" (Giesberg 18). As medical professionals, women physicians were well positioned to capitalize on the growing preference for reforms based in scientific rationales.

As outlined in the previous chapter, the public's perception of medicine as a profession, and of women as medical professionals, was complicated in the nineteenth-century United States. The strongest students tended not to pursue medical education: medical students had a reputation for being unruly, and proprietary schools often sacrificed quality education for profit. Historian John Duffy explains that medicine's reputation was particularly low in the 1840s and 1850s, and the average member of the profession did not achieve high social or financial status until well into the twentieth century (181–82). Although many nineteenth-century physicians earned a meager living, sometimes supplementing their medical work with farming or other jobs, there were some physicians who achieved a higher economic and social position; these elite practitioners "enjoyed both social position and wealth" (182). Duffy observes that physicians with higher standing shared a number of characteristics: they tended to come from affluent families, to have completed both college and medical school (a college degree was not a requirement for admission to many medical schools), to have extended their medical studies in Europe, to serve as professors at respected medical schools, to treat well-off patients, and, by the end of the century, to specialize in a particular branch of medical practice (182). Although the profession as a whole was not held in high regard, these well-placed physicians were highly respected. Women were not likely to attain the highest status according to these measures, since they were barred from teaching at men's medical schools, including the elite, well-funded schools. Women also faced ongoing resistance to their decision to pursue medical careers. However, based on the results of a survey of women physicians, Duffy observes that "in terms of income and membership in medical societies, female medical graduates would appear to have been doing better than their male counterparts" (291). He attributes women physicians' relatively high social and financial status to the more uniformly affluent and educated backgrounds of the women who pursued medical careers: "[Women's] success probably speaks more for the strength of character needed for women to enter medicine and their middle- or upper-class background than any other factor. The many semi-illiterate, lower-class males who had access to the medical profession at that time were not too likely to build a profitable middle-class practice" (291). Although simply practicing medicine was not enough for a physician to claim a high social status and the ethos advantages that accompanied it, formally educated women physicians tended to possess the characteristics of respected professionals.

Furthermore, even physicians in rural areas, who were not affiliated with the better medical schools and whose practices often did not contain the numbers of affluent patients needed to earn a substantial income, enjoyed a degree of respect in their communities. A physician could easily be the most highly educated citizen in his or her area, and physicians were often active participants in local political and social activities. In both community and individual affairs, physicians relied on their historical roles as moral advisors. Duffy explains that "the role of family doctor in Protestant America had always carried with it certain aspects of a father confessor and moral arbitrator. Many physicians happily accepted their moral obligations and used the authority of medicine to support the accepted middle-class moral values" (185). Even if nineteenth-century physicians were not respected as professionals in the sense that they would be in the twentieth century, they could still exert significant influence on their patients and communities; this may not have been the prestige of the expert, but it was an important ethos resource nonetheless. Influence over moral matters was compatible with the moral authority traditionally attributed to women and mothers, so this aspect of the physician's ethos was not a new ethos location for women physicians; instead, they were able to extend their virtuous ethos by adding their professional status to it.

Finally, despite the unevenness of the regard the public felt for the medical profession, a medical education and the out-of-doors career it made available to women provided them with rhetorical tools previously inaccessible to women. The advanced education many women physicians acquired made them experts when few women had access to higher education, let alone access to scientific knowledge, like human anatomy and physiology, that had previously been prohibited to them. Working among a wide range of people afforded women physicians a form of firsthand experience unavailable to women whose lives were largely confined to domestic activities. Although a medical career might not automatically earn one the respect of a community, an assessment of the rhetorical influence of the physician must consider the context. For women, working as physicians meant gaining access to new persuasive tools that they could only rarely acquire in any other way, while men could pursue multiple routes to education, wealth, and public status. Despite the complicated and evolving nature of professional respect in the nineteenth century, the women physicians who succeeded in their careers benefited from their professional status because of the rhetorical opportunities it opened up for them.

Developing ethos strategies for calling attention to women's professional status was a crucial development for women's rhetoric. Rhetors, male or female, who could present their assessments of situations from a position that the public understood as "expert" and who could ground their proposals in professional experience were likely to convince audiences to accept their plans. Such arguments did not have to be "scientific" in the twenty-first century sense, but instead had to be recognizable according to the multiple and evolving notions of "science" viable in the nineteenth century. Thus, in 1881 spiritualist, water-cure physician, and radical reformer Juliet H. Severance defended her right to speak on behalf of Free Love by reference to scientific objectivity: "Let this [Free Love] and all other subjects receive careful, thorough and impartial discussion and analysis. In this way we will show ourselves scientific investigators instead of bigoted ignoramuses" (11). Because the public turned to experts, including professionals, for leadership on critical issues, women who wanted to be listened to needed to shift the bases for their rhetorical authority from exclusive reliance on religion, morality, and familial relationships to include scientific professionalism also. If women had not claimed the expertise and social status of professionals, they would have had a much more difficult time making meaningful contributions to many of the turn-of-the-century social debates.

In her account of women's participation in the United States Sanitary Commission (USSC) during the Civil War,[5] Judith Ann Giesberg identifies a shift in the rhetorical methods of the women involved in the USSC: by the end of the war, these women "commanded the respect of commission men by appealing to them as colleagues, not as 'ladies' or moral superiors. Without abandoning sex-specific appeals and a separatist strategy, women at the commission branches adopted the rhetoric and tactics of male professionals and acted in distinctly political ways" (171–72). Women physicians, involved in the institutions and discourses of medicine, likely took a similar approach toward advocating social reform. Women physicians also reflected the late-century trend toward college-educated reform women who did not base their ethē or their arguments for reform primarily on maternity or domesticity (Ryan, *Mysteries* 166). Even though women physicians were not alone in their motivations or methods for reform work, they did still occupy social positions more strongly identified with scientific professionalism than did many reform-minded women. Because women physicians were professionals, they had access to different rhetorical resources than nonprofessional women did. Consequently, their arguments often relied on the appeals, evidence, and rationales appropriate to rhetors with the status, expertise, and experience of physicians.

Linkages between reform work and economic structures, such as professionalism, were important components of women's activism in the nineteenth-century United States. In her study of the 1850s women's rights movement, Natasha Kirsten Kraus draws attention to the ways that women's rights activists exploited the inconsistencies inherent in popular conceptions of *woman* in order to redefine that concept in ways that would allow women to participate in both politics and the economy (183). Kraus contends that women's political rights were only achieved through concomitant transformations in a network of concepts and institutions: "women could not have gained political rights such as suffrage unless a transformative disruption of social meanings and institutions of Womanhood, contract, the economy, and the nation had already occurred" (75). The women physicians who participated in social movement rhetoric benefited from and extended the work of earlier women's rights activists, who "refigured True Womanhood complexly, dovetailing popularly accepted social meanings of Womanhood with shifts in meaning that placed education, financial independence, and the right to contract at the center of a radically altered True Woman" (Kraus 169–70). Women physicians exemplified the educated, financially independent model of womanhood developed at midcentury. Seen through the lens of Kraus's analysis, women physicians' professionalism, which was in part an economic position, was interwoven with and necessary to their reform work, particularly their activism on behalf of women. They adopted a professional ethos and used the expertise associated with that role to authorize their reform arguments.

In order to achieve the popular persuasion essential to effecting social change, women physicians necessarily engaged in public rhetorical acts. Their reform activism, which took the form of convention speeches, formal addresses, books, and articles in newspapers and magazines, confirms Mary P. Ryan's assertion that "Contrary to common assumptions that women's place in nineteenth-century America was in the home, it is not difficult to locate Victorian women . . . in the public arena" (*Women* 3). Furthermore, Lindal Buchanan's observation that antebellum expectations for feminine domesticity varied across race and class might also be adapted to apply to women physicians during and after the Civil War: "antebellum women who worked outside the home, whether due to economics or enslavement, confronted markedly different gender norms and constraints than those encountered by more privileged women. The cult of true womanhood, therefore, chiefly affected the latter group's efforts to . . . speak in public" (27). Although women physicians often came from middle-class backgrounds, their work outside the home complicated their positions relative to traditional gender norms for their class. African American and American Indian women physicians, as well as white women physicians who turned to medical careers out of financial necessity, also spoke publicly from complex gendered, raced, and classed positions.

For all of these women, speaking and writing publicly as professionals were not only viable options, but also options that afforded women access to a range of persuasive tools previously unavailable to them. This chapter examines the strategic uses to which women physicians put their ethē as professionals in support of their reform commitments. In particular, I focus on nineteenth-century women physicians who connected their reform work to their medical expertise and experience, who saw their efforts on behalf of social change as extensions of their responsibilities as physicians. Unlike most of the (nonprofessional) women activists studied by rhetorical scholars, these women physicians relied on their professional status to authorize their rhetorical activity, rather than justifying it as an extension of traditional feminine roles. Acknowledging this aspect of women's rhetorical activity broadens our sense of the scope of nineteenth-century women's persuasive strategies. In particular, women physicians' reform rhetoric relied on *professional witnessing* as well as on *prescribing for society*, two ethos-based persuasive strategies that emphasized women physicians' authority *as physicians* to promote social reforms.

Professional Witnessing

Professional witnessing by nineteenth-century women physicians occurred when a rhetor described what she had seen in her professional practice to authorize her calls for reform. Operating at the intersection between ethos and logos, professional witnessing functioned both as evidence supporting a woman physician's argument and as reference to her experience and authority. Examining the role of women physicians' professional experiences in authorizing their reform rhetoric is one means of answering Julie Nelson Christoph's call "to ask how the personal affects writing that is less clearly personal" than autobiographical narrative incorporated into academic writing and research (661). Christoph argues that most scholarly attention to the personal in writing has a narrow focus, one that restricts our understanding of the range of rhetorical uses for the personal: "in limiting our explorations of the personal to explicitly autobiographical scholarly writing, we have missed many of the potential ways and settings in which writers invoke the personal" (660). Because extensive professional experience, measured in years of practice or in numbers of cases, was one of the qualities that garnered one respect as a physician, professional autobiography was already incorporated into the persuasive medical ethos operative in nineteenth-century America. In pointing to what they had witnessed and experienced in their professional roles, women physicians conveyed the sense that they had firsthand knowledge of the conditions they sought to reform while reminding audiences that they were objective medical professionals, not just ordinary individuals providing what might be a biased account of events. Even before medicine was recognized as a prestigious profession affording its members an authoritative and expert ethos, physicians could point to their wide experience as evidence and use that experience as part of their ethē. For women, who had historically lacked access to such rhetorical resources, the ability to ground their arguments in interactions with a wide range of people outside of their families and friends was an important addition to their persuasive practices. Near the end of the century, as medicine grew in prestige, women physicians were able to combine their experience with the authority and expertise associated with professionalism. Together, their professional experience and expertise suggested that women physicians had special insight into and an expert, objective perspective on the problems they sought to reform.

Because women physicians were committed to improving the lives of women and because they perceived their scope for doing so in the broad terms of nineteenth-century medical influence, some women physicians called for the ballot on behalf of the patients whom their professional experience led them to believe had been physically and emotionally harmed by their exclusion from the polls. For example, Harriot Hunt reported in her autobiography (figure 2.1) that when she revealed to her friends her intention to attend the 1850 women's rights convention at Worcester, they warned her that she might lose social standing by identifying with the suffrage movement: "I decided to go to Worcester—many of my friends regretted this—they urged that it would be ridiculous for me to identify myself with such a motley crew,—some scolded, some entreated, some said I should lose caste." Hunt went on to explain her reasons for ignoring her friends' counsel through drawing attention to the pain she had witnessed as a physician: "What was all this to one, who for fifteen years had been the confidant of woman, who had known that her diseases resulted in great measure from her position; who had sympathized with the heart-broken, prescribed for the penniless, and mingled her tears with the widow and the fatherless?" (*Glances* 250). Asserting a rationale based in her professional experience rather than in a conventional feminine role, Hunt explained her women's rights work in different terms than most nonprofessional women did. She protected her ethos from questions such as, "Then you wish to be a man?" and "So you are going to take man's place?" (*Glances* 256) and simultaneously presented herself as altruistic, as inspired by what she had witnessed in her medical practice to strive to benefit women.

Elsewhere in her autobiography, Hunt justified her work for greater political and occupational rights for women by reference to the lives of her patients: "How frequently I have heard that woman's sphere is at home, and, remembering the many women among my patients whose poverty denied them a home, felt the cruelty of this mockery of the poor!" (*Glances* 151). Hunt described her commitment to women's rights as growing out of her medical practice; at the same time, her practice provided rhetorical material that she could use as evidence supporting suffrage and occupational opportunities for women, material inaccessible to other women and to men physicians, in whom women were, it was believed, less likely to confide. Therefore, in addition to crafting a persuasive ethos built on her sympathy for women's plight, Hunt also presented herself as possessing special insight into the condition of women.

Just a few years later, Marie Zakrzewska adopted an approach similar to Hunt's, drawing attention to the fact that her career had exposed her to situations that other women had not witnessed. In *A Practical Illustration of "Woman's Right to Labor"* (1860), a sequel to Caroline Dall's *Woman's Right to Labor* (1860), Marie Zakrzewska drew attention to her unique position as a witness to social degradation. This approach to the question of the propriety of occupations for women outside the home contributed a different perspective

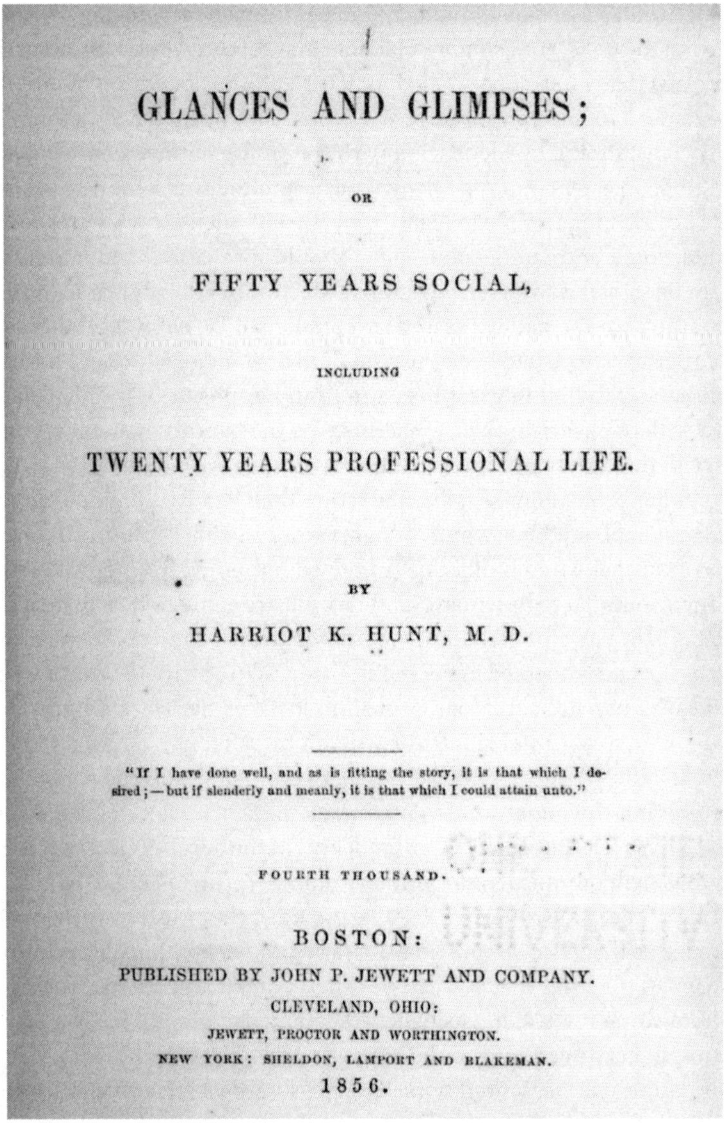

GLANCES AND GLIMPSES;

OR

FIFTY YEARS SOCIAL,

INCLUDING

TWENTY YEARS PROFESSIONAL LIFE.

BY

HARRIOT K. HUNT, M. D.

"If I have done well, and as is fitting the story, it is that which I desired;—but if slenderly and meanly, it is that which I could attain unto."

FOURTH THOUSAND.

BOSTON:

PUBLISHED BY JOHN P. JEWETT AND COMPANY.

CLEVELAND, OHIO:

JEWETT, PROCTOR AND WORTHINGTON.

NEW YORK: SHELDON, LAMPORT AND BLAKEMAN.

1856.

Figure 2.1. Title page of Harriot K. Hunt's autobiography, *Glances and Glimpses*, 1856.

to the ongoing debate, which more commonly focused on concerns such as women's physical and temperamental capabilities, the neglect of families believed to result from women's work, and the lack of options open to women compelled to work because of financial necessity. According to Zakrzewska, the opponents of women's occupations were reluctant to have women learn of the degradation that existed in society: "It is my honest and earnest conviction, that the reason that men are unwilling for women to enter upon public or business life is, not so much the fear of competition, or the dread lest women should lose their gentleness, and thus deprive society of this peculiar charm, as the fact that they are ashamed of the foulness of life which exists outside of the house and home. . . . If I could but give to all women the tenth part of my experience, they would see that this is true" (46). In asserting that the true reason women were limited to domestic work was men's embarrassment of "the foulness of life," Zakrzewska reminded her readers that as a physician she had witnessed aspects of humanity unavailable to most women and men. She suggested that any woman who had observed what she had seen would come to the same conclusion about the need for women's occupations that Zakrzewska had; this claim built identification with her readers, whom she implied would think as she did, and it insinuated that she was a reasonable person who drew logical conclusions from the evidence at hand.

Zakrzewska's story also included moments in which she explained how her professional experience informed her commitment to the cause of work for women. For example, she drew on the confession of a patient to explain women's poor health as a consequence of their financial dependence on and obedience to men: "I thank Heaven, my dear doctor, that you are a woman; for now I can tell you the truth about my health. It is not my body that is sick, but my heart. These flounces and velvets cover a body that is sold,—sold legally to a man who could pay my father's debts" (120). In recounting this exchange, Zakrzewska reminded readers that she possessed special insight into women's condition by virtue of her medical practice. Zakrzewska's narrative proved she was knowledgeable because her professional rounds brought her in contact with women in a range of circumstances—often poor, sometimes prostitutes, sometimes abandoned by lovers, sometimes in loveless marriages—and from these women she learned about lives unknown to many middle-class women.

As a woman who had herself pursued a nondomestic career, Zakrzewska was well positioned to argue for women's ability to reform society from outside the home: "Only faith in ourselves and in each other is needed to work a reformation. Let woman enter fully into business, with its serious responsibilities and duties; let it be made as honorable and as profitable to her as to men; let her have an equal opportunity for earning competence and comfort,—and we shall need no other purification of society" (46–47). Zakrzewska's experience as a feminine professional justified her proposal: "One fact I learned, . . . that men always sympathize with fallen and wretched women, while women themselves are the first to raise and cast the stone at them. Why is this? . . . The reason is, that men know the world; that is, they know the obstacles in the path of life, and that they draw lines to exclude women from earning an honest livelihood, while they throw opportunities in their way to earn their bread by shame. All men are aware of this: therefore the good as well as the bad give pity to those that claim it" (45–46). When Zakrzewska described what she learned while working as a midwife in Berlin and later as a physician in the United States, she relied on autobiographical experience to demonstrate her sympathy for women and her knowledge of the world outside the domestic sphere. Although other nineteenth-century women sought economic conditions that would provide options for women other than prostitution, most of them could not ground their arguments in professional experience. Unlike nonprofessional women, Zakrzewska was in a position to present her advocacy of broader occupational opportunities for women as an outgrowth of her professional experience combined with her concern for the welfare of women.

Professional witnessing was also used to refute claims made by opponents of suffrage. For example, in 1883, thirty years after Hunt grounded her commitment to women's votes in her professional experience, homeopath Clemence Lozier cited her professional experience as evidence in her refutation of former Surgeon General of the U.S. Army Dr. William A. Hammond's characterization of women as unfit to vote. Writing in the *North American Review*, Lozier first quoted Hammond, who claimed that "As woman cannot reason abstractly, neither can she reason exactly. . . . On account of her inability to be exact in regard to her age, the diseases she may have had, her mode of life, and other matters in which exactness is required, life insurance companies decline to issue policies to her" (516). In contrast, Lozier asserted, "The gentleman is wholly incorrect. Insurance companies insure women's lives at slightly advanced rates, because of childbirth risks. I myself was examining surgeon for the New York Globe Mutual for many years" (516). In this case, Lozier's professional background allowed her to present herself as more knowledgeable than her opponent and gave her access to information that she used to refute his claims. As a physician and former employee of an insurance company, Lozier could point to professional expertise and experience, crafting an ethos previously unavailable to women. She went on to suggest that Hammond's own professional experience might have clouded his opinions of women: "Perhaps Dr. Hammond's practice among sick, weak, abnormally emotional and artificially stimulated patients, forming a wealthy *clientèle*, accounts for his view of woman" (516). Pitting her experience against his, Lozier challenged Hammond's professional authority as only another physician could.

Lozier also proposed possibilities for future professional witnessing in her refutation of Hammond's antisuffrage arguments. In making his argument, Hammond had drawn on a line of research going back at least to the mid-1800s that ranked human beings according to brain size, finding that men of Western European descent were the most evolved and intelligent and that men of other races, particularly African Americans, were not as intellectually developed; women were less developed than men, though white women might outrank men of other races. Influenced by this work, Hammond claimed that women's brains were smaller than men's and so women were unfit to vote. Countering this argument, Lozier posed the possibility of other criteria for measuring intellectual capacity and thus suggested that one day the professional's knowledge might be different: "Perhaps some day a woman anatomist will dissect the brains of several men, and discover wonderful twists in their convolutions, or absence of them, or thickening of the cranial plates or diploë, which, in her estimation, will disprove their ability to vote or to rule" (514). Later, Lozier suggested an alternative interpretation of existing data about brain size: "We might more reasonably claim that woman's [brain] structure appears more complex than man's. Comparative anatomy demonstrates highest complexity as indicating highest type" (515). In proposing alternative interpretations of data and suggesting that scientific findings might depend on the gendered interests of the researcher, Lozier used her familiarity with science to remind her readers that science is always provisional, pending the next study, so claims about women's "nature" based in scientific measurements ought to be taken as tentative until more balanced research could be performed. Lozier's arguments depended on her ethos as a practicing physician and an examining surgeon for an insurance company and on her strategy of positioning herself as a professional witness.

Another example of professional witnessing can be found in the writings of American Indian physician Susan La Flesche (later Picotte), who relied on her professional experience to advocate for her fellow Omahas. La Flesche, the first American Indian woman to earn a medical degree,[6] had been supported in her medical education by the Connecticut Indian Association (CIA), a group of upper-middle-class white women committed to "reforming" American Indians through missionary work, education, and home building (Tong 61). After graduating from the Woman's Medical College of Pennsylvania in 1889, La Flesche frequently published letters reporting her observations among the Omahas in the CIA's the *Indian Bulletin* and in the *Indian's Friend*, the publication of the CIA's parent organization, the Women's National Indian Association.

In these letters, La Flesche addressed her audience of white women tactically, appealing to their cultural biases in order to ensure that they would continue sending supplies. She expressed appreciation for the money and materials provided for the Omahas by the women's societies and demonstrated that the donations were being put to what the members of the CIA would have perceived to be good use. La Flesche further appealed to her audience by representing the Omahas as eager to adopt a white lifestyle. For example, in an account from 1889, she described her extensive nonmedical work as including several educational activities that would have appealed to her audience: "Sometimes I give them lessons in English and in numbers; one evening, hymns, such as 'Nearer my God to Thee;' [*sic*] they are learning this in Indian, also 'My country 'tis of thee.' One evening is devoted to scrapbooks and all we can learn from them, another night they are taught how to march, etc. They are very backward in speaking English, so the English lessons will be a help to them, after they have them regularly" ("From Dr. Susan La Flesche"). These signs of "progress" would have been well received by the CIA and would have encouraged club members to send more money and supplies.[7]

La Flesche also reported on her medical practice, noting that the Omahas readily accepted her as a woman physician from among their own people: "They have not shown the least prejudice so far towards women physicians. Members of both political parties come to me, which surprises me, for some thought the 'Non-progressives' would not come for political reasons" ("From Dr. Susan La Flesche"). In fact, in an 1891 letter, she described her work as extending well beyond conventional medical practice: "Many come to my office not only for medicine, but also for help in daily business affairs of different kinds, some to ask to have a letter translated for them, or to have one written, and some want a little interpreting done." Like other women physicians, La Flesche characterized her professional experience as extending beyond the bounds of conventional doctor-patient interactions. Her reports of her broad involvement in the activity of her community helped position her as an authority on the condition and the needs of the people around her. La Flesche also cast herself as useful, reassuring the Connecticut women that their investment in her education was paying off, explaining, "I have had more work among the women than I ever thought I would, for they have called me in to attend them in cases where a white doctor was never called before among the real Indians" ("A Letter").

La Flesche reported on the general health of her community and recounted specific cases, often using professional witnessing to highlight details that suggested the worthiness of her patients. In an 1892 address before her alma mater, the Hampton Institute, La Flesche told a story that reinforced the lessons of "civilization" the students were being taught. Called to the home of a woman suffering from consumption and *la grippe* (influenza), La Flesche found her patient, who had herself studied at Hampton, lying in one corner of a one-room house. She called the scene "a pathetic sight," but reassured her audience that "no one at Hampton would need feel ashamed of that quarter of the room. Her bed had sheets and pillow-cases. . . . The girl and everything in her quarter of the room were clean and neat as could be" ("My Work").

La Flesche retold the story of this dying woman on several occasions; in her report published in the *Indian's Friend* in 1892, she noted the careful attention paid to the patient by her husband: "Her young husband was devotion itself. He was awake every night and listened for the slightest whisper, ready every moment to lift her to a more comfortable position, seeming to know what she wanted even before she spoke. He never left her side" ("Our Medical Mission"). Such a characterization may have been intended to counter what La Flesche termed "the absurd question" she was sometimes asked: "Do the Indians really love their wives?" In response to this question, she asserted that "The Indians are *human beings* just as the white people are, and there are Indian men who are just as careful, watchful and affectionate to their wives as any one would wish to see anywhere" ("The Home Life"). Surrounding her assertions of the humanity of the Omahas with descriptions of her medical work might have functioned to mitigate some audience members' tendency to distrust La Flesche's claims as subjective or biased as a result of her identification with the Omahas.

The broad experience of the late nineteenth-century professional combined with his or her supposed objectivity and commitment to scientific truth might have reassured audiences of the trustworthiness of women physicians as rhetors. An ethos built on professional experience, therefore, was one method women physicians—particularly those who faced the combined obstacles of speaking as women and as members of nondominant ethnic groups—used to establish effective ethē despite being denied access to many of the virtues associated with an ideal speaker in nineteenth-century America.

In addition to the devoted husband portrayed above, in 1892 La Flesche also described a husband who was so sensitive that, despite being "a strong muscular man," he could not bear to hold his wife's head while La Flesche extracted a tooth:

One day I had to pull a young woman's tooth, and as the husband
was a strong muscular man I was in hopes he would support her
head for me. He sent for his brother to do it and when he saw me
take the forceps up he beat a hasty retreat. I heard him walking
up and down in the other room, and when they told him I was
through he appeared with such a happy relieved look on his face
and thanked me so earnestly. I could not help but be glad for
him that she was through with her suffering. There are many
instances like this that I know of. Of course, there are some cases
entirely different, and where there is no happiness. But so we find
it wherever we go in this world. ("The Home Life" 40)

La Flesche's professional access to the breadth of Omaha society at crucial
moments in family life provided her with anecdotes and other persuasive
material that she could use through professional witnessing to reassure
the CIA of the humanity and the worthiness of her community, thereby
justifying their continued financial support. Employing professional
witnessing in this way also enhanced La Flesche's ethos by reminding her
readers of her professionalism, her expertise and experience in matters related to medicine and to the Omahas, and her position as an intermediary
between the CIA and the Omahas.

Not all the news from Nebraska was good, however. La Flesche frequently
expressed outrage at the lengths to which whites went to sell alcohol to the
Omahas, including holding Omaha voters hostage and bribing them with
food so that they would vote against temperance measures. In her letters,
including one published under the title "The Omahas and Citizenship" in
1891, La Flesche emphasized the good intentions of the Omahas: "It seems
hard that when these people are trying to save themselves from the danger
of intoxicating drink, that a white man comes to put a stumbling block in the
way. We do not blame the Indians, for they do not understand all the ways
and methods of the white man." In a letter to the Commissioner of Indian
Affairs published in *The Indian's Friend* in 1900, La Flesche noted a recent rise
in bootlegging on the reservation and asked for the reinstatement of a deputy
to enforce laws prohibiting the sale of alcohol to the Omahas. Referring to
her professional experience, La Flesche characterized the change that had
taken place since the deputy left the reservation: "For four years, from 1889
to 1893, I worked among the Omahas, night and day, attending the sick. At
first I went everywhere alone, at any time of night or day and felt perfectly
safe among my people, but intemperance increased until men, women and
children drank; men and women died from alcoholism, and little children
were seen reeling on the streets of the town; drunken brawls in which men

were killed occurred, and no person's life was considered safe, and no person could cross the reservation without protection or firearms" ("Another Appeal"). The scenes La Flesche witnessed as she made her medical rounds authorized her appeal to the commissioner. Ethos would have been crucial in such an appeal, and La Flesche's ability to write to the commissioner as a professional addressing another member of the middle class might have earned her a more attentive reading than she would have received had she not been a professional woman.

For their part, nineteenth-century African American women physicians who wrote or spoke in public forums focused at least as much on advocating for their race as they did for their gender. Writing of nineteenth-century professional African American women, Jacqueline Jones Royster observes that "In addition to their achievements in the professional arena, these women were remarkable in terms of their social advocacy and activism and the consistency with which they wrote and spoke in public arenas in the interest of social change" (*Traces* 200). Many African American women physicians fit this pattern of combining professional accomplishments with public advocacy, using their professional expertise and authority to comment on the "nature" of African Americans, particularly to counter the belief that their weak constitutions made them more likely than whites to die of a range of diseases and conditions. Speaking before the Alabama State Teachers' Association in 1892, Halle Tanner Dillon (figure 2.2),[8] resident physician at the Tuskegee Normal and Industrial school, presented physiological education as vital to improving the status of her race. Drawing on the medical discourse of her time, early in her speech Dillon referred to "the laws governing our bodies," "the laws of health," and the tenets of heredity as it was understood in the nineteenth century. She also cited statistics on infant mortality, fertility rates, and the number of deaths from tuberculosis to compare the health of whites and African Americans. For example, after citing a report on the vital statistics for the state of Alabama, she combined citing statistics with referring to health principles: "What appalling figures these, and what a tale do they unfold! 502 colored infants perished for want of what we firmly believe to be knowledge as to the laws of health on the part of the parents" (184). Dillon's use of discourse conventions associated with science and medicine grounded her argument for social reform in her professional standing and expertise. In addition, in citing the "vital statistics of the State of Alabama" (184), Dillon relied on a source that her audience would perceive to be unbiased and factual. She used the statistics as the basis for her call for reform: "Poverty with its twin sisters, ignorance and immorality, no doubt claimed a portion of these deaths, but these figures give us incontestable proof of the necessity of teaching the great mass of our people how to observe the laws of health" (184). The compilation of mortality figures by the medical community in Alabama (Dillon attributed the report to Dr. Hayes) was a form of collective professional witnessing that Dillon tapped into to demonstrate her connection to the medical community and to justify the educational reforms she sought.

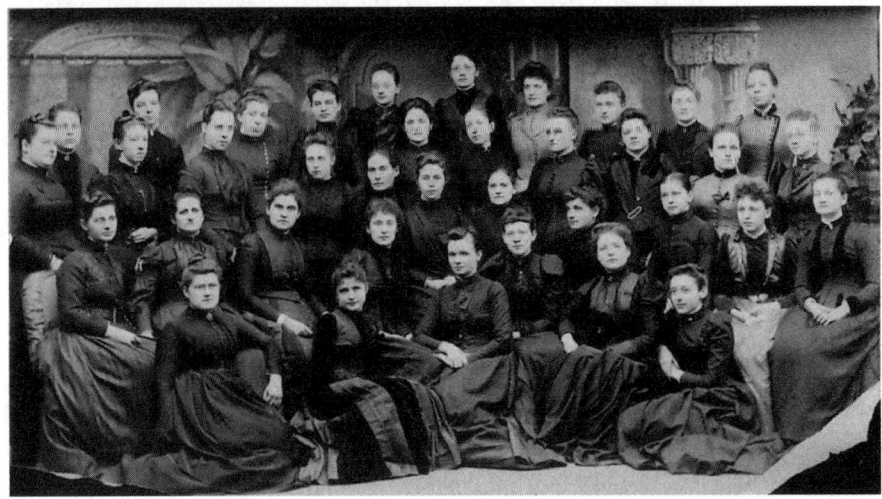

Figure 2.2. Woman's Medical College of Pennsylvania classes of 1891 and 1892. Halle Tanner Dillon is in the top row, right side. Courtesy Legacy Center, Drexel University College of Medicine.

Despite linking herself to the Alabama medical community, Dillon also distanced herself from white physicians by directly confronting their prejudices against their African American patients. After raising the question of why African Americans died at higher rates than whites, she referred to what she had witnessed as a professional among her colleagues, noting that "Our white physicians say that it is 'race characteristics chiefly'" (185). Rather than attributing the high mortality figures to the biology of African Americans as white physicians did, however, Dillon argued that it was "not so much race characteristics as race ignorance of the laws of health combined with race poverty." She went on to argue that if African American children enjoyed healthful surroundings as white children did, they would have similar chances of good health: "Where environments have been equal the colored boy or girl has shown the same, and often greater, ability to bear the ills of and combat with the various diseases than the white boy or girl" (185). Dillon made a related argument about adult women: "While white physicians look with pitying eye upon the black skin of their patients, thinking that certainly the 'race characteristics,' in which they believe so firmly, will surely prevent the wound from healing with the same ease as in the fairer skin, yet when both have the same antiseptic precautions the result is often more favorable for the sombre-hued patient" (185). Implicitly suggesting a controlled study of the effect of environment and medical treatment on white and African American patients, Dillon positioned herself as a scientific researcher, reporting on the positive results of cases she had witnessed in which African Americans enjoyed improved health when offered healthier environments and appropriate antiseptic measures.

In referring to statistics and to comparable patient cases, Dillon reached beyond the individual professional experiences relied on by other nineteenth-century women physicians in their professional witnessing. She pointed to more generalizable conclusions as evidence and authority supporting her claims: "Again, while white physicians claim the rapid increase and fatality of certain diseases among the colored race, such as affections [*sic*] of pregnancy, uterine and venereal diseases, statistics and clinical experience prove the opposite. In spite of the many hardships of our women, the degrading and debasing influences under which they struggled without a hand to help, they have been remarkably free from many complaints which the more carefully nurtured white woman suffers" (185). Dillon's access to "statistics and clinical experience" allowed her to challenge the assertions of white physicians, authorizing her to offer her own interpretation of statistics as well as her clinical experience to refute the explanations offered by white physicians. Relying on professional witnessing as an ethos strategy and for evidence supporting her claims, Dillon made use of persuasive appeals that were largely inaccessible to African American women before they entered the medical profession.

In addition to arguing that it was the physician's standard of care, not the patient's race, that determined the chance of recovery, Dillon emphasized the importance of physiological education in improving the health and consequently the social status of African Americans. Near the end of her address, she described for the teachers in her audience the kinds of lessons children should study: "Let [the student] find the radial artery, exercise the biceps, examine the tendons of the flexor muscles of the forearm. Get a calf's brain and let the scholars gather around the table and explain the hemispheres and convolutions of the brain. Procure a microscope and let them watch the blood corpuscles circulating in a frog's leg . . ." (187). As a physician, Dillon demonstrated her comfort with visceral studies of physiology and the vocabulary that accompanied them. In addition to lessons on physiology, she recommended instruction in diet, exercise, and hygiene, studies that also suggested her professional expertise.

Throughout her address, Dillon insisted that "it is not so much the inherent weakness of the race as its want of knowledge of practical physiology that makes the death-rate so high among us" (185). In calling for education and improved living conditions for African Americans, Dillon joined with other nineteenth-century African American women in promoting "racial uplift" as described by Shirley Wilson Logan. Advocates of racial uplift believed that "through education, economic independence, and sanitary living conditions, black people could thrive." According to Logan, for African American women involved in the racial uplift project, any "inferiority" attributed to African Americans was "a direct consequence of slavery, not ... an innate and indelible trait" (153). Like other reform-minded African American women, Dillon argued that African Americans' material living conditions, not their biological "nature," led to the patterns of poor health observed by the medical community. Although other African American women made similar arguments, as a formally educated and state-certified physician, Dillon enjoyed an especially strong ethos for making such claims. What she had witnessed in her role as a professional contributed to an authoritative, objective, scientific ethos that countered assumptions about African American women that undercut their efforts to create a persuasive ethos.

Rebecca J. Cole, the second African American woman to earn a medical degree,[9] also sought to improve conditions for African Americans by referring to what she had witnessed as a professional to challenge negative representations of their "nature." In a report on the October 1896 meeting of the Women's Missionary Society of Philadelphia, she cast doubt on statistics, provided by sociologist W. E. B. Du Bois, demonstrating that African Americans were more likely to engage in criminal behavior and to die of consumption than any other class of people. Describing those who developed the statistics as victims of "colorphobia," she challenged the idea that African Americans were disproportionately represented in these two groups, asking "And who makes up the police records? To what class do most of the men in this department belong but to Irish democracy? Who can tell how many white offenders go free, either by bribery or by their own aptitude to escape the consequences of their actions?" (5). Furthermore, Cole suggested, white physicians were too willing to diagnose African Americans with tuberculosis and, once that dire diagnosis was made, to allow them to die: "On the point of deaths from consumption, I would say this: hosts of the poor are attended by young, inexperienced white physicians. They have inherited the traditions of their elders, and let a black patient cough, they immediately have visions of tubercles. Let him die, and though in the case there may be good reason for a difference of opinion, he writes 'tuberculosis,' and heaves a great sigh of relief that one more source of contagion is removed" (5). In this passage, Cole relied on her experience as a physician to craft a persuasive ethos built in part on her inside knowledge of the medical profession and its practitioners. She also used her knowledge to support her skepticism of Du Bois's statistics and to indicate her identification with her audience, the readers of the *Woman's Era*, the official publication of the National Association of Colored Women. Cole's report adds another facet to professional witnessing, in addition to knowledge gained in the laboratory or from observing patients. The evidence she cited was her experience with white physicians: because she had seen white doctors neglect African American patients as a result of assumptions about their predisposition for tuberculosis, Cole was able to present herself as someone knowledgeable about the true causes of African American mortality rates.

Like Dillon's, Cole's plan for improving conditions for African Americans was based on health education: "We must teach these people the laws of health; we must preach this new gospel, that the respectability of a household ought to be measured by the condition of the cellar; that to prolong the hours of toil or study or pleasure habitually into the night, when we must be up betimes in the morning, is to rob our offspring of vitality, and invite epilepsy, consumption, and a train of other evils" (5). In this passage, "these people" refers to African Americans who had recently moved to Philadelphia. Cole's plan to educate recent arrivals was accompanied by a plea for laws to prohibit overcrowding in tenement houses, what she called "Cubic Air Space Laws" (5). Both ideas were frequently advocated by nineteenth-century women physicians, who, in addition to promoting health education, also taught the public about the importance of adequate ventilation. Instead of grounding her calls for less crowded dwellings in the health of individuals as many physicians did, however, Cole placed her argument in the context of the influences on public health that she had witnessed as a professional, resisting Du Bois's statistics demonstrating that African Americans were especially susceptible to disease by attributing their illnesses not to individual or biological weakness but rather to poor living conditions.

As professionals and as women, nineteenth-century women physicians were well-positioned to hear about their patients' problems and to use medical statistics, patients' stories, and the suffering they had witnessed in their professional rounds as proof of their knowledge and authority, as evidence, and as emotional appeals in support of social reform. In recounting anecdotes about patients and drawing conclusions based on years of professional experience, women physicians justified their reform work and drew on a source of rhetorical material inaccessible to most women and men. As a component of women physicians' ethē, professional witnessing reminded audience members of women physicians' unique access to knowledge while elevating their claims above those that might be dismissed as "merely" personal experience; a professional's autobiographical experience was more valued than most individuals' daily anecdotes, particularly those of nonprofessional women who might be perceived to be biased or overemotional. Because the professional had the authority to examine "the rich confusion of ordinary experience" (Bledstein 89) in order to "rearrang[e] reality" (90), the woman physician's interpretation of medical statistics as well as her patients' stories had the potential to change how people thought about the lives and rights of oppressed groups. The qualities attributed to the late nineteenth-century physician, including expertise, experience, authority, and concern for the wellbeing of others, constituted a persuasive ethos for reform work, an ethos women physicians reinforced through professional witnessing.

Prescribing for Society

In her refutation of claims about African Americans' "natural" tendency to contract tuberculosis and commit crimes, Cole offered a diagnosis and a prescription intended to improve living conditions for African Americans. She concluded her article by advising a course of treatment: "These are the things [health education and the reduction of overcrowding] that we can do to attack vice, disease and crime in their strongholds, for they have no complexion and they always yield to such and to no other treatment" (5). Cole constructed social problems as an illness that could be cured by following the specific plan she outlined. Mirroring the medical profession's new scientific search for universal causes of disease (for example, the search for *the* microbe that causes tuberculosis in all patients) rather than climatic, individual, or familial dispositions toward a given disease, Cole used medical epistemology and vocabulary to diagnose and prescribe for her community-patient.

In doing so, Cole reinforced her ethos and shaped audience reactions by asserting her professional status, a strategy that not only situated Cole as a physician authorized to advise the public but also simultaneously positioned the members of her audience as "patients," constrained by the doctor-patient relationship to obey her advice. Just as nonprofessional women extended their maternal or sisterly roles so that their public activism would be perceived as familial advice offered to the nation (O'Neill 353), some nineteenth-century women physicians constructed their public rhetoric as a form of doctor-patient interaction: the physician observed the symptoms evident in society, diagnosed the problem, and prescribed a cure that she believed would improve the health of the nation.

As a strategy for crafting an effective ethos, prescribing for society gained some of its influence from the authoritative connotations of professionalism by the end of the century; at the same time, it persuaded by suggesting an ethos for the audience that reinforced the rhetor's authority by overlaying the doctor-patient relationship on the reformer-public context. In this way, late-nineteenth-century women physicians' reform rhetoric demonstrates the reciprocity between rhetor and audience constructs involved in ethos formation: when women physicians constructed an ethos for themselves as professional authorities, the values represented by that ethos (expertise, experience, authority) imposed a reciprocal set of values on their audiences, implying that readers should demonstrate virtues such as obedience, respect for authority, and recognition of the incontrovertible knowledge of science. The reciprocal nature of ethos in nineteenth-century doctor-patient rhetorical exchanges demonstrates how ethos might be negotiated between the rhetor and the audience; it also suggests that an especially authoritative ethos might involve imposing a particular social location, such as *obedient patient*, on audience members.

Like Cole, Emma A. Reynolds[10] relied on medical concepts to mark her professional status in her advocacy of a plan that she believed would improve the health and the financial security of African Americans. In a letter to the *Galveston Daily News* in 1895, Reynolds encouraged young African American women to enter nursing school, a new educational opportunity that had only recently arisen with the establishment of African American hospitals and colleges; aspiring African American nurses were not permitted to study in white institutions. In 1886, a school of nursing was founded at the Atlanta Baptist Seminary (later Spelman College), and training programs associated with hospitals rather than academic institutions were established for African American women in the 1890s (Hine 6–7). Reynolds urged young African American women to take advantage of these opportunities: "In my observations both north and south I have been painfully impressed by the absence of young colored women from the [nurses'] training schools. Very few are found taking the course any place—none here. I suppose it is because no one has called their attention to the value of such a training, both to themselves and to the race. This apparent indifference is to be regretted, for among no other people is the need of trained nurses more urgent." Reynolds, who had herself studied nursing before entering medical school, believed that trained nurses would improve mortality rates: "The death statistics show that the mortality of the negro is fearful. It is also shown that the majority die from those diseases caused by surroundings which violate the laws of hygiene. With this etiological factor known a clew to the remedy is given, vis: Proper training in hygiene and care of the sick, cleanliness in the homes, proper ventilation in churches and school houses." Like Cole, Reynolds identified an etiology explaining problems that were simultaneously matters of health and of social conditions, and she offered a remedy for those problems appropriate not to individual patients alone, but to an entire community. Using the vocabulary of her profession—*mortality, laws of hygiene, etiological,* and *remedy*—to assert her place in it, Reynolds advocated a course of action intended to improve the physical and social health of her community. Notably, the "remedy" Reynolds prescribed was not a literal medical cure, such as a drug or surgical procedure; instead, Reynolds positioned herself as a physician prescribing a social remedy that would cure several interrelated problems affecting health, education, and living conditions. In prescribing a not-strictly-medical cure for a not-strictly-medical set of conditions, Reynolds asserted an ethos as a physician qualified and authorized to instruct the public. For the women who followed her plan, nursing school would mean "honorable employment at good wages," and for their community, the presence of trained nurses would result in an "incalculable benefit to the home-making of the race." Reynolds's plan, then, addressed both the individual patient conventionally imagined as the subject of medical care and the community that was collectively ailing. As a physician, she capitalized on the professional discourse and authority available to her to claim an ethos that empowered her to promote the reforms that she believed would benefit both individual patients and her community.

Cole and Reynolds relied on medical vocabulary to assert their professional status in their calls for actions that they believed would resolve problems that were both medical and social. Such a reference to their professional ethos extended the scope of the physician's influence beyond advising individual patients or making public health recommendations to include the social problems that often overlapped with the medical problems that constituted the physician's conventional sphere. Some nineteenth-century women physicians took this strategy even further, using the act of prescribing for society to call for reforms not directly related to individual or public health. For example, Hunt's "Address on the Medical Education of Women," which she delivered before the women's rights convention in Worcester, Massachusetts in 1850, "prescribed" women physicians as a cure for society's ills. This speech was peppered with medical imagery and terminology that reflected

Hunt's midcentury conceptions of the causes of and treatments for disease. In the introduction, after acknowledging that society was in a transitional moment, Hunt expressed her belief that it needed a systemic cure, not just superficial treatments: "Noble men and women have been working upon the outer skin, and thus preventing a palsy in the community; but still the *heart*, the central point of circulation has not been reached. Surface remedies have been applied, and irritants and stimulants have performed their uses; but now we need something internal, and therefore we demand equal freedom of development, equal advantages of education, for both sexes" (45). After this opening, when Hunt drew her audience's "attention to the professional sphere of woman, as a PHYSICIAN," she announced, "I speak from the experience of many years, and bear testimony to duties of vital importance. I have lived in this work, loved it, felt its power, enjoyed its privileges, [and] been sustained in it by kind and intelligent spirits" (45–46). Throughout this address, Hunt spoke as a professional, advising her public "patient" about the treatment that would cure its ills: the educated woman physician.[11]

As Hunt explained it, the "body" of nineteenth-century society was already struggling toward health; the physiological lectures that had been offered, the health societies that had been formed, and the medical information and advice books that had been published were all part of "a sort of spasmodic action [that] has seized the public," the efforts of a body to rid itself of disease. These spasms, however, could not effect a cure alone; a more radical treatment was necessary. She observed the "patient" and then commented, "this is a convulsion only which will do no good, unless we have medical knowledge for our sex, which may be appropriated day by day" ("Address" 49). Just as a nineteenth-century patient would slowly recover from an illness, society's wellbeing would improve "day by day" as the "treatment"—scientifically educated women physicians—took effect. Hunt's ethos in this speech rested heavily on her status as a physician, and she capitalized on that status by prescribing a cure for society's ills.

Two decades later, in 1871, Mary Edwards Walker positioned herself similarly to Hunt when she wrote the following in her book *Hit*: "As a Physician, the author believes that her duties are not *all* in the sick-room, for, after an experience of over fifteen years, she finds herself loudly called to diagnose the great body politic, more thoroughly than ever before, and her prognosis is, that *doubling* the dose at the Ballot-box will produce convalescence. Every one knows that the people are happier when well, than when sick, and after the important dose has been taken and health secured, the marriage relation will be something better than the least binding contract that is ever made"

(122). For Walker, the "medicine" she prescribed—women's votes—would cure the problem posed by unfair divorce laws (122–128). In this passage, Walker reminded her readers of her professional status ("As a Physician") and articulated an expansive sense of her professional responsibilities, which were "not *all* in the sick-room" but also involved "the great body politic." Such an assertion of Walker's professional status and the authority to advise the public that accompanied her status as a physician was an ethos strategy to which few women had access at the time. Although nineteenth-century women physicians prescribed for society on a range of reform topics, including dress reform, temperance, and social purity, those subjects might all be understood as having a direct connection to health; therefore, physicians would logically participate *as physicians* in those debates. When Hunt and Walker employed medical terminology and explicit reference to their status as physicians in advocating occupational and political rights for women, however, they extended their professional ethē into sites beyond the physician's conventional sphere of influence. Relying on their ethē as professionals provided women physicians with an opportunity not only to advise individual patients or to advocate public health measures but also to argue from a position of authority on issues that they cast as affecting the "health" of society, even when those issues were not directly related to health in the usual sense.

In the political and social reforms discussed here, rhetorically positioning oneself as the physician and society as the patient allowed nineteenth-century women physicians to claim rhetorical authority that did not derive entirely from their traditional feminine roles, although their femininity was always vital to their ethē. In one sense, women physicians did draw on their domestic authority, as they advocated "cleaning up" urban areas and educating the ignorant. In doing so, they acted in accordance with the model of feminine professionalism identified by historian Ellen S. More, who writes that "women physicians had molded their professional identity around a core of civic duty in the form of social housekeeping" (67). Yet women physicians' claims about what would benefit society derived at least as much from their professional expertise and the authority of medical-scientific epistemology as from their feminine moral authority. In prescribing for society, nineteenth-century women physicians claimed an ethos that reflected the growing influence of the expert and the professional, whose authority increased throughout the later decades of the 1800s and whose power is even more significant today. Women physicians' development of ethos strategies that signaled their professional expertise was a crucial turn in the history of women's rhetoric. Nineteenth-century women physicians' speech and writing demonstrate that historical women did not rely solely on "feminine" rhetorical strategies: in drawing on the rhetorical resources of professionalism, women physicians initiated a tradition of professional women's rhetorical practices, a tradition to which many modern women who speak and write as professionals today owe a great debt.

The Woman Physician as Reform Activist

The strategy of prescribing for society highlights the reciprocity between rhetor and audience constructs, especially the influence a rhetor's ethos has on the characteristics attributed to an audience. Such reciprocity is particularly important for rhetors advocating social reforms, because in order to achieve the reforms they seek, activist speakers and writers must alter the public's hierarchy of values, convincing them to privilege one set of values over another. This can occur through a reordering of priorities, as the audience is persuaded to adopt the virtues represented in a rhetor's ethos. For example, to persuade the public that women should be permitted to pursue a broader range of occupations, Zakrzewska sought to privilege the notion that women could "clean up" society over the notion that women should be protected from the degraded elements of society. Zakrzewska did this in part through her ethos as a feminine professional who had witnessed depravity and who was still respectable and even helpful to women in need. Extending Zakrzewska's ethos outward to the audience would shift social values from feminine virtues like delicacy and domesticity in favor of women's benevolence. Likewise, arguments about the "nature" of African Americans involved replacing the negative value attributed to African Americans because of their supposed biological weakness with a more empowering positive value attributed to the role of education in achieving good health and hygiene. African American women physicians' ethē contributed to this shift by drawing on their medical experience as witnesses of medical racism and of the consequences of ignorance and by presenting themselves as educated professionals. Nineteenth-century women physicians' reform rhetoric demonstrates the dynamic nature of ethos, particularly for those who seek social reform: women physicians did not merely reflect the values their audiences already held but also impressed upon their audiences their sense of what society's priorities ought to be.

In their speech and writing advocating social and political reforms, nineteenth-century women physicians invoked their professional status in contexts outside of typical doctor-patient or doctor-doctor communication. Even as the supposed objectivity of the professional was important to their ethē, women physicians blended positioning themselves as professionals with identifying themselves as women, as American Indians, and as African Americans, demonstrating that professionalism was not just one location but instead that it could be combined with the insight afforded to rhetors who identified with those for whom they spoke. Women physicians used sophisticated ethos constructions to intervene as professionals in the important issues of their time, speaking with authority and evidence unavailable to most nonprofessional women and extending the range of rhetorical practices accessible to nineteenth-century women.

3

Educating the Public:
Women Physicians' Popular Health Advice

Woman—God's best gift to man and the chief support of the doctors.

—the annual toast at medical conventions,
quoted in Anna M. Galbraith, *Hygiene and Physical Culture for Women* (1895)

As soon as nineteenth-century women physicians began learning anatomy and physiology, they felt it was their duty to share that information with the public, particularly with other women. Health lectures by women physicians were very popular in the mid- and late 1800s, so popular that many, including Elizabeth Blackwell and Anna M. Longshore-Potts, published their lectures for wider distribution. Health information lectures and texts were a means of fulfilling women physicians' promise to connect the professional medical community with the domestic feminine sphere. Blackwell acknowledged this promise in 1852 when she described her published lectures as "the first fruits of [her] medical studies," which she provided "as an earnest of future work" (*Laws of Life* n. pag.). For these women, the work of a physician—particularly a woman physician—involved rhetoric and education as much as it involved medicine and surgery. In 1860, Elizabeth and her sister Emily, who followed her into medicine, described a woman physician's primary duty as health instruction: "As teachers . . . to diffuse among women the physiological and sanitary knowledge which they need, we find the first work for women physicians" (10). Indeed, for some women physicians, health lectures served to fill their time and their pockets in the early years of their practices, when people were reluctant to put themselves under a woman's care.

Nineteenth-century women physicians' health information and advice books often reached broader audiences than women physicians could reach through their lectures or their practices. For some readers, such books represented their first interactions with a woman physician. Without firsthand knowledge of women physicians, readers must have relied on other cues to determine the ethos of the woman physician health writer. Some cues circulated in the popular media, such as this passage from a book published anonymously in Philadelphia in 1870: "It is clear that the female medical ranks must be filled by the disappointed, or the falsely ambitious; the weak-minded or the wrong-minded" (*Men and Women Medical Students: The Hospital Clinics and the Woman Movement* 16). Countering such negative portrayals were the ethos cues provided by the health information and advice genre itself. In a discussion of genres as responses to recurrent rhetorical situations, Carolyn Miller explains the effect genre has on audience: "Form shapes the response of the reader or listener to substance by providing instruction, so to speak, about how to perceive and interpret; this guidance disposes the audience to anticipate, to be gratified, to respond in a certain way. Seen thus, form becomes a kind of meta-information, with both semantic value (as information) and syntactic (or formal) value" (159). The instructive aspect of genre is particularly relevant to nineteenth-century women physicians' health information and advice texts: although readers might have been unfamiliar with and wary of women physicians, the writers' decision to publish in the genre of the health information book positioned women physicians as experts educating and advising the less informed. Predisposed by the genre to respond to the author as expert adviser, readers might have acquired an attitude toward women physicians that countered the negative caricatures circulated by opponents.

In this chapter, I explore how the nineteenth-century American women physicians who wrote health information and advice texts taught readers to perceive them as feminine professionals. After first describing the genre conventions and other common features of health information and advice texts, I demonstrate that women physicians used these conventions to assert their professional authority and their femininity simultaneously. Although the characteristics associated with *professionalism* and *femininity* evolved over the course of the century, both components of women physicians' ethos would be necessary if female readers were to accept them as health advisers. Relying on and adapting the genre of the health information and advice book, women physicians were authorized to inform their readers and to encourage them to be healthy, autonomous individuals who valued their own bodies enough to care for themselves properly.

The texts examined here represent a range of therapeutic schools, including regular, water-cure, botanical, and eclectic medicine, but all were intended to educate readers, primarily women, about human anatomy and physiology and the practices by which good health could be achieved. Although the educational purpose was common across these books, the authors sometimes articulated a complex attitude toward nonprofessional women's health education, demonstrating both a commitment to increasing their readers' knowledge and confidence as well as a desire for the professional to be recognized as the exclusive authority in matters related to health. In these cases, writers taught their readers that although nonprofessional women should be better informed about their bodies, their autonomy should be limited so that physicians could exercise their own ethos as authoritative professionals. The writer and reader roles implicit in the genre of the health information and advice book allowed women physicians to engage in complex constructions of their ethē as authoritative experts and, reciprocally, of nonprofessional women as intelligent and strong, but also properly subservient to the physician's greater expertise and authority.

Women Physicians' Health Information and Advice Books

Women physicians' popular medical books and lectures contributed to a longstanding tradition of advice for women. Alongside the volumes of domestic and social advice written for nineteenth-century women were numerous texts offering recommendations on subjects related to health, such as diet, exercise, and child care. Because of the history of women's exclusion from medical expertise, most of the popular health texts in circulation in the 1800s had been composed by men. Although many of these physicians wrote for both men and women, woman's perceived weakness and her primary role in reproduction and child care made her the intended audience of much medical advice. Because after 1850 *woman* was so often construed to mean a patient—"the chief support of the doctors" as one toast to her poor health described her (qtd. in Galbraith 207)—and as one who needed "scientific" approaches to health and household labor, the relationship between physician-writers and woman-readers was clearly one of authoritative experts speaking to uninformed laypersons.

When it came to educating women about anatomy and physiology, however, the traditional model of the male expert speaking to the uneducated female broke down. For many women, learning specific details about the body from a man produced intolerable embarrassment, a fact noted in the 1838 advertising for Mary Gove's[1] anatomy and physiology lectures: "Physiological facts of a delicate nature and which many ladies would not bring themselves to hear from a gentleman, but a knowledge of which is of great importance to the well-being of society and individuals, will be brought to view in these lectures" ("Lectures"). Yet until women began acquiring medical education at midcentury, few were qualified to teach other women about anatomy and physiology; consequently, women were left largely ignorant about the basic principles of health. As late as 1895, physician Anna M. Galbraith wrote in the preface to *Hygiene and Physical Culture for Women* of "the ignorance shown by the masses of otherwise well-educated women, in regard to all functions of the human body," ignorance that "render[ed] the woman's life well-nigh a burden" (vii).

Nineteenth-century women's strong desire for the information women physicians offered quickly made their lectures and books quite popular. One of the most successful medical speakers was Anna M. Longshore-Potts, who began lecturing shortly after completing her degree in 1852 as a member of the first class to graduate from the Female Medical College of Pennsylvania (which later became the Woman's Medical College of Pennsylvania). In the preface to her *Discourses to Women on Medical Subjects* (1887), she recounted the popular demand for her lectures:

> Soon after I entered this new field of useful labor, in the practice of the healing art, I resolved to devote a few months out of every year to lecturing upon medical subjects, and my first effort took place in the city of Philadelphia, where I gave several consecutive courses of lectures to women only; but after many earnest solicitations from the ladies in attendance to extend the lectures to the husbands and sons, I ventured upon one for a mixed audience. I very soon found, however, that one lecture would not suffice, so yielded to the further demands, until the number increased indefinitely; and from that great centre they were extended to towns and cities throughout the United States, the territories, and British America, also through the Colonies of New Zealand, Australia, and Tasmania; and the whole of England, including six months in London; and the principal cities of Scotland and Ireland. (viii–ix)

After describing the great demand for her lectures both at home and overseas, Longshore-Potts attributed her decision to publish her lectures to her audience: "Throughout all these countries and colonies there have been earnest entreaties from the large number of listeners, and from hundreds of grateful patients . . . for a book to read, from which could be gained a similar course of instruction to that to which they had listened in the public and private lectures, and to this general call I have yielded" (ix). Although Longshore-Potts's international tour was extraordinary, her story of receiving requests to extend and publish her lectures was common among women physicians. For example, Rachel B. Gleason (figure 3.1), an eclectic[2] and water-cure physician who ran a water-cure establishment with her husband in Elmira, New York, demonstrated the demand for her text in the introduction to her *Talks to My Patients: Hints on Getting Well and Keeping Well* (1870): "Many of my patients have requested me to put my 'Parlor Talks' in print, that they might have them for home reference." Even former patients who lived at a remote distance sought the publication of Gleason's advice: "Letters from the extreme East and the far West have come to me, asking for a book or some advice which should help them to understand and meet the infirmities and functions peculiar to womanhood" (v). The public's interest in health information and medical self-help advice supported women physicians' speech and writing on these topics.

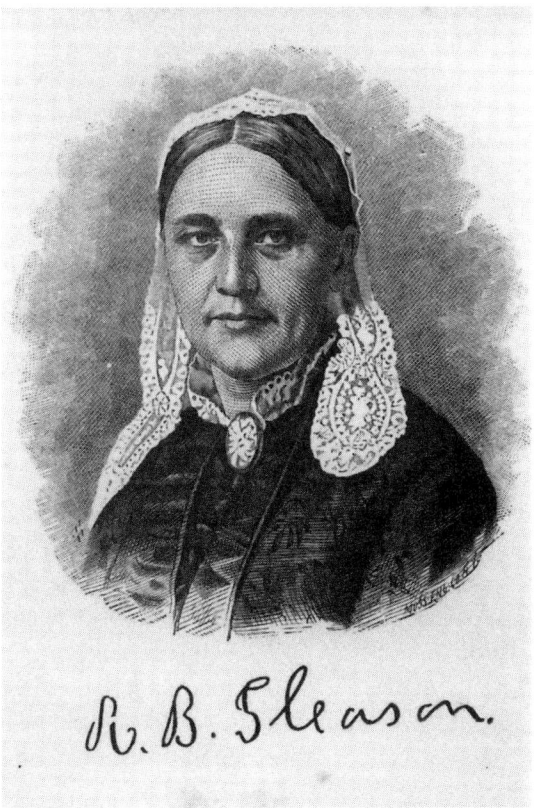

Figure 3.1. Rachel Brooks Gleason, frontispiece for *Talks to My Patients*, 1880.

Indeed, opportunities for health education were extremely popular and accessible to women, who participated as providers and recipients of medical information beginning near the middle of the century. Historians Anita Clair Fellman and Michael Fellman describe the popular appeal of health information in the nineteenth century:

> The interest in medical self-help was matched by the hunger for general information on anatomy, physiology, child care, physical education, and hygiene. The transmission of this knowledge took an even more popular form than writing—the public lecture. These lectures, which were a form of mass entertainment as well as instruction, attracted many people, including those whose religious backgrounds made them still wary of the theater. The health lecture was an appropriate outing for a polite woman and eventually became an acceptable occupation for a woman. From 1838, dozens of women lecturers covered New England and the West, enrapturing thousands of their eager sisters with talks on the "Laws of Life," which might somehow provide the key not only to the family's physical well-being, but to its emotional and moral health as well. (8)

Women physicians contributed to this popular culture of health education. Through their health lectures and the books based on those lectures, women physicians reached large numbers of people; this body of professional writing constitutes a significant contribution to the rhetorical activity of nineteenth-century American women.

Moreover, women physicians' medical advice and information texts represent an important development in rhetorical history. For the first time, women spoke and wrote to other women as scientific-professional advisers,[3] leaving men out of the professional-to-amateur medical advice exchange. For women physicians, the possession of health information was fundamental to improving women's quality of life, to improving popular attitudes toward women's minds and bodies, and to reforming society along hygienic lines. Many women physicians believed as Prudence Saur did when she wrote in the preface to *Maternity: A Book for Every Wife and Mother* (1891) that "The greatest need of the age is a better understanding of the laws of our being; it is a point upon which the future of our race depends. I believe in the enlightenment of mothers and daughters upon this, and all topics pertaining to the physical, mental and moral conditions of women, as the surest means of correcting the glaring evils which to-day embitter the lives of our sex" (iii–iv). Adopting the genres of the medical advice book and lecture allowed women to employ the persuasive strategies and genre conventions available to them as scientific professionals advising the public, extending the range of women's rhetorical activity. Women physicians used their new discursive position to provide women with an alternative to the advice offered by men and to intervene in contemporary social debates in the hopes of shaping the behavior and values of individuals and their communities.

In addition to educating their audiences about anatomy and physiology, women physicians addressed many of the reform issues of the post–Civil War era in their health information books: they unanimously opposed corsets, frequently using anatomical images to depict the damage done by tight-lacing (figure 3.2); nearly all condemned alcohol and tobacco; and some, particularly late in the century, promoted female and male sexual chastity, contributing to the social purity movement. Most writers advocated education and useful occupations for women, claiming that ennui was the source of many of women's health complaints. Exercise was frequently recommended for girls and women, although the writers' advice for women's activities often reflected a conservative sense of women's physical capacity. For example, in her *Hygiene and Physical Culture for Women* (1895), Galbraith endorsed bicycling as exercise for women, but she warned readers that "Hills should be taken quietly," and "When the rider cannot breathe easily through the nose and with the mouth shut, it is time to stop" (90). In using information about anatomy and physiology to justify political and social change, women physicians contributed to the body of "reform physiology" texts published in the nineteenth century. According to Wendy Hayden, "These texts, written by physicians, both informed their audiences about the body and exhorted audiences to advocate women's rights, creating a hybrid genre with specific rhetorical negotiations common to all of the texts, whether written by a male or female physician" (*Evolutionary* 84). Through "reform physiology" texts, science operated in the public sphere to influence attitudes toward a wide range of social issues. Women physicians writing about anatomy and physiology therefore gained a powerful rhetorical tool not only for educating readers but also for persuading them to support political and social reforms.

Women physicians' health information texts also addressed matters of individual behavior. Abortion, generally cast as the act of a selfish woman who preferred social pleasures over maternity, was said by some women physicians to be not only a sin but also to damage the reproductive system irreparably, resulting in a lifetime of pain and weakness. Readers were also advised not to overexert themselves while menstruating and to avoid cold, wet feet, often the result of staying out late at dances and wearing inappropriate shoes, because this condition was believed to interrupt the menstrual cycle. Some writers, such as Gove, recommended that readers avoid "the

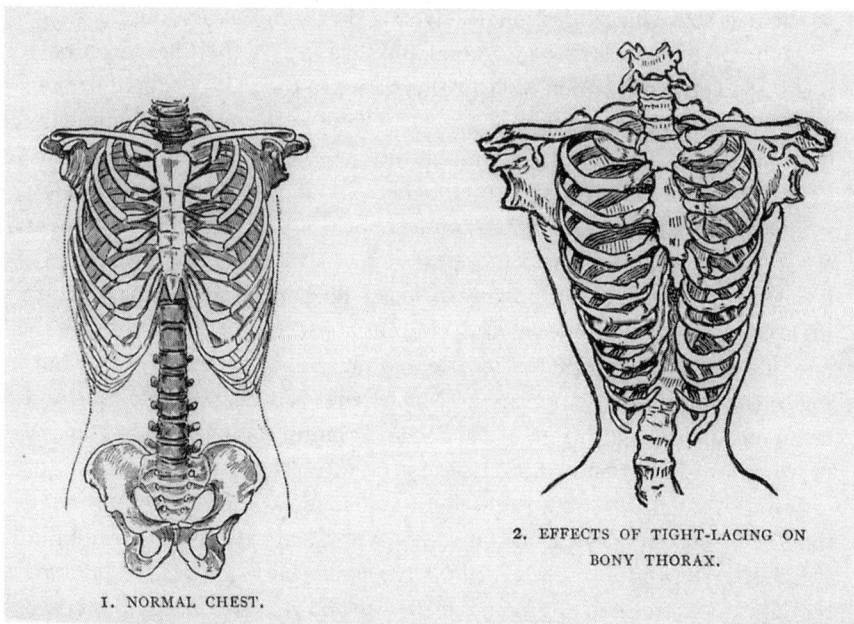

2. EFFECTS OF TIGHT-LACING ON
BONY THORAX.

1. NORMAL CHEST.

Figure 3.2. "Normal Chest" and "Effects of Tight-Lacing on Bony Thorax," *Hygiene and Physical Culture for Women*, 1895.

sensualizing effects of rich, stimulating food" (165). Instead, simple, nutritious diets were promoted. Writers also encouraged ample ventilation, and some, such as Mary Taylor Bissell, taught women how to select the most hygienic locations for their homes, considering air quality, soil composition, and the level of the water table (*Household*).

Like all genres, the health information and advice book might be defined as a set of "typified rhetorical actions based in recurrent situations" (Miller 159). The rhetorical situation that prompted health information and advice texts in nineteenth-century America included the perceived poor health of many women; widespread ignorance about physiology, particularly women's reproductive physiology; and a disparity between the health knowledge possessed by physicians and that accessible to the public. Health information books and lectures by women physicians filled a particular need, because they overcame some of the obstacles to women's health education. Women's access to health information had historically been limited by feminine modesty and reluctance to learn about the body from men, who until the nineteenth century were the nearly exclusive sources of scientific information about anatomy and physiology.

Women were especially eager for information and advice about pregnancy and childbirth. Relief from the complaints accompanying pregnancy and delivery was especially difficult to come by, however, because some men physicians were apathetic to women's concerns. The radical Chicago obstetrician Alice B. Stockham drew attention to women's frustration at the advice provided by men in her book *Tokology* (1883), which provided health information, instructions for avoiding conception, and advice for painless childbirth. In a section called "No Help from Doctors," Stockham positioned herself as one who could relieve women's suffering when no male physician would:

> In one of my conversational lectures a lady testified that for seven months before her child was born she never knew one hour's relief from nausea. . . . She consulted three different physicians, and each one told her nothing could be done except to wait for "nature's relief." She went home in despair and suffered to the end. When she heard the theories I teach, with suppressed emotion she exclaimed: "Thank God for the hope you give. To my dying day I shall use my feeble voice to promulgate these truths, that others may not grope in the valley as I have done." (40–41)

The woman quoted here sought help from men physicians; many women, however, were reluctant to ask men for help, particularly when the symptoms suggested a problem with the reproductive organs. Women physicians' lectures and books provided an avenue for women who wished to maintain their modesty while learning about their bodies.

Teaching Readers How to View Women Physicians

Risa Applegarth has called for "recasting *ethos* as *location within and among genres*," a reconceptualization that she believes "captures possibilities for as well as limitations on a rhetor's capacity to shape *ethos* strategically" (44). In choosing to write in the genre of the health information and advice book, nineteenth-century women physicians were able to capitalize on reader expectations for the genre to develop rhetorical characters as professional, authoritative, expert, and consequently due a significant degree of respect. However, the writers of these texts also had to provide evidence of their professional expertise in the texts themselves, in effect teaching their readers to view women physicians as knowledgeable and authoritative. At the same time, they had to reassure audiences that they were still respectably feminine.

For example, formal features common in health information and advice books, such as line drawings, were used by women physicians to teach anatomy and to demonstrate exercises appropriate for young women. Incorporating line drawings affiliated women physicians with scientists, who had long used such illustrations to represent the structures of plants and animals. Chapters devoted to each bodily system (digestive, respiratory, skeletal, etc.) and to classes of disorders (childhood illnesses, reproductive difficulties, the results of overwork, etc.) showed that the writers possessed a comprehensive knowledge of medicine. Other features, such as glossaries, indexes, and tables of contents demonstrated that women physicians intended these texts to be easy to use. Prefaces also indicated the authors' commitment to educating the public. For example, in her preface to *Familiar Lessons on Physiology, Designed for the Use of Children and Youth in Schools and Families* (1847), Lydia Folger Fowler[4] explained her purpose in writing the two-volume series: "The design of these two volumes, is, to present these subjects in a clear and familiar manner, to explain their general laws, to illustrate them by cuts and familiar examples, such as occur in every-day life, to impress the truths inculcated on the conscience, so that children may not only feel their importance, and that it is their duty to obey the laws of their being, but that they may also feel that they have responsibilities [for being healthy], from which they cannot free themselves" (v). Similar expressions of a desire to help women and children by providing straightforward health information appeared in several of the health texts written by women physicians. A woman with such generosity of spirit and goodwill toward women and children could not belong to the class an anonymous critic categorized in 1869 as including "the disappointed, or the falsely ambitious; the weak-minded or the wrong-minded" (16).

As even this short list of some of the conventions of health information and advice books suggests, genres respond to and manifest a complex set of situational features, including the audience's purposes in reading, its beliefs about the writer, the discourse that preceded the current text, the epistemology reflected in the text, and the writer's goals for the text. Ethos is one of those features, and Applegarth explains that it both affects and is affected by the genre in which it participates: "Because genres organize rhetorical resources as well as structure rhetorical constraints, genres significantly shape one's possibilities for *ethos*. Locating one's text—and oneself—in a genre begins the work of locating oneself relative to a particular audience" (50). Yet nineteenth-century women physicians could not simply locate themselves in the genre of the health information and advice text. A woman physician who merely adopted the ethos conventions associated with the genre would have been perceived as inadequately feminine by her audience. She would have found herself in a situation similar to that of early American women's rights activists as described by Karlyn Kohrs Campbell: "On the one hand, a woman had to meet all the usual requirements of speakers, demonstrating expertise, authority, and rationality in order to show her competence and make herself credible to audiences. However, if that was all she did, she was likely to be judged masculine, unwomanly, aggressive, and cold" (12). To succeed in addressing the public, a woman physician could not just build an ethos as a knowledgeable *physician*; she also had to build an ethos as a caring and concerned *woman*.

Another feature of the context that women faced in locating themselves in the genre of the health information text was public expectation: the supporters of women physicians believed they practiced a different kind of medicine than male physicians did. As one physician and supporter of women in medicine, Orin Davis, explained in 1881, "Woman's heart is always in the right place, abounds in marvellous sympathy, disinterestedness and faith, carries the joy of Eden to the languishing, and opens unto them the beautiful realms and treasures of her wondrous moral power. Professional knowledge only widens the sphere of her beneficial influence" (266). Nineteenth-century patients who selected women physicians likely also expected to receive more "feminine" treatment from a woman than they would have received from a man. Because a large part of the appeal of women physicians for supporters was precisely their differences from male physicians, practicing medicine "like a man" would have raised the question of why women physicians were necessary: if women physicians offered the public nothing new, why should it tolerate this innovation?[5] For a woman physician to have located herself within the existing genre of the health information book as it was authored by men would have been to abdicate one of the strongest justifications for her existence.

For these reasons, women physicians often emphasized their femininity in their health information texts, creating a new sort of ethos for the genre, one suited to the woman physician's location between medicine and femininity. One of the most direct means of building an ethos as simultaneously feminine and professional occurred on the title pages of health information texts. Frequently, the women physicians who could claim both social markers identified themselves on title pages with the abbreviations "Mrs." and "M.D." (figure 3.3). This style of self-identification told readers simultaneously that the writers were respectable married women (and probably mothers) and medical doctors. Another common strategy used by women physicians was simply affixing "M.D." or "Dr." to their given and paternal names, thereby identifying themselves as women through the use of their first names. Less common were strategies for masking the writer's gender or her name: on the title page of *Build Well: The Basis of Individual, Home, and National Elevation*

(1885), Cordelia Agnes Greene is listed only as "C. A. Greene."[6] Some women identified themselves only by their marital status, primarily when they were adherents of irregular therapies or when their husbands were well-known physicians themselves. For example, phrenologist Lydia Folger Fowler identified herself as "Mrs. L. N. Fowler," taking the initials of her famous husband, Lorenzo Niles Fowler. Mrs. Mott, who practiced botanic medicine alongside her husband, subtitled her book *Mrs. Mott's Advice to Young Females, Wives, and Mothers* (1834), identifying herself only with her husband's surname.

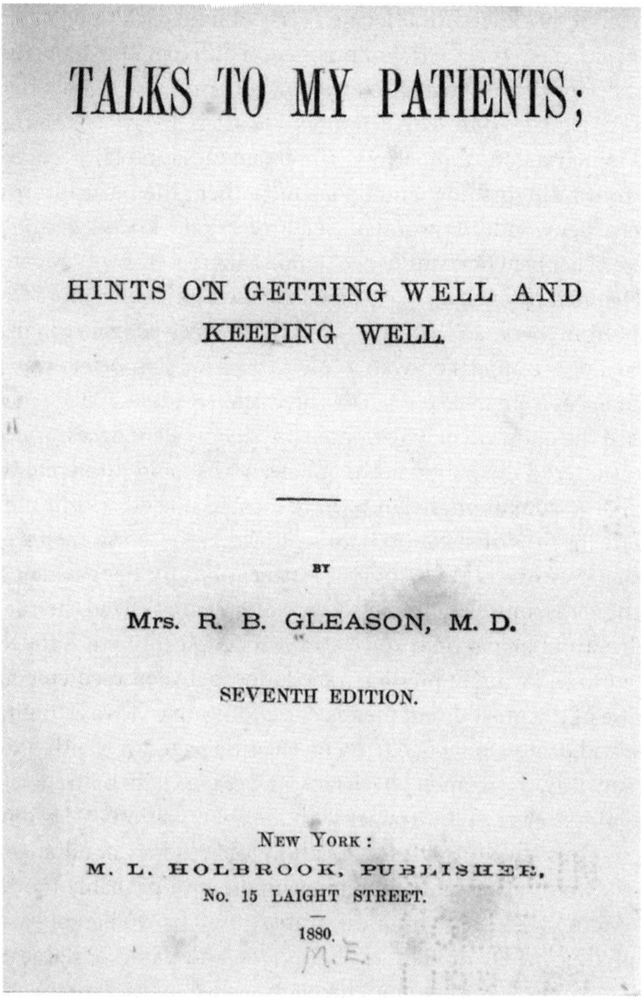

TALKS TO MY PATIENTS;

HINTS ON GETTING WELL AND KEEPING WELL.

BY

Mrs. R. B. GLEASON, M. D.

SEVENTH EDITION.

NEW YORK :
M. L. HOLBROOK, PUBLISHER,
No. 15 LAIGHT STREET.

1880.

Figure 3.3. Title page of Rachel Brooks Gleason's *Talks to My Patients*, 1880.

Title pages were also sites in which writers could enhance their credibility by listing their professional accomplishments. For example, the title page of *Hygiene and Physical Culture for Women* (1895) described Galbraith in these terms:

> Fellow New York Academy of Medicine; Attending Physician Neurological Department, New York Orthopedic Hospital and Dispensary; Late Attending Physician and Instructor in Diagnosis and Clinical Medicine[,] Woman's Medical College, New York Infirmary; Former Gynecological Clinician and Assistant Attending Staff for Diseases of Women, Woman's Hospital of Philadelphia, etc., etc.

Lists like these informed readers of the writers' expertise. Interestingly, facing some of the title pages was a frontispiece featuring a photograph or a sketch of the writer. This arrangement provided a visual representation of the balance between femininity and (masculine) medical expertise: the image of the woman's body (and her properly feminine dress) was visible to the reader at the same time her professional credentials were displayed along with her name, allowing readers to reassure themselves of the writer's femininity despite her accomplishments (or, considered from the other direction, to associate significant professional accomplishments with womanhood).

Some women physicians reassured their audiences of their femininity by characterizing their rhetorical activity as informal speech, often as a conversation that took place inside a home rather than a speech in a public venue.[7] Such a description grounded women physicians' speech and writing in conventionally feminine spaces and formats. For example, the title of Rachel B. Gleason's advice book, *Talks to My Patients; Hints on Getting Well and Keeping Well* (1870), reflects the work's original form, what Gleason termed "Parlor Talks" (v). In her introduction, she recounted her patients' requests for such a book: "Often young wives and mothers, who have been under my care during girlhood, have asked me where they could find a book which contained, in substance, what I had given in my informal lectures, adding, 'I am sorry I did not take notes of them; but, *then*, the need of much that you said seemed far away; now it is near, and I have no one at hand to give me the advice, no work to consult in reference to these matters of delicacy'" (v). In this passage, Gleason was careful to specify that her lectures were "informal" and not a more masculine form of speech. Furthermore, her inclusion of her patient's words suggested the need women had to find educated women whom they could approach informally on "matters of delicacy."

Another strategy nineteenth-century American women physicians used to assert their femininity in their health information and advice books was reference to the social roles and interests common among middle-class women. Because motherhood was consistently esteemed throughout the 1800s, when a woman physician referred to her own role as a mother, it typically strengthened not only her ethos but also the pathos of the argument, particularly when it came to moral, rather than strictly biological, issues. One such issue, which appeared in nearly all the popular medical texts published by women, was abortion, which until the 1830s was a legally and culturally accepted form of birth control in the United States, as long as the pregnancy was terminated before "quickening"—the time when the mother could feel the fetus moving. After midcentury, states passed a variety of laws intended to regulate and limit abortion (Brodie 254). Ultimately, regular physicians "became the most visible single group seeking to tighten the laws against abortion" (267). Combining medical opposition to abortion with late-nineteenth-century middle-class women's investment in strict sexual morality, women physicians in the 1880s and 1890s frequently spoke forcefully against abortion. In her 1885 book *Build Well: The Basis of Individual, Home, and National Elevation*, Cordelia Greene, who graduated from Cleveland Medical College in 1856 and went on to operate her own water-cure establishment in New York, referred to her responsibilities as a mother to emphasize her opposition to this procedure: "So great a crime is [abortion], so disastrous to the soul and body of the mother, aside from the sin against God and her child, that I would not, could not, cause abortion in the case of my own daughters to save them from shame—not even at six weeks of fœtal life. I could bow my head in anguish with them; I could help them rear and care for an illegitimate child,—but must not put upon them or take upon myself the guilt of murder" (82–83). In this passage, Greene demonstrated that she understood the emotional and material implications of an illegitimate pregnancy, but she argued that the moral and religious consequences of abortion were more severe. Modeling a mother's reaction, Greene refuted the popular rumors, articulated by George Ellington in 1869, that women physicians "attend[ed] to peculiar cases, such as all married women, and some single ones, are liable to. . . . They ask[ed] no question who a woman may be or where she comes from, so long as the money to pay expenses is forthcoming" (560); in other words, women physicians were believed to perform abortions. Drawing on her supposedly superior feminine morality and on her lived experience in feminine roles, Greene constructed her ethos as a principled adviser who was sympathetic to the sufferings, hopes, and fears of her female readers. This ethos position was not available in the preexisting masculine information and advice genre but was an ethos women physicians developed as particularly appropriate for them. In performing femininity in their health information and advice texts, nineteenth-century women physicians altered the genre, not only creating new possibilities for ethos within it but also opening up possibilities for emotional appeals and for the relationship between rhetor and audience constructed by the health information text.

Developing an ethos for health information and advice texts also required nineteenth-century women physicians to educate their readers about the relationship between feminine professionals and the public. The use of specialized terminology demonstrated women physicians' expertise and established a respectful distance between them and their nonprofessional audiences. Many of the women who wrote popular medical texts reassured their readers, as Mrs. W. H. Maxwell put it in 1860, that "[the author] has endeavored to avoid all terms that would be liable to confuse the unlearned reader, and she has given in plain language the results of her own experience" (7). Even so, simply naming and describing the organs and their functions required the use of scientific language. For example, in *Hygiene and Physical Culture for Women* (1895), Galbraith incorporated specialized terminology into her description of the respiratory system: "The lungs are the essential organs of respiration, or the ventilators of the body. They are two in number, separated from each other by the heart, are placed in a semi-distended state in the air-tight thorax, which we have seen, they, together with the heart and great blood-vessels, completely fill. The lungs ultimately consist of air cells, surrounded by [a] dense plexus of capillaries and nerves. The air cells communicate with the exterior through the bronchial tubes, trachea, and larynx" (186). Elsewhere, Galbraith referred to professional consensus to support her advice about allowing enough time for rest: "The amount of sleep required by the healthy adult is proportionate to the waste of vital strength, whether muscular exercise, intellectual labor, or emotional prodigality. The medical authorities today are pretty well agreed that eight hours of sleep is the minimum required for the maintenance of health. And all concede that the brain worker requires more sleep than the laborer" (285–86). As professionals, Galbraith and other women physicians made recommendations based not only on their own experience or on tradition, but based in the judgment of a community of experts. This source of authority not only differentiated women's medical advice texts from the advice offered by nonprofessional women but also established women physicians' professional ethos as more authoritative than that of nonprofessional advice authors.

As medical scientists, late-nineteenth-century women physicians also had access to the conventions of medical writing, and they employed them to inform readers and to remind them of the writers' expertise. For example, in 1891 Mary Taylor Bissell, who taught hygiene at the Woman's Medical

College of the New York Infirmary, made her description of excretion concrete through the use of numbers and measurements: "Some of these waste
elements are eliminated through the lungs in the shape of vitiated air to the
amount of seven or eight quarts per minute; some through the skin in the
shape of water and solid substances, from one to two pounds daily, and in
unusual exertion double that amount. The kidneys have carried off from three
to five pints of fluid in twenty-four hours" (*Physical Development* 12). If the
genre of the health information text prepared readers to accept expert advice,
this passage, with its precise measurements and technical vocabulary, would
have reinforced the readers' perception of the writer as expert, improving
popular attitudes toward women physicians as advisers.

Other references to professional medical writing occurred when women
physicians included synopses of experiments that supported their claims
about the means of achieving optimal health, as Galbraith did in 1895 in her
chapter on dress: "How seriously the corset interferes with the expansion
of the lungs is shown by some experiments of Dr. Sargent's. . . . He found
that the average lung capacity when corsets were worn was 134 cubic inches.
When corsets were removed the test showed a lung capacity of 167 cubic
inches—a gain of 33 cubic inches." Galbraith went on to interpret these findings: "That is, the woman who wears corsets cripples her lungs to the extent
of one-fifth of their entire capacity" (233). Numbers derived from scientific
studies constituted a relatively new form of evidence in popular rhetoric;
women physicians incorporated them into their medical information and
advice books to convince the women in their audiences to adopt beneficial
behaviors, most frequently healthy modes of dress, but they also had the effect
of reminding readers of the writers' expertise. In *Physical Development and
Exercise for Women* (1891), Bissell went so far as to include a description of
her own scientific experiment: "To ascertain in figures how much ordinarily
tight clothing interferes with lung expansion and freedom of the diaphragm,
the writer induced ten young ladies to allow themselves to be measured about
the chest both with and without a corset or waist, and noted the results" (34).
After reporting measurements proving the constriction caused by corsets,
Bissell concluded, "These figures point their own moral, and make comment
needless" (35). In performing her own research, Bissell not only proved to
her readers that corsets were unhealthful but also showed them that she
participated in science and did not merely repeat the findings of men.

As professionals, women physicians had another source of knowledge
and authority inaccessible to most women: their professional experience.
Even Mrs. W. H. Maxwell, M.D.,[8] who seems to have lacked a formal
medical education, noted the distinction between the professional and the

nonprofessional woman. In *A Female Physician to the Ladies of the United States* (1860), Maxwell explained that the practicing physician's broad experience authorized her advice: "she only whose experience has not been confined to herself and daughters, can be relied on for advice" (23). In fact, one of the most common strategies of self-presentation in women physicians' health information and advice texts was reference to the writer's experience in her practice. Greene's book, *Build Well* (1885), was full of instances of this strategy. For example, Greene wrote, "In some families whose history I have known for nearly half a century, I have been directly conversant with cause and result. In one case . . ." This opening was followed by the story of a family who suffered because the parents engaged in "Excesses in the genetic relations of marriage" (43–44). Statements such as this one suggested to the reader both the writer's medical knowledge and the experience she had gained through decades of practice; Greene invoked both the authority of expertise and the authority of wisdom. A few pages later, Greene referred to the breadth of her experience: "In my intimate acquaintance with many hundred families I have seen beautiful approximations to perfected love in home life in not a few instances, and its fruition is ever joy and peace" (48–49). Because Greene had established her length and breadth of experience, when she wrote "I have never failed to observe" (49), "I have never seen" (84), "I have never known more frightful or more certainly fatal hæmorrhages than" (85), and "I have never known an instance of cure in such a case" (99), the reader was likely inclined to believe her.

In addition to serving as evidence supporting a writer's claims about health, anecdotes drawn from professional experience could also be used to prove the writer's usefulness as a woman physician, reinforcing her ethos by demonstrating goodwill. For instance, in *A Book of Medical Discourses in Two Parts* (1883), African American physician Rebecca Crumpler[9] warned her readers to avoid administering catnip tea, which was supposed to produce sleep, to babies. She told the story of being summoned to treat a three-day-old infant. When she arrived, she "suspected that catnip tea had been around," though no one would admit it. Crumpler reported that she "staid [*sic*] by the little victim fifteen hours without sleep, finally succeeding in . . . saving the child's life," at which point "shame caused the disclosure of the cause of the mischief," which was indeed catnip tea (26). Crumpler's story of her determined efforts on behalf of this child not only conveyed the dangers of catnip tea, but also illustrated women physicians' commitment to their patients. Earlier in her book, Crumpler criticized men physicians for leaving women too soon after childbirth—"as soon as the navel cord is severed" (11); in contrast, her willingness to spend fifteen consecutive hours on one infant suggested that women physicians possessed greater devotion to the well-being of women and children.[10]

Reference to her professional experience also justified Crumpler's claims to originality—often a component of a scientific ethos—in treatment. In a chapter titled "The Better Mode of Washing the New-Born," she declared that "Washing is the name given to the old method. Cleansing is the proper one for the new" (14). After describing the procedure for cleansing a newborn, she compared its effects to those of washing: "It often happens that, after 'washing' and dressing by present methods, blood oozes from the cut end of the cord. Seldom does this happen by the new method,—I should say, my method" (16). Alluding to her experience, Crumpler could point to what "often" occurred with the old method of bathing a newborn and maintain that her own method was safer.

As in Crumpler's work, many of the advice texts by women physicians used references to medical practice both to support the arguments the writers made about diseases and their treatments and to enhance the writer's medical authority. For example, in her 1887 text Longshore-Potts stated, "In a large and varied practice, extending over a quarter of a century, we have found the majority of these obstinate cases of 'irritable bladder' are the result of the causes just stated" (208–9). Likewise, in 1891 Saur wrote, "My belief is that the sulphuric acid in the mixture is a specific in scarlet fever, as much as quinine is in ague, and sulphur in itch. I have reason to say so, for in numerous cases I have seen its immense value" (431). Although ordinary women had long been able to claim the authority of their experience as mothers and grandmothers, women physicians' rhetoric was authorized by their professional experience with a variety of patients over several years.

Men had traditionally enjoyed the authority that came from reference to professional experience, and they used it in composing books directing girls' and women's education, deportment, and health care, ultimately restricting women's activities on the basis of their accumulated professional experience. Edward H. Clarke's *Sex in Education* (1873), one of the most influential nineteenth-century books by a physician about women's abilities, depended on the cases Clarke had seen over the course of his career to demonstrate that women suffered from attending school continuously, that is, from not taking time off for menstruation. Of course, this argument had implications for the levels of education women could attain and the kinds of careers believed biologically appropriate for them. When women physicians could claim years of professional experience, they too claimed the authority to make statements about the "nature" of things—men, women, health, society—and about how they ought to be.

For example, Greene, who wrote her *Build Well* in 1885 after nearly three decades of practice, frequently referred to the knowledge she had gained over those years in order to advocate the behaviors that she believed would improve the physical and moral health of individuals and society. In discussing the optimal conditions for conception, for instance, Greene stated that she had "many illustrative instances of the effect of temporary sickness or disordered conditions transmitted from parents to children," but that she "will give but one or two" (39). Greene's instructions to avoid conceiving a child while either parent was in any way sick, intoxicated, or systemically "depressed" (40) implicitly gave women greater control over marital sexual activity. Later in her book, Greene complained that, though the "marital rights" of husbands were frequently insisted upon, "the marital rights of wives, . . . strange to say, are rarely mentioned, and only properly considered, by comparatively few husbands." She went on to argue that "These rights should certainly be, at least, half the choice in regard to the time of intercourse and maternity" (71). Like men physicians, women were beginning to use their professional experience to advocate behaviors that affected not only the health of those immediately involved but also gendered social dynamics.

Women Physicians and the Professionals' Prerogative

Although some nineteenth-century American women physicians advocated medical self-help and contributed to popular efforts to teach members of the public to prevent and treat illness on their own, many of the women who wrote medical advice and information texts used them to exert their authority as professionals. As the authors of these texts constructed ethē that demonstrated their expertise and usefulness to the public, they also developed their own sense of professional identity and of the desired relationship between the physician and her patient. As expert advisers and as new members of a profession, women physicians negotiated their new roles, balancing their goal of educating the public with the professional's interest in monopolizing specialized information. Although the nineteenth-century women who wrote popular medical texts frequently expressed their desire to share physiological information with women, and in fact built part of their case for women's medical education on women's need for such information, these physicians were still professionals who thought of themselves as a distinct class. As professionals, women physicians benefited from possessing specialized knowledge inaccessible to the public, and they firmly believed that some information was best kept out of the public's hands. The complexity of women physicians' ethē is apparent in their health information and advice books, where they balanced demonstrations of goodwill (sharing medical information) with reminders that they possessed expertise that they would not share. Enhancing the woman-physician ethos through a straightforward display of goodwill toward the audience in the form of sharing all of the writers' knowledge was probably not possible, given the technical nature of medical expertise. Even if it were possible, however, such free sharing would have undercut the goals of those women who wished to claim the social and rhetorical advantages of professionalism.

In their medical information and advice books, several women physicians acknowledged that they were withholding information, explaining that some conditions were too serious or complicated to be treated by anyone but a physician. For example, in 1870 Gleason opted not to describe specific causes or treatments for conditions preventing conception, stating that "they can only be detected or corrected by the experienced physician having the patient in charge" (171–72). Even Maxwell, whose advocacy of abortion placed her outside the bounds of mainstream women physicians, preserved some areas of medical care for the professional. In her "Introductory Remarks," she explained that her purpose in writing *A Female Physician to the Ladies of the United States* (1860) was to provide women with basic information, particularly about menopause: "As a popular work, it cannot be expected that this book should be a *perfect* treatise on the subjects under discussion. The causes and treatment of the various diseases can be spoken of only in generalities, as too much minuteness would defeat the object of the writer. The broad land marks that are familiar to every eye, and the hidden points of disease are in the one case well known, in the other too obscure to be rendered cognizable to any other than a professional reader" (11). Elsewhere, Maxwell insisted on complete deference to the physician, instructing her readers that for some conditions, "implicit obedience to the orders of the medical adviser is absolutely imperative" (61).

Achieving professional status allowed women to become advisers to the public with an authority that other women who wrote popular advice texts—about health, conduct, or domestic matters—lacked. This authority was validated by membership in a recognized profession, by experience working at a career, and often by extended formal education. It also put women in the position of protecting their status and claiming that some information and some therapies were best handled by a professional, so they had to develop rhetorical means for sharing some, but not all, of their knowledge. For many of the women who published popular medical texts, this maneuver was accomplished in promises to the reader that the book would be scientific, but not overwhelmingly so. For example, early in her book, Gleason described *Talks to My Patients* (1870):

> This is not a medical book, not a learned book, not a show of science, and I trust not *un*scientific. It will savor little of the library, more of every-day life. A simple compend of such motherly hints as seem to be needed, and such as, from my long care of the sick, I have found available.
>
> The book will offer no new theory as to the cause or cure of diseases, but merely practical suggestions how to relieve pain, or, better still, to avoid it; such means as we have for many years found efficient in our infirmary. (vi)

The practices nineteenth-century women physicians developed for negotiating the competing demands of educating the public while asserting the exclusivity of the profession suggest a high degree of reciprocity between ethos and genre: the genre of the health information text attributed a great deal of authority to the physician-writer; at the same time, the physician's desire for a privileged professional identity along with her perception of her readers' intellectual capacity affected the genre's conventions, limiting the information provided to the most basic descriptions of anatomy, physiology, and illness.

Because nineteenth-century women physicians justified their books by arguing that women needed some physiological information to fulfill feminine roles successfully, the writers could focus on what they believed a wife and mother needed to know to care for her family. Women physicians did not always have an easy time determining the extent of the knowledge that women needed, however. Saur, for example, seemed to vacillate between her commitments to women and to her profession. In *Maternity* (1891), her discussion of dysentery revealed her conflicting priorities: "Now with regard to medicine. I approach this part of the treatment with some degree of reluctance—for dysentery is a case requiring opium—and opium I never like a mother of her own accord to administer. But if a doctor cannot be procured in time, the mother must then prescribe, or the child will die! *What then is to be done?*" (338–39). In the next chapter, Saur seemed to come to a compromise between physicians' desires for professional control over health care and mothers' desires to help their children:

> A mother should be made acquainted with the symptoms of the serious diseases of children. I am not advocating the doctrine that a mother should *treat serious* diseases; far from it; it is not her province, except in certain cases of extreme urgency, where a doctor cannot be procured, and where delay might be death; but I do insist upon the necessity of her knowing the *symptoms*

> of disease. . . . If she were better acquainted with these matters, how much more useful would she be in a sick room, and how much more readily would she enter into the plans and views of the physician. By her knowledge of symptoms, and by having his advice in time, she would nip disease in the bud. (398)

Saur explained that mothers should know about disease not so that they could treat serious conditions themselves, but so that they could be better nurses who were more compliant with physicians' orders. In constructing distinct roles for the mother and the physician, Saur mirrored domestic advice literature, such as that by Catharine Beecher, who "distinguished crucially between mothers and physicians" (Baym 175). Nina Baym, in her study of nineteenth-century women's affiliations with science, observes that Beecher limited mothers' practice of domestic science and health care: "The mother's work was to prevent illness by constructing the home as a healthy physical container for the bodies it housed; when illness struck, she was to follow the doctor's orders" (175). When women were themselves physicians, however, the overlapping roles of *mother* and *physician* posed a conflict of interest, one that Saur negotiated, between the professional's claim to monopolistic expertise and the mother's impulse to help her children. Saur reinforced the notion that authority and specialized knowledge were components of the physician's ethos; reciprocally, Saur constructed the mother's ethos as reflecting virtues such as obedience, helpfulness, and devotion to children.

Other nineteenth-century women physicians seemed to recognize the physician's prerogative but were uncomfortable withholding advice from their readers, expressing fear that a physician might not always be immediately available, as Saur did, or that his or her prescriptions might not be practical. For example, in chapter 7 of *A Book of Medical Discourses* (1883), Crumpler expressed her reluctance to undermine the authority of an attending physician: "I do not wish to be understood as usurping the power of other physicians; each has his or her own method of procedure" (31). Elsewhere, however, she complained of "the expense of the [dietary] articles mostly ordered by physicians" and suggested that there were other foods that could improve a child's health (65). Her concern for families who could not afford to follow a physician's instructions put Crumpler in a difficult rhetorical and professional position: as a regularly educated physician, she valued her profession, but at the same time she understood the impracticality of some of her colleagues' prescriptions. In contrast to the physician who thoughtlessly instructed his patients to follow an expensive diet, Crumpler enacted the ethos of a sensible woman physician, one who was sensitive to her patients' financial constraints and who understood practical domestic matters, such as the price of food.

When women physicians published medical advice texts, they engaged in a discursive performance of professionalism. Although they believed women would benefit from accessing some of the information historically withheld from them, they also needed to show the public that they were themselves professionals and so possessed specialized knowledge and skills incomprehensible to the nonprofessional. By distinguishing themselves from silly, ignorant women, by insisting on the patient's obedience to the physician, and by withholding some details of physiology, etiology, and treatment from their readers, nineteenth-century women physicians assumed the role of professional expert. This was a significant social and rhetorical development, because for the first time, women could claim a professional prerogative, deciding on behalf of their audience members what specialized information would be appropriate for them. Although medicine's control over information has been criticized for limiting patients' abilities to make decisions and for reifying the profession's own power, for women not to have adopted the rhetorical role of professional who determines the public's access to information would have barred them from one of the most authoritative discursive stances of the last 150 years. Moreover, with women in a position to decide which facts to share and which were best kept in the hands of professionals, for the first time women's interests were considered in that decision.

Health Education and Woman's Place in Society

Even though nineteenth-century women physicians deemed some vocabulary and some facts beyond the reach of ordinary women, they perceived women to be so lacking in basic facts about anatomy and physiology that they assumed the information they did provide, limited though it was, would have a liberating effect on women. In 1895, in a chapter condemning corsets, Galbraith described a myth that she sought to dispel: "[Woman] was led to believe . . . that she was a victim of her functions; a woman, ergo, an invalid" (224–27). Many of the health information and advice texts authored by women drew attention to the consequences of women's ignorance of anatomy and physiology, ignorance that affected entire families as mothers made uninformed decisions about their children's health or became invalids themselves and so were unable to perform domestic labor. In her preface to *Maternity* (1891), Saur emphasized her belief in the propriety of women's study of health and hygiene: "The important object of this work is to show that [women's] universal suffering *is not* the result of excessive mental development, but a lack of *physical* culture" (iii). Countering the conventional medical opinion that intense study was a cause of women's diseases, Saur argued instead that women were weak because of their ignorance of anatomy and physiology. Once women were educated about these sciences and arranged their lives according to scientific principles, she wrote, "a higher type of womanhood will be developed" (iv).

Teaching women about anatomy and physiology involved encouraging them to be mindful of the choices they made that affected their bodies. Saur defined the "lack of *physical* culture" on which she blamed women's poor health as "a want of balance between excitement and rest, especially before maturity has been reached, improprieties of dress, and sedentary habits of life" (iii). Many nineteenth-century women physicians advocated an active life for all girls and women, constructing women as inherently healthy. Because of women physicians' medical education, they were well positioned to counter existing medical constructions of the female body as weak and prone to suffering. They did so by arguing that civilization, not biology, caused most of women's ailments; "natural" women, they claimed, did not suffer as "civilized" women did. For example, Bissell began one of the chapters in *Physical Development and Exercise for Women* (1891) by lamenting the effects of civilization on girls' physical health: "That we should be obliged to sit down and seriously consider how our girls can find sufficient exercise to promote their development and to gratify their natural love for physical sport is a commentary upon our distance from nature" (79). Modern-day girls, she wrote, no longer worked outdoors; instead "school-life absorbs most of a young girl's vitality, and society (even for the tiniest) what remnant remains." Consequently, girls' "muscles cry out for activity, and the nerves play their pranks in sheer desperation; and our girls are often thin-limbed and hollow-chested, and in a word lack robustness" (80). Women were not inherently weak or nervous, Bissell implied, and rather than reducing girls' access to education as some commentators suggested, Bissell advocated restructuring girls' schools to allow for more physical activity. In fact, she claimed that the very activities deemed by some to be dangerous or inappropriate for women—including playing tennis (81–83), swimming (83–84), and exercising in a gymnasium (89–108)—would produce stronger women. In their health advice books, women physicians argued that the source of woman's suffering was not her reproductive system but her behavior, much of which was a matter of social convention. This meant that, rather than being doomed by biology to invalidism, women could live active and healthy lives if they were properly educated about anatomy and physiology and learned correct habits.

When nineteenth-century women physicians took on the role of popular health adviser, then, they sought to alter popular conceptions of the potential of the female body to be healthy. Some women physicians even made overt links between physiological knowledge and greater respect for women. In her *Lectures to Ladies on Anatomy and Physiology* (1842), for example, Mary Gove identified ignorance of physiology as the greatest obstacle to human progress and to women's advancement in particular:

> With what pleasing and joyous anticipations do the friends of science look forward to that period when this black night of ignorance shall be chased from our beloved land, and light be poured in, even to every dark corner.
>
> How can the dawn of this day be hastened? I answer, by the efforts of woman: let woman use her energies, let her attain that moral and intellectual elevation which is her right. Let her attain that height where men *cannot* look down upon her, if they *would.* Let her repudiate at once and forever those sickly tales of fiction that enervate the mind, without informing or improving. Let her nobly resolve that she will have science, that she will be no longer a plaything, a bauble. When woman thus arises in the greatness of her intellectual strength, then there will be a new era in the history of our world. (57)

Like Gove, Gleason also expressed concern for popular perceptions of women as ignorant. Writing in 1870 of the patients admitted to the water-cure establishment she and her husband ran in Elmira, New York, Gleason suggested that uneducated women not only suffered physically because of their ignorance, but also appeared ridiculous. In a section titled "Imaginary Prolapsus," she explained that nearly all of the women who came to her complaining of "falling of the womb" had incorrectly diagnosed themselves: "During the last twenty years, of the many women who have consulted me for this infirmity, not one in ten were suffering from uterine displacement" (43). Gleason then attributed women's tendency to think that all pelvic pain resulted from a uterine prolapse to their lack of anatomical knowledge:

> Is it strange . . . that women, to whom the pelvis is a sort of unknown country, save that they know from personal experience that it is a locality as productive of misery as a Western marsh of ague—is it strange, I say, that they are often mistaken as to whether it is a mal-position or a mal-condition of the parts which induces the pain?
>
> I could fill this little book with cases having a strange mixture of the sad and the ludicrous to illustrate this one point. (43–44)

Whether women lacked health information because it was withheld from them by men or because there was no one to whom their feminine modesty would allow them to turn before women became physicians, women

93

physicians believed their sisters were suffering as a result of their ignorance. As the passages from Gove's and Gleason's books suggest, some writers seemed to believe that women's ignorance and poor health were detrimental to the reputation of all women. Women who studied the information provided by women physicians would learn how to be healthy, strong, physically competent for the demands of their daily lives, and educated in the sciences of anatomy and physiology. All of these traits might contribute to increased opportunities for women.

Taking a different approach to altering perceptions of female health, some women who wrote health information and advice texts contested popular medical and religious notions of the body's, especially the female body's, weakness by drawing together the physical and the spiritual, by describing the body as unified with the soul and as a valuable component of Creation. Elizabeth Blackwell stated this philosophy most clearly in 1852: "In the wonderful whole of creation no part is separated from the rest, mind and matter, body and soul, substance and form, are essentially related. The creation is filled with the Creator!" (*Laws* 61–62). Linking body, mind, and soul perhaps came naturally to nineteenth-century women, who had been entrusted with the responsibility for the physical, intellectual, and spiritual development of children. In the context of women's own health, however, unifying the body and the soul made the body worthy of attention and care. If women came to understand that their bodies were "filled with the Creator" and that physical health was a prerequisite for achieving more perfect spirituality, they might be more likely to take better care of themselves. Blackwell informed her readers that "We cannot separate the body and soul—the health of one must, as a general rule, be based upon the other; fresh air and exercise are singularly conducive to virtue" (*Laws* 167). Likewise, in *Physical Development and Exercise for Women* (1891), Bissell compared the effects of exercise on the lungs to the role of moral training in shaping the character: "Now, exercise acts upon the lungs as moral training does upon the character,—gradually accustoming them to prepare for and meet the emergencies of sudden exertion with calmness" (71). In making this comparison, Bissell associated the recognizable good of moral training with the less agreed-upon good of exercise for women. Constructing physical well-being as contributing to virtue and as a moral good in its own right countered negative views of the female body and placed physiological study firmly within the category of activities appropriate for pious women.

Finally, women physicians sought to alter attitudes toward the female body by challenging constructions of the body and its functions as dirty and unladylike. They attributed much of this attitude to women's ignorance of anatomy and physiology. The women physicians who wrote medical information texts spent a great deal of time expounding the wonders of bodily systems and explaining how the various organs and processes worked together and influenced each other. For example, in educating readers about the digestive system, few writers failed to instruct women to establish a regular bathroom regimen, emphasizing the importance of waste removal to overall health. To make the subject more palatable to her readers, Galbraith (1895) likened the human digestive system to a domestic furnace:

> Every housekeeper knows that, although her furnace is in perfect working order, the draughts good, and it is supplied with coal, if it is allowed to become clogged with cinders or choked with ashes, the fire instead of burning gradually dies out. And the only way to procure a good fire is to have the cinders and ashes *regularly* removed, at not too long intervals. . . . Yet, strange to say, while a woman would consider herself an incapable and shiftless housekeeper did she not bestow all this care on her furnace, . . . she forgets that her own physical machine must be quite as carefully looked after if it is to be kept in good running order. . . .
>
> The refuse matter which collects in the lower bowel must be evacuated *once every day*. (152)

If women who, as Saur said in giving advice similar to Galbraith's four years earlier, "fail to heed the demands of nature" due to "a sense of false modesty" (86) could begin to think of their obligations to care for themselves in the same terms that they thought of their domestic duties, they might feel less shame about their bodily functions. Women physicians thus sought to alter not only public attitudes toward the female body, but also women's attitudes toward their own bodies, instructing women to attend to, respect, and even admire their own physiological processes and capabilities.

In relying on their ethē as authoritative experts to promote a positive, healthy model of femininity for women and in insisting that women were not inherently weak, nineteenth-century women physicians paved the way for women to be taken seriously. Even as women physicians described their audiences as currently ignorant, weak, and suffering, the writers simultaneously constructed their readers as potentially informed, healthy, and active in promoting the health of their families and their communities. Galbraith articulated such a transformation in her preface: "This little book will have accomplished its end if it arouses woman to extend her studies on the subjects discussed [hygiene and physical culture], and to bend her thoughts and energies to the emancipation of her sex from the bondage of invalidism" (viii).[11] Resisting the notion that nearly all women were doomed to the silly, morbid, or pathetic invalidism envisioned by so many novelists and social commentators, women physicians used their professional ethos and the genre of the health information and advice book to offer a model of femininity in which women were respected for their intelligence and common sense and strong enough to act on their knowledge and beliefs.

Relying on a genre and a related ethos that highlighted the writers' expertise and their authority to advise the public, nineteenth-century American women physicians interrupted the conventional male-to-female flow of medical advice. They used the health information and advice genre to speak directly to women about their health, their interests, and their fears, offering their audiences a new kind of advice: advice that came from someone who understood them, who shared the embodied and the social experience of life as a woman. Women physicians' health information and advice texts demonstrate how feminine professionalism authorized their advocacy of better care for female bodies at the same time that it allowed them to withhold medical information from women. The complex and sometimes contradictory rhetorical practices of professionals were evident in early women physicians' speech and writing, serving as a reminder that even as nineteenth-century women physicians constructed a healthy, respect-worthy ethos for their female readers and even as the writers themselves benefited from the strong ethos their medical careers enabled, women physicians also participated in a discourse that excluded some of the very people they sought to help.

4

Teaching Women to Talk about Sex

> If our own minds are filled with the purity of truth we shall
> be able to present it in the beauty of its purity.
>
> —Mary Wood-Allen, *Teaching Truth* (1892)

Nineteenth-century Americans, and women in particular, were eager for scientific information about sexuality and reproduction, information that would affect the moral tone and the physical health of the nation. The vulgar connotations surrounding these subjects near the end of the century, however, made them difficult for respectable women to study and discuss, so there was great call for "pure" sources from which children and adults could learn about sexuality. As temperance leader Lillian M. N. Stevens stated in her commendation of the Self and Sex series of books, "There is great need of carefully, delicately written books upon the subjects treated in this series"[1] (figure 4.1). Nineteenth-century American women physicians, especially Emma F. Angell Drake and Mary Wood-Allen, sought to fill this need, publishing books that readers accepted as "pure" because of the writers' combination of middle-class respectability, feminine morality, and medical expertise. These women physicians believed it was vital for women not only to study but also to speak about sex and reproduction. To this end, women physicians relied on their ethos as feminine professionals to alter the vulgar connotations surrounding sexuality so that the subject could be discussed, in Wood-Allen's words, "in the beauty of its purity" (49).

The sex-ed texts written by nineteenth-century women physicians constitute a subset of the medical advice and information texts discussed in chapter 3. Some writers, such as Wood-Allen, published books in both categories. Others, such as Elizabeth Blackwell, wrote health advice books that contained a strong emphasis on subjects related to sex (see, for example, *Laws*

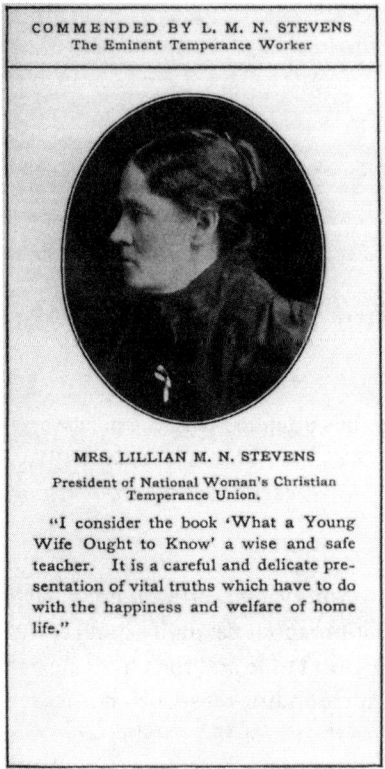

COMMENDED BY L. M. N. STEVENS
The Eminent Temperance Worker

MRS. LILLIAN M. N. STEVENS

President of National Woman's Christian
Temperance Union.

"I consider the book 'What a Young
Wife Ought to Know' a wise and safe
teacher. It is a careful and delicate presentation of vital truths which have to do
with the happiness and welfare of home
life."

Figure 4.1. Commendation of the Self
and Sex series by Lillian M. N. Stevens,
accompanying books published in the
1890s and 1900s.

of Life). Because of the overlap between authors and subjects, many of the
rhetorical features of medical advice and information texts also appeared
in sex-ed texts. Women physicians' books about sex and reproduction also
participated in the rich context of advice appearing in marital manuals,
etiquette books, religious pamphlets, and guides for health and hygiene. For
example, *Aristotle's Master-piece*, which was first published in England in the
mid-seventeenth century and circulated in later editions in the United States
well into the middle of the nineteenth century, provided basic information
about human reproductive physiology, advice for conception, guidelines
for diagnosing and treating reproductive disorders, and instructions for
midwives. This book cast women as passive participants in sexual activity:
"in man [the venereal appetite] proceeds from a desire of emission, and in
woman from a desire of reception" (51). This supposedly innate behavior in

men and women was said to be reflected in their reproductive cells: "In the generation of the foetus there are two principals, active and passive, the active is the man's seed elaborated in the testicles . . .—the passive is an egg impregnated by the man's seed" (13). The assumption in the 1817 edition of *Aristotle's Master-piece* that "a young couple . . . naturally desire[s] children" (10) was a bit less certain later in the century when Dr. John Cowan published *The Science of a New Life* (1869). Cowan felt the need to remind his readers that "The originating of children in God's own image should be an intensely active, lovable desire on the part of both man and wife" (131).

Cowan was not alone in his concern. In their study of nineteenth-century American medical advice literature, Anita Clair Fellman and Michael Fellman note that with the shift from home production of food and goods came a change in the size and purpose of families: marriage was no longer a primarily economic arrangement, and large families were no longer necessary for the labor that used to be performed in homes and on farms. Fertility rates, especially among middle-class Americans, declined. All of these changes led to questions about the purpose of marriage and of the role of sex within marriage; these questions were fodder for many medical and social advisors (79). According to some commentators, modern civilization and the unnatural habits of living it fostered increased sexual desire beyond "natural" levels (98). Both feminists and promoters of Free Love insisted that women should have the right to determine if and when they should conceive (84). At the same time, women's rights advocates also expressed concern that if sex were separated from procreation, "in a society of inequality between the sexes, women could only lose an important source of economic support, indeed of leverage in conjugal relations, if the marriage relation were no different than legalized prostitution" (80). Consequently, many advisers promoted "marital continence" as a strategy for limiting the number of children without the use of contraceptive methods, which, it was believed, would "debase the quality of the moral relation between husband and wife, would license promiscuity, and would lead to marital breakdown" (80). For example, Cowan advised couples to sleep in separate beds, if not different rooms, until the day they had selected (and spent four weeks preparing for) for the conception of their child (171).

The attitudes of sexual-advice writers toward women's rights were complicated. On one hand, according to Fellman and Fellman, some commentators perceived women's reluctance to bear large families as another example of women's "insubordination": "Women's refusal to honor their marriage relation when it did not please them, to carry on the reproduction which traditionally had been expected of them, to take their doctor's advice on these subjects, and, in general, to accept their lot in life provoked many advisors" (83). On the other hand, some writers encouraged women to pursue rights and opportunities. Cowan advocated women's rights in order to produce more perfect citizens: "Keep a woman—a mother—in bondage, and the low conditions that spring from a life of bondage will develop themselves in her sons—the future men of the nation" (380). Elsewhere, Cowan wrote that a better generation of men and women would be raised if women had the rights to suffrage, property, participation in government, occupation, education, and "her own person" (380–81). Cowan's assertion of a woman's right "to her own person" resonated with women writers who understood a wife's right to decline her husband's sexual advances as an extension of women's efforts to control their bodies and to increase opportunities for self-development free of the burden of unwanted children.

Nineteenth-century women physicians' sex-education books entered into this extensive cultural conversation, typically reflecting the middle-class values of their writers as well as a commitment to women's rights to their bodies. Although their vision of human sexuality does not differ greatly from other books written around the end of the century, these texts are of interest to scholars of women's rhetoric because of the attention they give to women as speakers. In their sex-ed books, women physicians taught non-professional women how to talk about sex: they modeled conversations with children about basic reproductive anatomy and physiology, offered young women reasons they could use to influence the behavior of young men, and encouraged women to speak with their fiancés about their beliefs about the purposes for and the appropriate frequency of sexual activity. Given the "delicacy" of these topics, the historical proscriptions against women's speech on these matters, and the crucial role human sexuality plays within families and in society more broadly, the rhetorical advice women physicians provided offered an important step forward for women.

Women physicians who wished to discuss human reproduction and sexuality, however, faced the additional challenges posed by writing about "delicate" subjects. For example, Alice B. Stockham faced legal action according to the 1873 Comstock Law, which made it illegal to use the mail to convey contraceptives or information about contraception. Her two very popular books, *Tokology* (1883) and *Karezza* (1896), offered not only instructions about the diet that Stockham maintained would result in painless childbirth but also advice for avoiding conception. An advertisement in the *Woman's Tribune* claimed that *Tokology* had reached a circulation of two hundred thousand copies by 1892 and had been translated into Swedish, German, and Russian, and was soon to be translated into Japanese ("Tokology Encircling the World" 163). This book was in publication until 1916, released at least eighteen times in English. Yet in 1905, the U.S. Post Office censored the Free Love periodical *Lucifer, the Light Bearer* after it published parts of Stockham's *Tokology*. In another incident, Stockham herself was arrested in Chicago and fined two hundred fifty dollars for distributing a pamphlet titled *The Wedding Night* (Brodie 284).[2]

Other women physicians who wrote about sexuality and reproduction avoided Stockham's legal troubles by addressing less controversial subjects; descriptions of the body and its functions were typically acceptable, especially late in the century, as was advice that confirmed conventional attitudes toward sexuality and maternity. Indeed, some of the books by women physicians about sex and reproduction were well received. A review of Wood-Allen's *Almost a Man* (1895) stated that it sold twenty-five thousand copies in the first two years after its initial publication ("Book Reviews"), and an advertisement for her *Teaching Truth* (1892) called sales of this book "immense" (Teaching Truth). Even late in the century, however, publishers and promoters of sex-ed texts went to great lengths to assure readers of the decorum of the writers and the purity of the material they presented. Nineteenth-century women physicians' sex-ed books often demonstrate the phenomenon Vicki Tolar Collins calls "rhetorical accretion," which she defines as the "process of layering additional texts over and around the original text" (547). Rhetorical accretion has the potential to refine, enhance, or degrade a rhetor's ethos: "With each accretion to a text, the speaker of the core text is respoken. Respeaking can be a way for the production authority to modify the ethos of the original speaker or call into question something in her text" (548). In the case of women physicians' sex-ed books, rhetorical accretion was used to reassure audiences of the femininity and propriety of the writers, despite the risqué subjects they addressed. Advertisements and book reviews praised the writers for handling their subjects reverently, chastely, and without any shade of prurience.

The most thorough effort at enhancing women physicians' ethos through rhetorical accretion accompanied books in the Self and Sex Series. Edited by minister Sylvanus Stall,[3] this series consisted of eight books, four targeted to men (written by Stall) and four to women (two by Wood-Allen and two by Drake) addressing specific life stages (girl/boy, young woman/man, young wife/husband, and middle age). Bound with the books and preceding even the title page was a set of "Commendations from Eminent Men & Women." Contributed by ministers, authors, teachers, and physicians, these testimonies, which were generally accompanied by a photograph of the well-known person recommending the book, vouched for the book's purity, its readability, and its practical usefulness. For example, Mrs. M. W. Sewall, identified as

"The Eminent American Educator," wrote of Wood-Allen's *What a Young Woman Ought to Know* (1892), "I am profoundly grateful that a subject of such information to young women should be treated in a manner at once so noble and so delicate that any pure-minded teacher or mother may read or discuss its pages with young girls without the slightest chance of wounding the most delicate sensibilities, or by being misunderstood." In the same text, philanthropist C. N. Crittenton praised Wood-Allen's "remarkable gift in the facility and refinement with which she is able to approach the most delicate subject without arousing a single morbid and sensitive impulse."

Other evidence of the worthiness of the writers and the material they presented was incorporated into the text. For example, in her preface to the 1899 edition of *Almost a Man*, Wood-Allen referred to "the innumerable letters from boys whose hearts were so filled with gratitude" after reading an earlier edition of the book "that they could not refrain from sending a word of thanks to the one whom they felt had done so much for them" (5–6). Women physicians used the need for widespread knowledge about sexuality to defend their decisions to write on such delicate subjects as reproduction, premarital sex, and prostitution.

In this chapter, I demonstrate that through books and pamphlets covering the topics of puberty, sexual behavior, reproduction, and menopause, nineteenth-century women physicians redefined human sexuality in terms that made the subject accessible to women and appropriate for women's rhetoric. Improving the connotations surrounding sexuality was not only necessary to protect the reputations of women physicians themselves but also to justify nonprofessional women who wished to participate in public discussions about sexuality and all the subjects related to it, including social purity, temperance, heredity, abortion, and child development. Adopting a "pure" attitude toward sexuality also established grounds on which women physicians could encourage women to take better care of themselves. For example, Wood-Allen encouraged the young women who read *What a Young Woman Ought to Know* (1892) to consider their influence on future generations: "Young women may feel that their individual violation of the laws of health is of no importance, but when they realize that the girls of to-day are the mothers of the future, and that the physical strength or weakness of each individual girl affects the average health of the nation, not only now, but it may be through her posterity for centuries, we can see that each girl's health is a matter of national and of racial importance" (219–20). As this quotation suggests, one strategy women physicians used to justify their discussion of sex was revising the discourse of sexuality and reproduction to describe these subjects as matters of social importance rather than individual pleasure. This rhetorical strategy and others described in this chapter allowed nineteenth-century women physicians to discuss sexuality while maintaining respectable ethē. Modeling for nonprofessional women approaches to discussing sexuality that relied on a tactful, maternal, scientific ethos, women physicians encouraged their readers to address subjects previously considered inappropriate for respectable women.

Persuading the Maternal Rhetor

Much of women physicians' encouragement to speak about sexuality was aimed at mothers, whom women physicians believed should be educated in order to discuss sexuality and reproduction with their children. In focusing their efforts on mothers, women physicians reflected what Nan Johnson describes as "the widely held nineteenth-century view that the most important rhetorical role for American women was their healthy moral influence over domestic life." According to Johnson, speaking from their domestic roles capitalized on women's greatest persuasive strengths: "For eloquence, no one could match the devoted mother instructing her children or the wise and loving wife counseling her husband" (118). Such rhetorical acts were complicated, however, when the subject was human sexuality; even though the domestic venue and interpersonal nature of the discourse suited beliefs about women's strengths as communicators, the topic of the conversations was something with which many women were uncomfortable. In order to achieve their goal of increasing the number of mothers who spoke with their children about sex and reproduction, women physicians first had to teach women about the subject and convince them not only that was it acceptable for a mother to speak about sex but also that it was her duty to do so.

Wood-Allen was the most prolific promoter of mother-child conversations about reproductive physiology, publishing at least fifteen titles, many of which went through multiple editions and were translated into several languages; however, women physicians as early as Blackwell (*The Laws of Life*, 1852) and Mrs. W. H. Maxwell (*A Female Physician to the Ladies of the United States*, 1860) implored mothers to speak with their children about the dangers of adolescence. Many women, however, were uncomfortable with such a rhetorical task because they were ill-informed on the subject and perceived it to be indecent. Some women were concerned about the effects possessing knowledge about sexuality would produce in children: in *Teaching Truth* (1892), Wood-Allen acknowledged that "Parents . . . sometimes fear that information will arouse wrong thoughts," but reassured her readers that "This will depend upon the manner in which knowledge is imparted" (47–48).

Women physicians sought to overcome women's reluctance by arguing that mothers were the ideal people to teach children about sexuality. For example, Wood-Allen drew on the characteristics of ideal maternity, particularly a child's implicit trust in her mother and her perception of her mother as the promoter of virtue to demonstrate that women could positively influence their children's attitudes toward sexuality. Wood-Allen's book *Child-Confidence Rewarded* (1903) featured a poem by the author that opened with a series of childlike questions, including "why is it that the sun / Shines only in the day?" and concluded by reminding mothers of the consequences of avoiding children's questions:

> And there's some other sorts of things
>   I'd like to ask about,
> Only you always say, "Hush, hush!"
>   And so I can't find out.
> The boys at school they tell me tales
>   That don't seem nice and clean.
> I wish you'd tell me, so I'd know
>   What these things really mean;
> Because you see, I know, mamma,
>   You never, never, lie,
> So, if you 'splained it, why 'twould be
>   The really reason why. (4)

The child in this poem would rather learn about sex from his mother than from the boys on the playground because she is such a good mother; he trusts her as a source of information, and he knows she is honest.

When mothers avoid questions about reproduction, Wood-Allen explained in the accompanying text, children learn that their mothers are embarrassed by the subject and so are more likely to believe the impure stories they hear at school: "[If a mother] is so far enlightened as to believe that some time [her child's] query must be answered, she postpones, as long as she possibly can, what, to her, seems an evil day. And, while she waits and trembles, some one less scrupulous than herself, has volunteered the desired information, and she has reason to tremble at the thoughts which have been insinuated into the innocent mind" (6). In another text, published in 1892, Wood-Allen encouraged mothers to educate their children by invoking her sense of her own maternal responsibility, telling readers, "I would rather tell a child the truth a year before it is really necessary, than to postpone it until five minutes after some one else has sown tares of evil thought in the virgin soil" (*Teaching Truth* 25). Not only might children hear impure things about human reproduction from their peers that would forever taint their attitudes, but they might, through accident or the influence of friends, fall into the vices of "self-pollution" or licentiousness. According to nineteenth-century medical and social thought, both vices weakened the vitality, and that weakness along with any diseases contracted sexually would condemn the next generation to poor health.

As evidence that mothers had a responsibility to be their children's teachers on this subject, Wood-Allen quoted boys who believed they would have been not only healthier, but also more virtuous, if their mothers had spoken with them before they developed bad habits: "I have often thought of the sadness that would fill a mother's heart could she know that the pale, blotched countenance, the clammy hands, the listless gait, the weakened memory of her son were evidences of solitary sin, and could she hear him say, as the truth comes home to him that he has wasted his vigor and defrauded himself, 'If my mother had told me what you have told us today, I should now be a stronger and a better boy'" (*Teaching Truth* 87). Women physicians argued over and over again that if adolescents knew about their bodies, about reproduction, and about sexuality, they would have a better chance of being healthy adults, remaining chaste, conceiving under the most pure and healthful conditions, and establishing an ideal home. Although Wood-Allen imagined a domestic context for women's rhetoric about sex, the subject itself and the significant influence over behavior that the writers attributed to mothers would make such conversations rhetorical breakthroughs.

Reforming Attitudes toward Sex

In addition to convincing women to speak with their children about sex, nineteenth-century women physicians also had to make women believe that they could have those conversations with propriety. As John S. Haller and Robin M. Haller note, "Discussions of sex predisposed the Victorians to an assortment of inferences in which sexual urges were somehow at variance with the search for morality and the proper definition of virtue" (91); therefore, before human development and reproduction could be discussed without the shadow of prurience falling over the conversation, women physicians had to disconnect *knowledge of sexuality* from *immorality* in their readers' minds. Such a shift in values would make it possible for women to discuss human sexuality without risking their respectability. Because women physicians sought to alter their audience members' values and to create an ethos for the nonprofessional woman that would allow her to speak about sex, women physicians who wrote sex-ed books could not simply demonstrate their allegiance to the audience's values. They needed, in fact, to alter the audience's values and by extension, its ethos. Craig R. Smith proposes a model of ethos that takes into account both the rhetor's and the audience's ethos. In his interpretation of Aristotle's *Rhetoric*, Smith suggests that "*ethos* dwells not only in the speaker . . . , but also in the audience" (6). In its most basic form, acknowledging that ethos dwells in the audience reflects the fact that the audience is the source of the values an effective rhetor chooses to demonstrate. In more complex instances of ethos negotiation, however, the suggestion that this appeal is located in both the rhetor and the audience implies that the rhetor can influence the ideals that the audience values: "An audience has character or characters; it has an *ethos* of its own to which speakers must attend. In adapting, they enhance their own *ethos*; if they fail to adapt, their *ethos* will be diminished. Beyond that, however, speakers can move the audience to conform to the speaker's *ethos* and modify the audience's habits and values. Such identification with a leader is difficult to achieve, but when accomplished, is the most powerful kind of persuasion" (13). The women physicians who wrote sex-ed books capitalized on the potential of ethos to influence their audience's values by presenting themselves as moral, scientific, respectable women. In not only arguing for the virtuous discussion of sexuality but also enacting it through their own ethē, women physicians created an opportunity for nonprofessional women to adopt a similar ethos and set of values.

Shifting the beliefs and values of the women in their audience was crucial to accomplishing women physicians' goal of widespread sex education provided by mothers. In *Teaching Truth* (1892), Wood-Allen stated that in educating children about reproduction, it was first necessary to "begin the instruction with the mother herself" (26), who "has, perhaps, no very exalted idea of the reproductive function, and feels that subject is surrounded with an atmosphere of indelicacy" (25). At the 1895 National Purity Congress, she expressed a similar sentiment: "the education of the child *must* begin in the *minds* of the parents" ("Moral Education" 233). In suggesting that mothers should change their ways of thinking about sex, women physicians implicitly argued for a new definition of feminine virtue, one that separated *ignorance* from *innocence*, and that made *virtue* the consequence of *knowledge*. Even the radical Mary Edwards Walker[4] associated knowledge with improved morals in her 1878 book on sexual morality: "Knowledge must ever be the basic principle upon which the purest morals are founded" (*Unmasked* 2). In order for women physicians and nonprofessional women to speak comfortably about sex, the ties between ignorance and innocence had to be broken. Insisting that education about such matters would improve the moral quality of the public simultaneously constructed women physicians as contributors to the progress of humanity and reshaped notions of proper femininity: knowledge about the body and about sexual behavior became a tenet of pure woman-hood, not cause to label the writer disreputable or scandalous.

In demonstrating that sexuality could be studied without moral taint, women physicians informed readers that even if the writer discussed taboo subjects, she and her book were still pure. Over Wood-Allen's career as a physician and reformer, she developed a reputation permeated by purity. According to the title page of *What a Young Woman Ought to Know* (1892), she held the position of "National Superintendent of the Purity Department [of the] Woman's Christian Temperance Union" (figures 4.2 and 4.3), and her obituary in the *Journal of the American Medical Association* (1908) listed her title as the "world's superintendent of the moral education department of the Woman's Christian Temperance Union" ("Mary Wood-Allen" 636). Wood-Allen's prominent position in the WCTU combined with her status as a degreed physician (Ann Arbor Medical School, 1875) afforded her both respectability and authority, qualities she needed to sanction the numerous sex-ed texts she wrote.[5] She was a strong proponent of the idea that information purely given was pure, and she often instructed women that human development and sexuality could be viewed in a pure light.

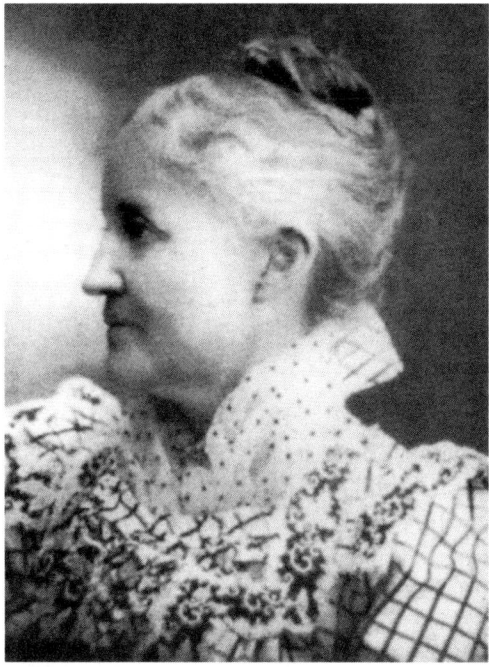

Figure 4.2. Mary Wood-Allen, frontispiece for
What a Young Woman Ought to Know, 1898.

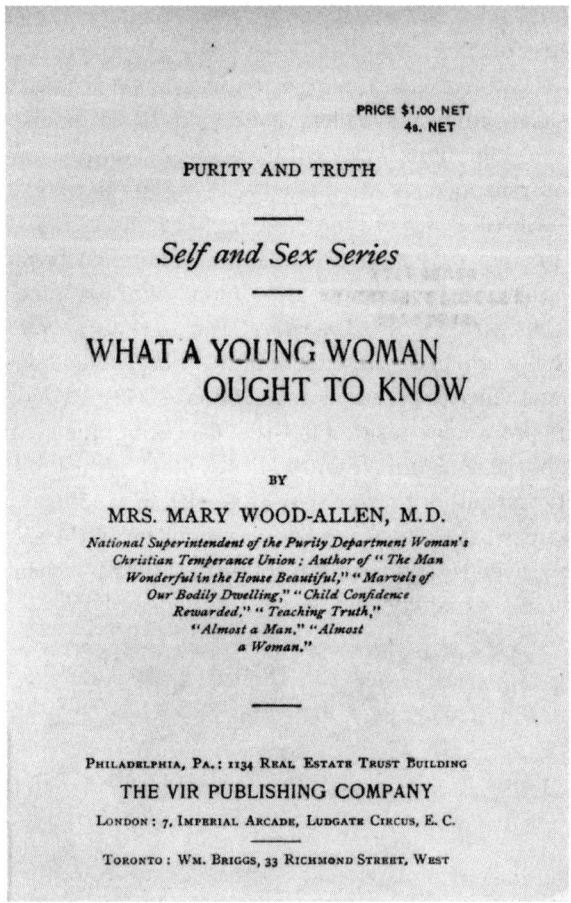

PRICE $1.00 NET
4s. NET

PURITY AND TRUTH

———

Self and Sex Series

———

WHAT A YOUNG WOMAN OUGHT TO KNOW

BY

MRS. MARY WOOD-ALLEN, M.D.

*National Superintendent of the Purity Department Woman's
Christian Temperance Union ; Author of " The Man
Wonderful in the House Beautiful," " Marvels of
Our Bodily Dwelling," " Child Confidence
Rewarded," " Teaching Truth,"
"Almost a Man," "Almost
a Woman."*

———

PHILADELPHIA, PA.: 1134 REAL ESTATE TRUST BUILDING

THE VIR PUBLISHING COMPANY

LONDON : 7, IMPERIAL ARCADE, LUDGATE CIRCUS, E. C.

———

TORONTO : WM. BRIGGS, 33 RICHMOND STREET, WEST

Figure 4.3. Title page of Mary Wood-Allen's *What a Young Woman Ought to Know*, 1898.

For example, in *Teaching Truth* (1892) Wood-Allen recounted her experience talking with a university senior who sought Wood-Allen because "She felt that she ought to know more of life." After the young woman told Wood-Allen that she would understand if the doctor found the topic too embarrassing to discuss, Wood-Allen exclaimed, "Dear child, it will not embarrass me in the least. I am only going to tell you of God's laws." The student, who came expecting an uncomfortable conversation, "looked up with tears in her eyes" when Wood-Allen had finished her explanation and said, "How beautiful it all is. I had nerved myself to endure knowing something that I felt I ought to know, but I had not the slightest idea that it could be made so beautiful, so ennobling" (79). Wood-Allen's insistence on the purity of information given purely was as much a prerequisite of her own respectable ethos as it was an argument intended to convince women to speak to their children. Before she and other women physicians could write publicly about human reproduction, they needed to develop a position from which a respectable woman could speak on such matters. By casting reproduction as part of God's plan, they could discuss this topic without sullying their reputations. In essence, women physicians told readers that if they saw something lewd in their discussions of reproduction, it was because *they* thought of reproduction impurely. Those wishing to accuse women physicians of impropriety risked facing that accusation themselves.

Identifying the Divine in human reproductive physiology was an important part of women physicians' argument that sex could be thought of in pure terms and represented an extension of the recuperation of the body evident in their general medical information and advice texts. For example, in Wood-Allen's *Almost a Man* (1895), the fictional Dr. Barrett taught young Carl to respect sexuality and reproduction because "If we are to think God's thoughts after him we must come to look upon sex as something to be thought of and spoken of only with reverence, never to be jested about or debased in any way" (23–24), because, through procreation, humans share in Creation and have the opportunity to "realize, even dimly, the yearning, tender love of their heavenly Father who had granted to them to know by experience his feelings towards his children" (38). Wood-Allen made embarrassment about sexuality seem ridiculous and replaced it with awe at God's wisdom and grace. What Dr. Barrett asked of Carl is what Wood-Allen asked of her readers: to forget the impure notions of sex learned from friends and to learn to think of it as part of God's plan. In this book as well as in her other sex-ed texts, Wood-Allen sought to shift the connotations surrounding sexual information, so that she could be perceived to be discussing a "pure" topic, not a "dirty" one.

In addition to situating sex in the Divine plan, Wood-Allen also described the division of humanity into sexes and the reproductive physiology that resulted from that division as fundamental to social institutions: "It is because of sex that we are gathered in families and enjoy all the delights of home. It is because of sex that we have ties of kindred, brothers, sisters, father, mother, uncles, aunts and cousins. Think of the pleasant home gatherings at Christmas or Thanksgiving, or upon family birthdays, with all the relatives, old and young, meeting in love and sympathy; think of the sweet prattle of children in the home; think of the tender ministrations of mother or sister in times of sorrow or illness or death, and remember that these are possible because of sex" (20–21). Dr. Barrett went on to tell Carl that literature, the great stories of history, and the wonders of the natural world all depended on sex (22–23). In this explanation, Wood-Allen described sex not as a matter of individual physical appetites and pleasure but as a feature of humanity central to social organization and expression.

Insisting that sex be viewed in the context of noble cultural institutions—religion, family, and home—allowed Wood-Allen to claim sexuality as a topic that a woman could discuss while maintaining a respectable ethos. Significantly, those institutions were also gendered feminine in their social context, so women physicians' redefinition of sex and its purposes combined with their scientific instruction gave women authority on sex and related subjects, such as heredity, alcohol consumption, and women's rights within marriage, subjects that women sought to influence in the nineteenth century. In fact, the implications for social morality and the family made sex a topic a woman had a duty to discuss, at least with her daughters.

Encouraging Nonprofessional Women to Speak

In addition to making sex an accessible topic for women's speech and writing, situating sex in the context of familiar institutions also cast sexuality as a social concern rather than a matter concerning only the couple involved. Although some nineteenth-century women physicians who wrote medical information and advice texts mentioned sexual pleasure (Saur 17; Greene 15, 76), it was more common for writers to discuss the potential parents' responsibility to conceive a child under optimal conditions and their opportunity to improve the physical and moral tone of future generations through following the guidelines suggested by the science of heredity. According to the nineteenth-century Laws of Heredity as women physicians explained them, a child inherited not only what we would today call genetic traits, but also the temperamental, vocational, and physical tendencies the parents cultivated prior to the conception of their child.[6] The fictional mother in Wood-Allen's *Almost a Woman* (1897) explained heredity to her daughter by describing what she had inherited from each of her parents: "Heredity means the passing on of traits or talents from parents to children. Now, your eyes are like papa's. They are a part of your heredity from him. You have other features like him, and you have many of his traits. It has been easy to teach you to be orderly because you have inherited his love of order. Then, too, you have many of my characteristics. My hair, my love of music, [and] my quick temper" (72). After the daughter asked if her children would also inherit a quick temper, the mother told her that she could, through conscious effort, provide her children with milder temperaments: "By controlling yourself you will have given them greater power of self-control; that is worth working for, isn't it? If, when I was of your age, I had begun to govern my temper, I should have been helping you. So it is in every field of effort. . . . Now, in your young girlhood, you are working to help future generations" (73). The Laws of Heredity provided women physicians with a scientific reason to direct individual behavior. Their feminine concern for future generations and their authority as physicians concerned about public health opened the scope of their influence well beyond the health of the individual. Because they believed that children could inherit personality traits, emotions, and interests that their parents cultivated long before conception, physicians were justified in encouraging their patients and the public to alter their behavior, to control their emotions, and even to take up edifying hobbies.

According to the Laws of Heredity, when and with whom one decided to have a child had significant implications for the health and moral quality of future generations. This aspect of scientific thought had direct implications for the temperance movement. Women physicians overwhelmingly advocated the prohibition of alcohol, expressing pity for the women who were forced to bear the children of drunken men. In *Build Well: The Basis of Individual, Home, and National Elevation* (1885), Cordelia Greene asked, "How may a wife reverence a degraded, besotted husband?" and then recounted the story of a man whose drunkenness produced children who were "cut short in all the rightful gifts of being." Because of the father's use of alcohol, only three of the eight children possessed respectable characters; Greene attributed the respectability of those three to their "patient, saintly mother" (24–25). According to nineteenth-century models of heredity, the children of intemperate men were condemned to a life of poor health and weak morals. Through teaching the scientific principles of the Laws of Heredity, women physicians gave the large number of women committed to the temperance movement a medical justification for their temperance rhetoric. Furthermore, women physicians' lessons about the damage to future generations caused by conceiving a child with a drunken man provided women with arguments they could use to control the conditions under which they engaged in sexual activity.

Arguments similar to those about the implications of drinking for future generations were applied to other vices, such as smoking. For example, in a chapter titled "Preparation for Fatherhood" in her 1901 book *What a Young Wife Ought to Know*, Emma Drake[7] warned readers that "The use of alcoholics and tobacco enfeebles the mind and constitution, and this enfeeblement accentuated is transmitted to the next generations. Many wives are struggling along in ill health that is directly traceable to the inhaling, night after night, of the breath of the husband, poisoned with nicotine" (118). The children produced in such a union, Drake explained, would forever be weak and would likely adopt the addictive habits of their fathers at an early age: "Many a little one is wailing through its infancy, and if it have strength sufficient, inherited from its remote ancestors, to pull it through, yet will it all its life suffer from its antenatal and postnatal poisoning; and the chances are that as soon as it is old enough it will take up the habit which is already acquired, to pass down along the line a more and more enfeebled heritage" (118). Drake charged women to protect themselves and their future children from the poisons of alcohol and tobacco even before marriage. Modeling a conversation between a young woman and her suitor, Drake asked, "How many times when the escort asks, 'Is tobacco offensive to you?' have our thoughtless girls answered, 'Oh, no,' when at heart it was repulsive and sickening." Instead of being accommodating, Drake would have young women invoke their scientific knowledge of the physical consequences of smoking to ensure the health of all involved: "When our dear girls have strength of character sufficient to say in response to such a query, while lifting frank honest eyes: 'Shall I answer your question honestly? then I must say, it is very offensive to me; for I know it does you harm, and I know as well that I cannot breathe the fumes of it *even* for an hour without physical harm to myself.'" Drake concluded this imagined exchange by reassuring the young women in her audience that their suitors would not be annoyed or offended, but would "rejoice in the courage of such a girl" and brag to their friends about her confidence and assertiveness (118–19).

Suggesting that a woman who confidently declared her true opinions could influence young men and even win their respect promoted women's engagement in health rhetoric with their peers, not just with their children. Although for the most part women physicians did not encourage women to speak or write publicly on the basis of their new knowledge about sexuality and reproduction, the rhetorical acts they did advocate should not be overlooked. Even young women, they claimed, who might otherwise appear frivolous and unaware of larger social issues and who lacked the authority of a matron or mother, could influence their social circles because they possessed physiological knowledge, particularly knowledge about heredity. In *Ideal Married Life* (1901), Wood-Allen emphasized the importance of young women's premarital conversations with their future husbands: "The woman who marries a man without having learned the ideas of her future husband in regard to the marital relation and without having expressed her own views on the subject has virtually expressed acceptance of the prevalent ideas concerning this relation. By her silence she has led her husband to suppose that she is willing to be responsive to the demands which to him shall seem reasonable" (213). In calling on young women to assert themselves, to resist the tendency to go along with their male companions' wishes, women physicians asked women to claim a voice that had largely been silent and gave them scientific reasons to use when they did so.

Once women were persuaded of the importance of talking with their children, their suitors, and their husbands about sex and of the possibility of discussing the subject in a pure manner, they needed a stance from which to engage in these conversations. Women physicians offered their readers components out of which they could build a respectable ethos for such discussions. One such component was a vocabulary untarnished by impure attitudes toward sex. As educated professionals, women physicians could offer their readers the language of science as a means of discussing sex purely. The mother in Wood-Allen's narrative sex-ed text *Almost a Woman* (1897) was not reluctant to use medical terminology, including *uterus* and *vagina* (47) and *ovum* and *spermatozoa* (62); in fact, she articulated her preference for scientific language. As the mother and daughter discussed female reproductive anatomy, the mother explained that *womb* and *uterus* refer to the same organ but that they are derived from different languages. The daughter expressed her preference for *womb*, and her mother agreed, but said that "as scientists use the Latin word we shall use that, so that we will know how to talk on these subjects scientifically" (47–48). The mother also taught her daughter using pictures of female reproductive organs (46) and male reproductive cells (62). The scientific terminology used throughout the mother-daughter conversation may have been meant to give mothers language with which to discuss human development and reproduction with their daughters, providing mothers with an alternative to the impure language with which they were probably familiar, thereby purifying the connotations surrounding talk about sex.

Wood-Allen's *Almost a Man* (1895) posed a more difficult rhetorical challenge than her other books, which focused on conversations with daughters or very young boys: how could a woman speak to a teenage boy (Carl, the young man in the story, is nearly fifteen years old) about puberty and sex? In this narrative, it was not a mother, but a woman physician who discussed sexuality and reproduction with Carl. Although *Almost a Man* covered much of the same material addressed in *Almost a Woman*, the approach was somewhat different. Possibly because Dr. Barrett was a physician, and possibly because Carl was a boy, Dr. Barrett did not use the domestic analogies used by the mother in *Almost a Woman*; instead, she explained reproduction through a scientific classification of life forms, starting by asking Carl (and the friends he brought along for their second conversation) "What is life?" (46) and then moving through protoplasm and single-celled life forms (48), to asexual reproduction (49) and sexual reproduction (49–50). In the course of her conversation with Carl, Dr. Barrett gave him a book about heredity and the damage parents who used alcohol and tobacco inflicted on their offspring. Wood-Allen avoided any appearance of impropriety, first by having Carl bring friends for the second (more "delicate") conversation; second, by speaking in terms of science—a language that allowed Dr. Barrett to speak "objectively" about this delicate subject; and third, by having Carl and his friends learn some of their lessons about the implications of reproduction from a book and not from Dr. Barrett directly.

Having access to scientific vocabulary, images, and studies was vital to women physicians' efforts to redefine *sex* in pure terms. Because, by the end of the century, scientific words were associated with objectivity and expertise, with the bright, clean laboratory where truth was discovered, and with progress and a higher quality of life, they were perfectly positioned to combat attitudes toward sex that cast it as shameful, disgusting, and the cause of suffering. Some nonprofessional women found courage to speak in women physicians' scientific explanations of sexuality, as did the writer of a testimonial letter included in the appendix to Wood-Allen's *Ideal Married Life* (1901): "There was no subject on which [my fiancé and I] could not converse, for we both had read your books carefully, and had thus gained a scientific vocabulary; and each knew that the thoughts the other held were *absolutely pure*" (426). Scientific vocabulary, images, and studies provided women with authoritative material that they could use in their discussions with their husbands and children, recreating the wife and mother as well-informed and authorized to influence her family's attitudes toward the purposes of sex.

Women physicians' sex-ed texts demonstrate that the writers expected women to use the information they provided as the basis for rhetorical action. Just as many nineteenth-century women physicians believed their medical education obligated them to share physiological information with other women, they also believed that nonprofessional women should translate their health instruction, even on the delicate topics of sexuality and reproduction, into rhetorical action. Anticipating her readers' reluctance to engage in premarital conversations about the role of sex within marriage, Wood-Allen wrote: "Some may object that such discussion before marriage would be indelicate. To my mind the indelicacy is in marrying ignorant of each other's views. If the two are intelligent, conscientious, pure-minded and by scientific study well-prepared with a good vocabulary they will be able to discuss this matter with all the freedom necessary to a clear understanding of each other and with added respect for each other. . . . Why should it be more modest to avoid the discussion of the relationship than to speak purely concerning it, to learn each other's views and thus be prepared for harmonious co-operation?" (*Ideal Married Life* 214). Much of women's speech about sex would take place in private, in conversations between parents and children or between wives and husbands, but even those private discussions would have been significant rhetorical acts, considering the negative connotations surrounding sex and the obstacle feminine modesty posed to any woman who wished to study or speak on the topic.

In order to overcome the discomfort women might feel in talking about sex, in addition to providing them with a model of an educated, tactful, responsible mother, Wood-Allen also offered her readers rhetorical strategies that could be used to make such conversations less embarrassing. The choice of a conversation, rather than a lecture, as a means of conveying information about sexuality was one measure that likely would have made women more comfortable. Jane Donawerth identifies the conversational form as particularly influential for historical women who theorized and practiced rhetoric (xxxviii–xl). This is true for nineteenth-century women physicians, who primarily imagined conversations for which there was little precedent: conversations about sex in which women were scientifically informed, in which they relied on an understanding of sex as part of the Divine plan and as an act with social consequences, and in which mothers participated as confident, informed speakers.

The sex-ed books could themselves have served as a starting point for conversations between parents and children, particularly texts such as *Almost a Man* and *Almost a Woman*, which were short books written using narrative and simple language that was accessible to children. Women physicians encouraged their adult readers to lay the groundwork for conversations about sex well before their children were old enough to read these books, however. For instance, in 1903, Wood-Allen encouraged mothers to cultivate their children's confidence so that they would be comfortable asking their mothers about reproduction as their questions arose: "The question of how to meet the absolute confidence of the little child is one worthy of our deepest thought. Shall we reward his trust in us with censure, with falsehood, with procrastination, or with absolute truth?" (*Child-Confidence Rewarded* 6). She showed mothers how to begin these conversations by discussing nonreproductive physiology. In 1896, she, like other writers of the time, compared the human body to a house, with a framework (skeleton), electrical apparatus (nervous system), and watchmen (the senses) (*The Marvels of Our Bodily Dwelling*).[8] When it came time to discuss reproduction, the characters in her stories modeled the use of flowers[9] and household occurrences, such as the preparation of a hen for dinner, to introduce children to male and female sex cells. All of these resources were familiar not only to children, but to their mothers as well.

Furthermore, these metaphors served to domesticate the body, converting viscera into objects that could be discussed without awkwardness or embarrassment. For instance, in their conversation about the "bodily house," the mother in *Almost a Woman* (1897) described the pelvis ("the lower story" [45]): "The pelvic cavity contains the bladder . . . and the rectum. . . . But it contains more than these. It is here in the pelvis that these organs of which you have not heard are located. You remember when you asked me about yourself and how you came into the world I told you of a little room in mother's body where you lived and grew until you were large enough to live your own independent existence. Did you ever wonder where this room is?" (46). Wood-Allen demonstrated that reproductive organs could be discussed openly, in terms familiar to both women and children. As their conversation continued, the mother, extending the bodily-house metaphor, explained the harm of tight-lacing: "Don't you think it strange that we never want little rooms with furniture huddled close together, except in our bodily dwellings? The Divine Architect has given us grand apartments, with all the machinery harmoniously related, and we think we improve things by putting everything into the closest possible quarters and disturbing the harmony!" (56). Putting serious medical advice in terms a child could understand, the mother in this story modeled the application of physiological facts to the social issue of dress reform.

As this example illustrates, a scientific understanding of sex and its role in social progress provided nineteenth-century women—both physicians and nonprofessionals—with persuasive material supporting certain reform measures. Women could use medical theories, scientific knowledge, and their informed observations of individuals and families to develop arguments for social reform. For example, in *Unmasked, or The Science of Immorality* (1878), Mary Edwards Walker used her expertise as a physician to speak directly to men about dress reform and prostitution. Writing of the latter subject using one nineteenth-century biological theory, she explained that men absorb "magnetisms" from the women with whom they are intimate so that "no matter how low or degraded [the women] may have been," the children men later father with their wives "will inherit the traits and often the looks of their mistresses" (24–25). Walker argued that men's ignorance of these and other biological "facts" led them to continue their risky behavior, and she noted her own role in alleviating this ignorance: "Prostitution will never be stopped until men are educated on these points, and it is because we so fully realize this that we have done what no other woman has dared to do, lectured and written to men exclusively on these important subjects" (25). For Walker, the social progress that would result from men's better-informed decisions about their sexuality justified her unprecedented step of directly addressing men on such a delicate subject.

In fact, Walker believed that scientific education was the best means of correcting most of the moral problems evident in society: "Science knows no false modesty. Much of the social evil is far beyond the sphere of legislation, but can be reached and the wrongs thereof righted through knowledge in youth" (*Unmasked* 78). Not only would the physiological education of children prompt them to make better decisions as adolescents, young adults, and potential parents, but, Walker implied, because science does not suffer under the false modesty that other social institutions bear, a scientific education might lead to more accurate truths and thus more beneficial behavior than any legislation could enforce. According to Walker, the physicians and nonprofessional women who took up the responsibility of educating children about sexual physiology could effect more substantial social change than could be accomplished by the men in the legislature.

Although Emma Drake adopted a much more conventional feminine ethos than Walker did, both shared the belief that education was the key to correcting the moral failings of society. Like many nineteenth-century women physicians, Drake maintained that ignorance, not inherent immorality, was the source of most depraved behavior. In *What a Young Wife Ought to Know* (1901), Drake advocated strict control over sexual activities, forbidding sex simply to satisfy lust, when either husband or wife was unwilling to conceive a child, during pregnancy, and any time the wife was disinclined to participate. Although she criticized the misuse of sex harshly, she acknowledged that many young people, particularly young men, were unaware of the proper role of sex within marriage, stating that "Ignorance and misconception are at the bottom of all that is wrong in the marital relation" (95). As a medical adviser, Drake attempted to enlighten her readers. This effort involved her in discussing topics which she "approach[ed] . . . with a degree of reluctance" (79), but through frequent reference to the Divine plan for marriage and scientific conclusions about the misuse of sexual functions, she addressed a wide range of delicate subjects. For example, Drake explained the purposes of Christian marriage in order to instruct readers on the appropriate frequency of marital sexual activity:

That while God ordained the marriage relation primarily, for the purpose of the perpetuity of the human race, as his first command to the pair in Eden would indicate, "Be fruitful, and multiply, and replenish the earth." . . .

Therefore when I say, that every young person should be taught before marriage, that the closest conjugal relation should never be allowed, without a willingness on the part of both that parenthood should follow, I mean simply what I hope I shall make clear throughout my book; that there should be no pandering to sexual indulgence, while there is unwillingness to bear as many children, as a proper manly and womanly Christian temperance in these things will allow. (86–87)

In educating readers about God's intentions for marriage, Drake sought to relieve young couples' ignorance about the purposes of marital sexual activity, thereby clearing the way for them to behave in accordance with the highest moral and religious principles.

In addition to referring to religion as many nineteenth-century women did in advocating marital chastity, Drake also used the scientific explanations available to her as a physician to combat young couples' ignorance of the proper role of sex in marriage. Relying on an understanding of the human system as an interconnection of physical, mental, and moral elements, Drake argued for sexual self-control: "There is a vast amount of vital force used in the production and expenditure of the seminal fluid. Wasted as the incontinence of so many lives allows it to be, and prostituted to the simple gratification of fleshly desire, it weakens and depraves. Conserved as legitimate control demands it to be, it adds so much, and more to the mental and moral force of the man, because it lifts him to a higher plane of being, and gives to the mental and moral the vital force otherwise wasted" (88–89). Using terminology, such as "seminal fluid," available to a medically educated professional woman, Drake taught women medical and moral reasons why marital sexual activity should be restricted. She was particularly concerned with women's right to decline their husbands' advances. Countering popular rhetoric about the marital rights of men, she argued that "the marriage relation is not one of license, but of liberty—liberty for both equally. Not liberty for one, and the grossest bondage for the other. Nowhere does the wife's opinion deserve greater respect and tolerance than here. Nowhere should her negative be so willingly accepted" (88). Given her desire to ensure women's rights to their own bodies, her lessons about the physical, mental, and moral consequences of excessive sexual activity could have validated women's right to choose when to engage in sexual activity.

Drake also offered women her medical opinion on the cause of what she believed was men's excessive sex drive: "The sedentary life of many men renders them a prey to the gratification of their lower natures. To all such men exercise becomes a religious duty, and should be practiced most persistently until their physical natures are well tired, and the sexual nature will not then dominate the finer and nobler instincts of their being" (94). Countering the notion that men naturally desired or required more sexual activity than women, Drake used her professional expertise to propose another, controllable, reason for men's interest in sex: their lifestyles and occupations. As a physician, she was assumed to be knowledgeable about the qualities and needs of the human body, and attributing men's "deviant" behavior to modern civilization—something Drake's readers would have been likely to mistrust anyway—allowed her to argue for less frequent sexual activity while avoiding blaming men directly. As professionals, Drake and the other women physicians who wrote about sex could participate in the discourse of marital advice from an objective, scientific, and moral standpoint. Their conclusions about the role of sex in marriage provided nonprofessional women with persuasive arguments for reducing the frequency of sex, potentially offering them more control over their own bodies.

As a physician, Drake was in a position to warn readers of the medical consequences of improper views of marital relations. She listed numerous diseases to which the children of ignorant or immoral parents were believed to be prone: "The world is full of dwarfed minds and bodies, dwarfed by their loveless and unwilling conception; paronoiacs [*sic*], cranks, feeble-minded, idiotic, epileptic, diseased children, for whom their parents are in great measure responsible" (89). Marriage for social connections, for financial security, or any reason other than love was likely, in Drake's professional opinion, to produce children who were sick in body and mind: "And this state of things will obtain just as long as marriage is made a marketable thing, and not the heart union of two lives" (89–90). Because she possessed physiological knowledge and professional standing, Drake's ethos authorized her to describe the repercussions of unintentional conception in terms other than the sentimental language often used to describe love and marriage. She could also argue that a bad marriage had consequences beyond those faced by individual women: the fates of the next generation and the whole of society were imperiled by loveless marriages.

For nineteenth-century women physicians, writing about the role of sex in morality, heredity, and health was something they felt that their medical expertise obligated them to do. For her part, in 1878 Walker justified her decision to address topics generally not discussed in polite company, especially by women, through reference to her sense of duty toward women and men: "If silence could do the work, all christendom could not open our mouth, but as nothing but an *exposé* of the wrongs to woman and the wrongs to pure manhood can be rightened and prevented, all christendom can not close our mouth" (*Unmasked* 110). Even though she wrote about subjects no "respectable" woman would take up, Walker claimed that she served a higher good in doing so. Although few of the women physicians who published books about sexuality were as risqué as Walker, all believed that women and children, and through them future generations of humanity, would benefit from frank discussions of sex, discussions that situated sexuality in scientific, divine, and familial contexts.

Acknowledging Women's Silences

Alongside of their arguments that women should use their scientific knowledge to speak about sex and related subjects, nineteenth-century women physicians also acknowledged the deep silences surrounding such topics. Greene, who in her 1885 book *Build Well* sought to teach the public about the true uses of sex and sexual pleasure, alluded to the confidences physicians kept about the consequences of the misuse of sexuality: "The sad living records [of the abuse of 'creative power'] are carefully concealed, not only in our hospitals and dens of infamy, but in some of our fairest homes, and known by few save the wretched victims and their trusted physicians" (17). Writing specifically of adultery, which she defined broadly to include sexual thoughts, masturbation, and the improper use of sex within marriage, Greene marked another silence: "Were I to repeat here the startling revelations of the misery and degradation resulting in individual life, and in some respectable homes, from disobedience to the seventh commandment, I should fill a volume several times larger than this. The thought of so much needless suffering is pitiable, but the unwritten records of mental and physical anguish from this sin are countless" (168). Greene's allusion to the confidential information physicians were privy to in their professional encounters suggested that she had ample evidence supporting her views on sex, even if she chose not to detail that evidence in writing.

Greene's reference to the silent suffering caused by the misuse of sexuality highlights the importance of women's learning to speak on this subject, to argue for what they believed were the proper attitudes toward sexuality and to intervene in the public debates that were directly or indirectly related to sexual behavior. As professionals with a scientific education and extensive expertise, late nineteenth-century women physicians had access to knowledge and discourse that allowed them to discuss sex with the appearance of objectivity. As women, and often mothers, they could infuse their discussions of sex with a moral and religious light. Both the scientific and the moral facets of women physicians' discourse about sexuality went a long way toward reconstructing sexuality as a topic that could be addressed by respectable women, even if they lacked the benefits of professional standing. Late-nineteenth-century women physicians offered nonprofessional women a reputable ethos through modeling conversations, providing scientific vocabulary, and suggesting arguments based in human physiology and heredity. Women physicians' authorization of ordinary women's speech and writing about sex suggests that ethos can manifest a dynamic relationship between speaker and audience, one in which the speaker not only reflects the audience's preexisting values but also promotes alternative values, which audience members can use to shape their own ethē in future rhetorical acts. Breaking the connection between innocence and ignorance and arguing that knowledge was a prerequisite of virtue, women physicians called for women to speak up and take greater control over their own sexuality, exert stronger influence over the choices made by their children, and participate more assertively in the wide array of social decisions related to morality.

5

Developing Collective Ethos in Medical Editorial Writing

> We are largely rated at our own valuation, the coy and shy
> manner may be very attractive but it is not business, and
> the profession of medicine in a large degree partakes of this
> element. . . . [I]t is not right to hide our experiences within
> ourselves. The profession of medicine is more than any other
> profession reciprocal, those who practice it are interdepen-
> dent, each on the other, and all available light is needed, [and]
> the women, no more than the men, have any moral right to
> withhold the smallest ray.
>
> —"An Epidemic of Aphasia," *Wom-*
> *an's Medical Journal* (1897)

Recognizing the importance of professional rhetorical activity for women's
success in medicine, in 1897 the editor of the *Woman's Medical Journal*
(*WMJ*) expressed concern at the absence of women's names from medical
conference programs and urged women not "to withhold the smallest ray" of
their experience ("An Epidemic of Aphasia" 280). By this time, several women
physicians had spoken and published in professional venues; some, such as
Mary Putnam Jacobi and Mary Dixon Jones, had produced a large body of
professional rhetoric. By the 1870s, and increasingly in the 1880s and 1890s,
even less famous women physicians engaged in several forms of professional
medical discourse: they presented papers at local, national, and international
conferences that were often reprinted in American medical journals; they edited and published articles in their own professional periodical, the *Woman's
Medical Journal*; and they published reports of cases, argued for the benefits
of particular treatment plans, discussed the role of the physician in civic life,
and debated professional issues in letters to the editors of mainstream medical

journals. In this chapter, I examine the editorials and letters to the editor published by women physicians in medical journals in the 1880s and 1890s, two decades in which a substantial number of women—leaders in the field as well as less-famous physicians—contributed to editorial discussions. Despite the relatively large number of women practicing medicine at this time, the question of women in medicine was not settled, and this debate intersected with debates about medicine's professional identity and about women's capabilities and their proper roles. I focus first on the *Woman's Medical Journal* and then on women's letters to male-edited, regular and homeopathic journals, paying particular attention to the ways women physicians constructed a collective professional ethos for themselves and their sister practitioners.

The *WMJ* was edited by and for regular women physicians, and after its first few issues, nearly all the contributing authors were women.[1] Elmina Roys-Gavitt (figure 5.1), an Ohio physician, served as editor-in-chief of the

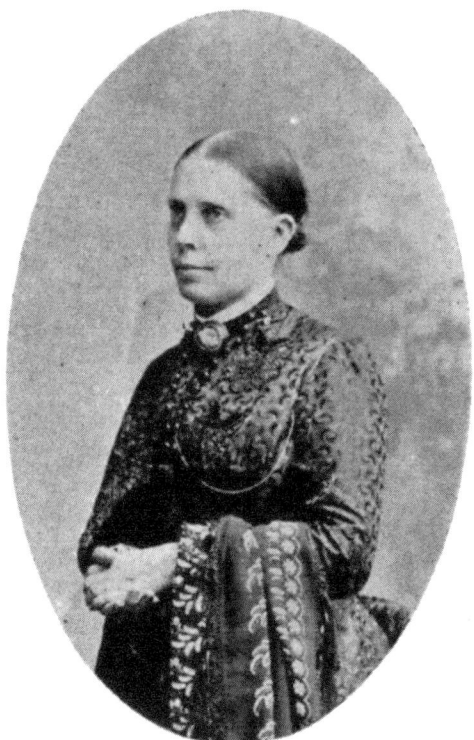

Figure 5.1. Elmina Roys-Gavitt, *Woman's Medical Journal*, 1898. Courtesy History and Special Collections for the Sciences, Louise M. Darling Biomedical Library, UCLA.

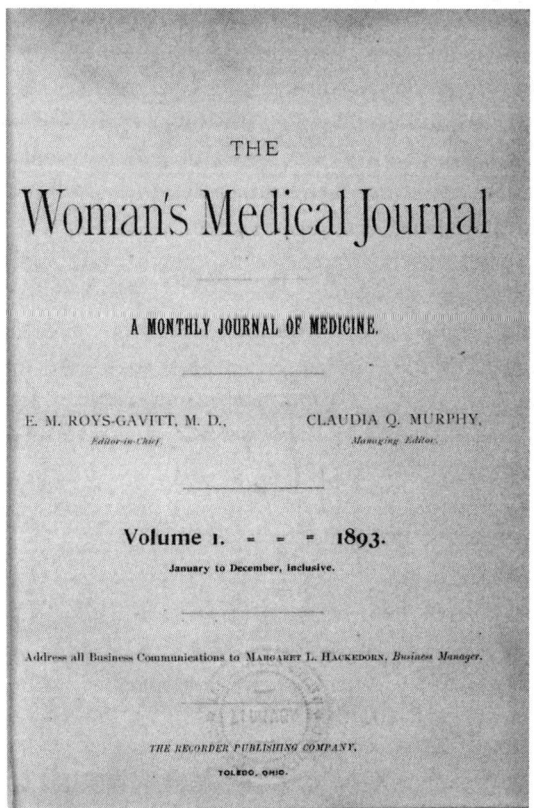

THE

Woman's Medical Journal

A MONTHLY JOURNAL OF MEDICINE.

E. M. ROYS-GAVITT, M. D.,
Editor-in-Chief.

CLAUDIA Q. MURPHY,
Managing Editor.

Volume 1. - - - 1893.
Januury to December, inclusive.

Address all Business Communications to MARGARET L. HACKEDORN, *Business Manager.*

THE RECORDER PUBLISHING COMPANY,
TOLEDO, OHIO.

Figure 5.2. Title page of the first volume of the *Woman's Medical Journal*, 1893. Courtesy History and Special Collections for the Sciences, Louise M. Darling Biomedical Library, UCLA.

journal beginning with its founding in 1893 until her death in 1898 (figure 5.2).[2] The establishment of the *Woman's Medical Journal* was an important step in confirming women's place in medicine, because sustaining a monthly publication with quality material submitted almost exclusively by women would demonstrate that women were regularly and scientifically educated and that they could make significant contributions to the field. As the editor of the *American Medico-Surgical Bulletin* noted, "Unlike many other medical publications, this one [the *WMJ*] has a *raison d'etre*. It has a live question behind it. If it demonstrates that women can successfully edit a medical journal, that will be so much argument of woman's fitness for the medical profession" (qtd. in "Pertinent Phrases" 278). The *WMJ* was conscious of its role in representing women physicians, and it frequently reminded its readers of their responsibility to each other and to future women physicians, encouraging them to behave in ways that would benefit the women's medical movement.

In the *WMJ*, nineteenth-century American women physicians cultivated a model of the woman physician as a rhetorically active professional—one who understood the work of a physician to involve not only daily rounds among patients but also speaking and writing in professional forums. In order to participate in professional discourse, women physicians needed to overcome the masculine profession's hostility to their presence in the field, the obstacles posed by conventional women's rhetorical practices ("the coy and shy manner" criticized by the *WMJ*), a lack of professional rhetorical training, and the absence of a longstanding tradition of women as medical rhetors. In editorial rhetoric, women physicians worked directly to solve these problems. Unlike research articles, which could only model appropriate rhetorical behavior, editorials and letters to the editor often spoke specifically about professional rhetorical activity and values. In their editorial writing, nineteenth-century women physicians engaged in a form of what Kimberly Harrison calls "self-rhetoric": "Self-rhetoric posit[s] the self as a site for rhetorical negotiation of competing ideologies and material conditions that allow for possibilities and limitations of self-definition and presentation. The term implies the personal rhetorical negotiations that then result in the public presentation of self. . . . In constructing one's sense of self in response to social, cultural, and material forces, the rhetor relies on self-persuasion to internalize and reconcile new and perhaps conflicting views of identity" (244). Although the *WMJ* was not a private discursive space like the diaries Harrison analyzes for evidence of self-rhetoric, it was a relatively enclosed discursive space, one in which women physicians wrote for one another, working together to determine the best strategies for defining the "woman physician" and for presenting that identity to the world.[3] Nineteenth-century women physicians faced "conflicting views of identity" as they negotiated what it meant to speak and write as professional experts and as women. By engaging in collective self-rhetoric in the *WMJ*, women physicians articulated for each other the strategies for effective rhetorical performance as professional women addressing a range of audiences, including individual patients, the public, and the masculine medical profession. The complex negotiations nineteenth-century women physicians had to manage in presenting themselves as professionals are evident on the editorial pages of the *WMJ*, where women physicians collectively negotiated an ethos appropriate for medical discourse by instructing their female colleagues on the behaviors and virtues expected of feminine professionals in the last few years of the nineteenth century.

Developing a Collective Ethos
for Women Physicians

One feature of professional behavior about which the *WMJ* was quite naturally concerned was women's participation in medical discourse. Of course, not all nineteenth-century women physicians possessed the confidence and verbal forcefulness necessary to speak and write as experts to large audiences of professionals who were accustomed to using journals and conferences as sites of assertion, criticism, argument, and knowledge-building. Women needed support and guidance to learn to be comfortable in such rhetorical situations, yet few models of rhetorically successful women physicians existed. Filling this void, the *WMJ* served as a discursive space in which women physicians articulated for themselves and each other how to behave rhetorically as medical professionals. The editors of the *WMJ* used their editorials for purposes similar to the identity-building Harrison identifies in Confederate women's diaries: "As they wrote about what they should and should not say and about how they appeared to themselves and to others, women diarists envisioned and fulfilled new roles. They coached themselves to speak and act effectively in their new contexts. . . . Whatever the context, women diarists relied on self-rhetorics to navigate identity conflicts resulting from clashes among former self-views, harsh realities that challenged self-perceptions, and cultural norms regarding gender and class that persisted in spite of war" (246). Like Confederate women who still felt bound by conventional femininity even as they took up previously "masculine" behaviors after their husbands left home, nineteenth-century women physicians used self-rhetoric to negotiate the conflicting demands of speaking as a woman while speaking as a professional expert.

One form the *WMJ*'s self-rhetoric took was the periodic update on the journal's success. An editorial in June 1894 commented on the journal's achievements in its first eighteen months, noting that it had doubled the number of pages of "reading matter" and that it now had subscribers in every state and some foreign countries. The editor called the journal's growth "little less than phenomenal" ("Just among Ourselves" 136). Eighteen months later, the editorial pages again noted the *WMJ*'s expansion: it had, in just three years from its initial publication, nearly tripled the number of nonadvertising pages. By this point, the editors were pleased to report, all the articles published in the journal were original and had been contributed by women. They claimed that the *WMJ* was "in the front rank of medical journalism" and that it had gone from being unknown to being "quoted today in every land" ("Just Three Years Ago" 323–24). If confidence is a requirement for rhetorical activity (Shaughnessy 85), the *WMJ*'s reports of its success combined with editorials characterizing it as "your journal" may have contributed to women's rhetorical activity simply through building the collective confidence of all of its readers ("The Old Year" 233).

In addition to recognizing the journal's accomplishments, the *WMJ* also pro-actively supported women's rhetorical activity by calling for them to write and speak, drawing attention to women's professional successes, and arguing that rhetorical activity was an inherent part of a medical career. The editors encouraged women to engage in medical rhetoric primarily through seeking a range of contributions for publication, naming "Short Practical Communications on topics of interest," "papers read at the various medical meetings," and "Reports of proceedings of all Woman's Medical Clubs" as materials it would be pleased to receive.[4] The journal also sought "contributions by Continental authors written in French, German, Swedish or Italian," reflecting a desire to access the international news that many prominent medical journals carried.[5] An 1893 editorial emphasized the communal nature of the *WMJ* and its readers' collective responsibility for its success: "If you have an interesting case report it. In brief, use your journal and help to make it what you desire it to be" ("The Old Year" 232–33). In another effort to draw women into medical publication, the *WMJ* published a series of papers written by students at Northwestern University Woman's Medical School in 1899. These papers, all of which traced embryonic and fetal development, provided no new information for readers, but they did get several aspiring physicians in print early in their careers (see, for example, MacKay; Russell). The *WMJ*'s active encouragement of women's professional rhetorical activity was a form of collective self-rhetoric that emphasized medical publication as an aspect of the woman physician's professional ethos.

In addition to calling for submissions, the *WMJ* also encouraged women's professional rhetorical activity through running notices of presentations by women at medical conferences, showing its readers that it was possible for women to read papers successfully before medical societies. For example, immediately below the masthead of the July 1899 issue, the editorial column announced that "Dr. Eliza H. Root, editor of the Obstetrical Department of this Journal, read a paper entitled 'Study and Teaching of Obstetrics in our Medical Schools,' at the recent meeting of the American Medical Association held in Columbus, Ohio" ("Dr. Eliza H. Root"). Four months later, the *WMJ* shared the news that "Dr. Marian K. Bowles of Joliet, Ill., was the only woman to present a paper to the Mississippi Valley Medical Association at its recent meeting held in Chicago" ("Dr. Marian K. Bowles"). The *WMJ* was not only a space for announcing women physicians' professional rhetorical achievements, however; it was also a space in which the exact nature of those rhetorical acts was articulated. The novelty of women speaking from a medical standpoint made their lectures and articles delicate performances of femininity and professionalism. Women physicians used the *WMJ* to work out the boundaries of appropriate speech and writing for themselves, as an editorial exchange from 1893–94 indicates. In December 1893, the *WMJ* ran a notice of lectures before the Nurses' Training School in Philadelphia by Clara Marshall, who was at the time Dean of the Woman's Medical College of Pennsylvania. The notice concluded, "Her subjects [are] the anatomy and physiology of the pelvic organs of women. Dr. Marshall states that her audience, among whom are 65 men, is most attentive and courteous" ("Dr. Clara Marshall"). The next month's issue contained this letter from Marshall: "I beg to correct an error in [a] statement in the WOMAN'S MEDICAL JOURNAL of December 1893, page 238. I did not state that my audience included '65' or '650' men, and I beg further to state that no men were present" ("A Misconstruction"). Marshall's desire to correct the misinformation about her lectures suggests that she believed speaking on women's reproductive anatomy before an audience that included men was inappropriate for women physicians, and she was eager to have her colleagues understand that she had not crossed the boundaries of appropriate feminine rhetorical behavior.

On several occasions, the journal reprinted the texts of conference presentations; this was common practice in the journals edited by men as well, but in the *WMJ* it served the important function of recognizing women's professional rhetorical achievements and of modeling medical discourse for readers. Other times, the journal bemoaned the absence of women from conference programs. One editorial in 1897 offered a mock diagnosis of the problem: "We seem to be afflicted with aphasia the moment a meeting is announced" ("An Epidemic of Aphasia" 279). In another issue, after noting that Dr. Marian K. Bowles "was the only woman to present a paper to the Mississippi Valley Medical Association" in 1899, the journal complained, "Several women are members of this society, but here, as in other medical societies, women are backward in writing papers, although fully capable of doing so" ("Dr. Marian K. Bowles"). The *WMJ* cast women's silence at conferences as a matter of choice rather than ability, and it ignored other factors that might work against women presenting at professional meetings, such as the reluctance a woman might feel to address a roomful of men and the scarcity of women who could support and model rhetorical activity in some local societies. Instead, the journal insisted on the necessity of speaking and writing for professional audiences, and it never allowed women to think that their gender was an adequate reason for avoiding the press or the podium. Across its editorial pages, the *WMJ* engaged in collective acts of professional ethos building through self-rhetoric: encouraging rhetorical activity, printing and praising successful papers, and teaching women how to be medical professionals.

The *WMJ*'s promotion of women's professional rhetorical activity was important because conference presentations and journal publications would secure some women relatively high status in the field. After the years women spent struggling merely to be accepted as physicians, such an accomplishment can hardly be overstated. What was perhaps more significant for the history of women's rhetoric, however, was the expansive rhetorical scope the *WMJ* suggested was available to all women physicians. In describing the sharing of professional experiences and information as a significant part of medical work and in encouraging readers to think of the journal as a forum that belonged to all women physicians and that would welcome any woman's contribution, the editors of the *WMJ* extended the reach of women's rhetorical activities. Whereas examining patients in homes or private offices and engaging in individual conversational exchanges were relatively compatible with conventional notions of femininity, the idea that a woman physician was expected to speak at medical society meetings and to publish in national journals pushed women into a broader rhetorical sphere, one in which they could influence not just one patient at a time but potentially a significant portion of the leading members of the profession.

The *WMJ*'s model of rhetorical professionalism was not exclusively public, however. Editorials also taught women how to handle requests for advice on uncomfortable topics. In December 1896, after noting that "'What would you do, doctor?' is a question that must be replied to—and silence somehow is construed into an answer" ("A Grave Responsibility" 309), the editors reassured readers that they were capable of advising their patients because the woman physician represented the pinnacle of medical development: "As time went on, the evolution of the doctor progressed, crude at first, but ascending a higher plane with each generation, until a few years ago the chrysalis opened and a young woman graduated" (310). The woman physician had, according to this narrative, always been "a purveyor of morals as well as of health" (310), but her feminine sensibilities might be disturbed by some of the questions put to her. To overcome this obstacle, the woman physician must "realize that she is a doctor as well as a lady. . . . By maintaining a purely professional attitude, never for a moment laying it aside, she will construct around herself a wall of reserve that cannot be shocked nor sundered" (310). Aware that private medical conversations involved the physician in both speaker and audience roles, the editors advised readers not only on the appropriate ethos to adopt when speaking, but also on strategies for maintaining an effective ethos while listening.

A woman physician's reaction to an uncomfortable or delicate question would affect her reputation as a woman and as a physician. As feminine professionals, women physicians represented morality merged with expertise, and so "many young men and young women present themselves for counsel," believing "the axiom that to the pure all things are pure," and as a result, "the young woman [physician] is disturbed" (310). In drawing "fine lines . . . between morality and immorality, between good and bad" (309), a woman physician had to be vigilant in maintaining her ethos as a feminine professional. In its advice on reacting to patients' questions, the *WMJ* counseled women to select some characteristics associated with femininity and to avoid others: a woman's "sympathy, foresight and perception" (309) made her the ideal physician, but she must not succumb to feminine shock at her patients' confessions or to hesitation when asked for advice. The woman physician must be firm and confident in her conversations with patients, adopting "a purely professional attitude" (310) that would allow her to maintain her dignity, which the *WMJ* asserted was "one of the essentials of men as well as of women in medicine" (310). The editorial concluded by reassuring readers that "by holding ourselves up we shall not lose in public regard or private estimation" (310). In this way, the editors reminded readers of the rhetorical advantages of relying on their professional identity, even when patients came to them seeking relief from "an aching heart, a conscience sick and sore, [or] a moral turpitude that sits like a pall," not just the treatment for "aching bodies" (309) more commonly thought to be the doctor's duty.

The editorials in the *WMJ* reveal an acute awareness of the intense scrutiny nineteenth-century women physicians faced as precedents. In one 1895 editorial, after pointing out that not all men who called themselves physicians were fit for their work, the writer called for greater fairness in judging women's standing in the profession: "Because one man or a score of men fail does not make all men a failure, so also with women" ("A Most Learned Judge!" 208). Likewise, in 1899, after reporting on the sentencing of an uneducated woman who performed abortions while claiming to be a physician, the editor pointed to the unfairness of all women physicians being condemned on the basis of this example and contended that reputable women physicians had an obligation to prevent such judgments:

> [J]ust such women do much to hurt the legitimate woman physician. It is a noteworthy fact that if a woman fails in any one particular line, other women in business or the professions fails [*sic*] equally. The individuality as to error, as well as to praise,

allowed men, not being accorded to women. While we deplore this condition, that very condition should stimulate us to renewed efforts to so raise the status of women physicians as to make such occurrences as the above, a case of individual error, and not one that will be used as a weapon against the honorable, honest woman physician. ("Dr. Mary Aiken" 246)

Interestingly, the *WMJ*'s response to women's being judged as a group rather than on an individual basis was a call for cooperation, a call for collective ethos building that would "raise the status of women physicians." Women physicians, particularly the "good," scientifically and regularly educated readers of the *WMJ*, had no choice but to be responsible for each other—their mutuality was, in part, imposed from the outside, by those who were still evaluating women physicians as an ongoing experiment. The collective nature of the *WMJ*'s self-rhetoric was thus both a result of opponents' tendency to class all women physicians together and a strategy with the potential to ensure that readers conformed to a set of characteristics that the *WMJ*'s editors believed were most likely to win acceptance for women physicians. As the *WMJ* encouraged professional rhetorical activity in women, it also directed them toward a particular kind of ethos performance, supporting women's forays into new discursive venues while also prescribing the shape their rhetorical character should take in those ventures.

Argumentative Strategies for Medical Editorials

In their contributions to the editorial pages of the *WMJ*, women physicians developed what Maud J. Frye[6] called "the courage which dares" (284). Speaking to the alumni of the Buffalo University Medical College in 1897, Frye explained that most women physicians would pursue careers in keeping with the conventional feminine temperament, but some would choose a more radical path: "The woman who gains wealth and fame in the practice of general medicine or of surgery will be the woman who possesses, without necessarily losing anything of her outward womanliness, the masculine type of courage. She will be the woman who would rather be wrong than not try" (285). Frye's "courage which dares" was reflected in the ethos nineteenth-century women physicians developed for their professional rhetorical activity. To convince *public* audiences of the propriety of women's medical practice, women physicians relied on the positive characteristics of femininity, such as nurturance, knowledge of domesticity, and sensitivity to women patients' modesty. In contrast, in their writing for *professional* audiences, especially texts composed later in the century, women physicians tended to present themselves as assertive, confident, witty, and logical. Taking this approach in their defenses of women's medical practice demonstrated to their readers that they understood the tenor of published professional debate, particularly the value of repartee, clear reasoning, and the absence of emotion.

Disputes about the propriety of women in medicine were often instigated by journal editors who wrote brief pieces disparaging women physicians. When women physicians submitted letters refuting negative characterizations of women and women physicians, however, the men who edited the regular journals expressed little interest in continuing the debate; in fact, they occasionally thanked the women for their well-presented views. For example, in 1890 the *Medical Record* published an editorial criticizing Johns Hopkins University for accepting the $100,000 it needed to complete its medical college from a group of women who stipulated that in exchange for the donation the college would accept women students on the same terms as men ("The Temptation of Johns Hopkins"). In the next few issues, Mary Putnam Jacobi and Emily Blackwell both responded to the editorial, defending women's medical education and criticizing the "ungenerous editorial" (Putnam Jacobi, "The 'Temptation'" 589) for the "sneers in which the writer . . . indulge[d]" (Blackwell 650). In response to Putnam Jacobi's letter, the editor commented, "Our talented correspondent has ably presented her side of the argument. We are always pleased to hear from her on these questions" (589). Likewise, the editor expressed appreciation for Blackwell's letter: "We are always pleased to give a hearing to the other side, and welcome Dr. Blackwell's criticism accordingly. No one is better able to speak for women than she who has herself done so much to advance female education, and there is none whose opinion is entitled to more respect" (650). Despite publishing an editorial arguing that the admission of women to Johns Hopkins would diminish the institution's prestige, the editor of the *Medical Record* seemed to have little interest in engaging women physicians in a debate over the propriety of women's medical education.[7]

Given the positive editorial commentary on Putnam Jacobi's and Blackwell's letters, one might question the sincerity of editors' attacks on women physicians and suspect that they were intended to stir up controversy in order to draw more readers to their publications. In 1895, the *WMJ* attributed male editors' criticism of women physicians to another source: boredom.

> There is no work which falls to the lot of the managing editor [of the *WMJ*] that gives such unalloyed pleasure, as watching the medical press and reading the learned lucubrations anent Women in Medicine. When our brother editors have nothing else to do, no

other topic to disturb the serenity of their cerebral development, they take up the theme of woman and sing it to many tunes. It may be grave or gay, still the theme is the same, and the moral is always deftly hitched on to the end. If there is anything in this world that women *do not* lack, it is advice—gratuitous advice, and should we attempt to follow it, our existence would partake of the manner of the shuttle-cock—forever going out and coming in. ("A Most Learned Judge!" 206)

After creating an exaggerated image of the erudite male editor, the *WMJ* undercut the opinions he offered, not only by describing them as products of boredom, but also by casting them as inconsistent and frivolous, like a game or a song. The editor[8] of the *WMJ*, in contrast, described herself (and, implicitly, the other women physicians for whom she stood) as amused by his advice but not subject to his vacillating recommendations; she is steady and consistent and follows her own conscience. In this way, the editor of the *WMJ* reversed conventionally gendered characteristics and claimed the most professionally suitable ones—consistency, independence, and strength of will—for herself. Making light of men's criticisms of women physicians suggested that late nineteenth-century women physicians were confident enough of their place in the profession that the disapproval of a few men did not bother them. In fact, the *WMJ* editor's bemused appraisal of male editors' comments indicates that she believed herself too wise to take the men's editorials too seriously.

Some late nineteenth-century women physicians went beyond insinuating that men's criticisms were illogical, choosing instead to highlight their adversaries' logical inconsistencies directly in order to cast opponents as lacking in professional values such as rationality and a scientific mindset. Because she was capable of noting and correcting those logical faults, the woman physician cast herself as more rational and more scientific than her detractors, thereby enhancing her own ethos while overturning gendered assumptions about women's weak intellectual abilities. One example of this strategy can be found in Mary A. Spink's 1894 rebuttal of a paper titled "Woman is Not Fit for the Practice of Medicine." Spink, an associate editor for the *WMJ*, wrote, "we can readily believe [this paper] was never intended for publication, so absolutely bare is the article of either logic or scientific fact" (15). Because medical professionals were supposed to think logically and scientifically, Spink's critique challenged not only the paper's conclusions, but also the writer's claim to his professional identity.

Further evidence of women physicians' logic and wit could be found in the *WMJ*'s responses to several editorials in mainstream medical journals, including the *Medical Record* and Louisville's *Medical Progress*. In both of these responses, the editors of the *WMJ* seemed to delight in pointing out the logical flaws in the men's editorials and in exhibiting their own precise logic. For example, in "Forward! Forward!" (1894), the editors took issue with the *Medical Record*'s criticism of women physicians as "too ready to attach themselves to the numerous fads and dogmas which run so closely to charlatanry" (qtd. in "Forward! Forward!" 11). The *Medical Record* based this complaint on an article published in a previous issue of the *WMJ*. The editors of the *WMJ* refuted the male editor's criticism while appearing generous by acknowledging that he might be correct; however, they demonstrated that his evidence was faulty: "There *may* be truth in it [the belief that women physicians are too willing to adopt medical fads], but we desire to say that the editor did not look closely to the name affixed to the article, or he would have noted that it was written by a brother practitioner, and *not by a woman*" (11). The *WMJ* continued by defending its decision to publish an article advertising a medical product by asserting that it "was such an article as most journals of the country carry. In fact all journals do this" (12). Refusing to accept the *Medical Record*'s implied expectation that women physicians adhere to higher standards than men physicians, the *WMJ* suggested that the ethos of that journal and its readers was comparable to that of journals edited and read primarily by men.

Some editorials incorporated wit alongside of their logical critiques of the opponents of women physicians, particularly when they could show that the statements made against women actually cast doubt on men's professional abilities. Such an approach was taken in "Our Quondam Friends" (1894), in which the editors quoted at length what was supposed to be a defense of women physicians written by the editors of the *Medical Progress*. After acknowledging that they believed women could "make an average, and occasionally more than an average, success" as physicians, the *Progress*'s editors insisted that "From a moral standpoint medicine is of course out of woman's sphere," but that for those women who could not or would not marry, a career was an acceptable alternative (97). The editors of the *WMJ* focused particularly on the final paragraph, which they italicized: "*She* [the woman physician] *never becomes eminent because she invariably lacks one essential faculty, a mental momentum, an art of reasoning, an originality which one must possess in order to prevent the study and practice of medicine from becoming routine or a mere code of dogmas. However, as the world stands at present, woman has come into medicine to stay, and men in our profession can no longer be sluggards and drones, but must look to their laurels or she will surpass them*" (98). The *WMJ* called this paragraph "a gem of logic and erudition," and then pointed to the inconsistency in the *Progress*'s argument: "We never become either average practitioners or eminent BUT men must look to their laurels, else we surpass them. Verily this is tough on our brother practitioners, 'damning with faint praise['] as it were" (98).[9]

Rather than focusing exclusively on the less-than-flattering portrait the *Progress* had painted of women physicians in its supposed defense of them, the *WMJ* drew attention to the editorial's implied misgivings about men's abilities. In their conclusion, the editors of the *WMJ* insisted that women and men should both be judged on their individual merits, not as classes: "The real truth of the matter is that women as well as men will find their level in the profession. If they are not competent, no amount of sentiment will bring them success. If they are capable, discerning and skillful, no amount of vituperation will keep them down. The old theory of survival of the fittest will prevail and the best will eventually triumph" (98). As in this passage, late nineteenth-century women physicians frequently cast medicine in Darwinian terms because of the freedom from social prejudice implied by natural selection. For women physicians, applying the concept of "survival of the fittest" to their careers meant that they would be judged objectively, by the same standards as men physicians. In other words, reference to "survival of the fittest" revealed women physicians as eager to be tested and confident in their abilities, not in need of the protection of chivalrous men. Calls for consistency in the evaluation of men and women physicians served two argumentative ends: first, they grounded women's professional claims in scientific objectivity and evolutionary theory, indicating their adherence to professional values; second, they suggested that women's presence in the field would not "feminize" it because women intended to compete for their places in medicine.

Turning Outward: Reshaping Medicine's Attitudes toward Women

According to Harrison, the ultimate goal of self-rhetoric is a successful rhetorical performance addressed to others: "The personal spaces of women's diaries provided room for rhetorical rehearsals and allowed women to persuade themselves that they could and should take on the new roles thrust upon them. Once *they* were convinced they were acting and speaking properly, they could present to their public—whether family, local community, or enemy soldiers—an ethos that accounted for the often conflicting demands of wartime culture" (260). For nineteenth-century women physicians interested in contributing to the medical literature, turning their rhetoric outward and testing their new professional ethos meant contributing to the medical journals historically edited and read by men. Letters to the editors of those journals provided the greatest opportunity for women physicians to make their case for women in medicine to members of the profession. Even before the *WMJ* began publication in 1893, women physicians submitted letters to the editors of medical journals, rebutting the criticisms of male editors and commentators. Examining these letters alongside the *WMJ*'s editorials reveals a relatively consistent pattern of argument and ethos building.

As I described above, one strategy the *WMJ* used to defuse male criticism while presenting women physicians as logical and witty was making fun of the editors of medical journals run by men. This strategy was also evident in women physicians' letters to editors. In her 1892 letter supporting women physicians' appointments to insane asylums, Sara Kime[10] characterized the *Medical Record*'s opposition to the proposal as desultory. She wrote that "the editor of the MEDICAL RECORD takes occasion every now and then to condemn" women's appointment to asylums. Such a dismissal of editors' hostility to women physicians not only suggested that the resistance was merely superficial but also implied that the editors were driven by a need for copy or controversy rather than a deeply held professional or personal belief. Whether or not the editors and the men reading the journals truly opposed women in the profession, women physicians' characterization of their criticisms minimized the threat they posed by attributing them to whimsy, boredom, or misplaced priorities. In contrast, Kime's support of women physicians' appointment to insane asylums was grounded in evidence. Noting that the Pennsylvania Medical Society had recently approved resolutions in favor of women's appointments, she wrote, "Coming as [the resolutions] do from the profession of a State where women have been successfully tried in this capacity, shows that the need has not been over-estimated and that women physicians have proven their qualifications and abilities to be nowise inferior to those of male physicians." Because a large number of women had graduated from the Woman's Medical College of Pennsylvania, Kime argued, the physicians of Pennsylvania had had ample opportunity to test the abilities of women physicians. That the medical society of that state supported women's appointment to insane asylums constituted proof that women physicians were qualified for such positions. As Kime's letter indicates, efforts to diminish the force of male criticism were often accompanied by demonstrations of women's own logic. Given the "intertwined" nature of ethos, pathos, and logos (N. Reynolds 327), Kime's logical argument reinforced her ethos as an intelligent, rational professional. In contrast to what she cast as the arbitrary comments of male editors, Kime and other women physicians presented themselves as logical, consistent, and firmly established in the field.

Women physicians would not have had access to the editorial pages of medical journals without the professional status that they had recently achieved. Their access to this discursive space was important because it represented the first time significant numbers of women were in a position to alter professional attitudes from within. Occasionally, women physicians took advantage of their new status as professional insiders to offer alternative explanations and viewpoints to those asserted by men in the field, particularly those that revealed negative attitudes toward women. For example, in a letter published in the *Medical Record* in 1883, Caroline Pease[11] developed an ethos based in rationality and justice in order to challenge the writer of a previously published report from Canada who disparaged the medical education of women. She quoted "his gravely expressed foreboding that 'there cannot be any doubt in the minds of all who think calmly on the matter, but that these young female doctors will locate on our streets, and in our villages and towns.'" Striving to make the presence of women physicians concrete to readers, the Canadian correspondent had implied that they posed a threat to men physicians' incomes and to the respectability of their neighborhoods. Rather than directly refuting these accusations, Pease shifted perspectives and showed readers the situation from the point of view of a woman with few financial opportunities: "And pray what if they do [open practices near men physicians]? Will the public morals be wrecked in consequence? The social scientist, if *he* 'think calmly on the matter,' will doubtless tell us society is better for a young woman 'locating on our streets' to practise legitimate medicine, than if forced by the closure of all avenues of respectable work she 'walk' that same street for bread." Invoking the expertise of social science, one of the newest professions, and one that might have a broader and less-biased view than the self-interested physician, Pease insisted that women's developing professionalism should be viewed not as an incursion into the masculine professional world but as a means of self-support for women that would ultimately enhance social morality.

Later in her letter, Pease took up the common criticism that women physicians pursued their careers to satisfy their greed. She answered this complaint by demonstrating women's need for an income and by noting the double standard inherent in calling a woman, but not a man, greedy for desiring to earn a respectable salary: "I can only say that whenever society reaches that happy stage of gallantry to our sex that the tradesman and artisan refuse to accept from us an equivalent of 'dollars and cents' for their work and their wares, doubtless the percentage of women who practise medicine from philanthropy, pure and simple, will more nearly approximate that of the men in the profession who decline all fees." Just as she shifted the perspective in her response to the threat of women physicians opening practices near men, Pease also presented an alternative perspective on women's behavior when she countered the representation of women physicians as greedy by reminding readers that not all women could rely on male relatives to provide for them financially. What the Canadian correspondent perceived as extra income, money that was not needed and so was sought because of avarice, Pease cast as necessary for daily expenses and as a just reward for professional work.

In addition to suggesting that women ought to have the right to respectable means of earning their livings, Pease also claimed that women could have higher moral purposes than those of idle domesticity, pointing to the large number of women physicians who had put their medical education to work in missionary fields. The medical missionary, Pease wrote, "has found her work, and is doing God and humanity better service than by devoting her immortal energies to making rick-rack trimming for her dresses." Again Pease offered an alternative representation of women, this time suggesting that it was not the conventional domestic woman, engaged in frivolously decorating herself, who represented the ideal woman, but instead it was the woman who traveled abroad—far outside the home—to relieve suffering and save souls, who best performed her duties as a religious human being. Pease capitalized on the ethos she had demonstrated throughout her letter as a writer who valued logic and justice in order to present an alternative to the virtues conventionally believed to be appropriate to women; a reader persuaded by Pease's ethos might be moved to accept her privileging of usefulness, piety, and professionalism over domesticity and fashionableness as virtues to be valued among women.

Another instance of relying on a rational and just ethos in order to offer alternative explanations appeared in the *Journal of the American Medical Association* in 1897. This letter, signed "An old Subscriber and Constant Reader of the JOURNAL," was written in response to an editorial titled "The Despised Office of Motherhood," which had appeared ten months earlier. The editorial had decried affluent women's lack of interest in maternity, attributing it to the preference for social over domestic activities and to the physical damage done to women's reproductive organs by late nights spent dancing. The response of the "old Subscriber," published under the same title as the editorial that prompted it, indicated that the writer was a woman, and in contrast to the original editorial, which blamed young women for the declining birthrate, this writer attributed at least some of the responsibility to men, and to physicians in particular. She referred to her practice as evidence: "I have had a large experience with women, as patients as well as every other relation of life.

I can assure you I have had more women come to me to ask me to aid them in securing good healthy children than to prevent or destroy them. Now, please make that fact as emphatic and prominent as you have the converse, if you will be just" ("The Despised Office" 375). After insisting on a balanced representation of women, the writer reminded her readers that not all men were prepared to be fathers, particularly those who contracted a venereal disease before marriage. She asked her readers, "How many, on an average, of the men you are personally acquainted with and can vouch for, are fitted, mentally, morally and physically to become ideal fathers, particularly with that old effete idea, 'That boys must be boys and sow their wild oats?' Too well do we, as physicians, know the harvest such a sowing produces" (375). Challenging a popular view of young men's liberties by invoking the profession's shared experience with the consequences of male promiscuity, the writer both resisted the blame the original editorial placed on women and reminded her readers that she shared their identity as physicians.

In fact, the writer suggested, the very women whom the editorial scorned for claiming that they were not interested in children might have been protecting their husbands. Referring to a recently developed diagnostic device, she offered this alternative to the representation of childless women as selfish: "It is high time we have some X rays (so to speak) on the conditions of the opposite sex. Women are proud and loyal as a class. When they have made a bad bargain they try to shield those who have wronged them; and declare they did not wish children, when they learned to their sorrow they could not have them, through the incompetence of their husbands the result of youthful dissipation. Such sublime heroism merits a better fate" (376). The writer's mention of X-rays, which had been developed as a diagnostic tool only two years before this letter was published, positioned her as a professional who kept up with recent scientific discoveries. Furthermore, the potential of radiographs to provide more accurate images of conditions not readily visible suited the writer's purpose of offering alternatives to men's explanations of women's actions. Just as a radiograph might help a physician diagnose a patient's condition, the writer's alternative viewpoint might more accurately explain declining fertility rates. Referring to X-rays functioned simultaneously to enhance the writer's ethos and to provide a metaphor supporting her argument that women did not despise motherhood. According to the writer's reasoning, not only were women not to blame for their childlessness, but they should actually be praised for disguising their husbands' indiscretions.

Elsewhere in the letter, the writer observed that in her experience, the strongest resistance to procreation came from men: "Every case that ever insulted me with the desire for assistance in destroying the product of conception, was urged and backed by the man in the case—married or single—almost without an exception" (375). Her concluding paragraph plainly countered the argument of the original editorial, demanding a more just examination of the situation: "If you canvass fairly you will find the male sex are keeping the children in abeyance. . . . And I am sorry to say it, many of our profession are in the category" (376). In this passage, the writer turned the original accusation back around to men in general, and she pointed in particular at some men in the profession. Even if her readers had not attempted to avoid children themselves, they might have contributed to the missteps of their patients through inadequate attention to women's health. The writer asserted, "We want physicians as a class to interest themselves in pregnant and parturient women. Instruct them and help them to accomplish this grand work with safety and comparative comfort, and then there will not be the aversion to it that is claimed" (375). Implicitly condemning men physicians for not paying enough attention to women's health concerns, she blamed them for women's difficulties in pregnancy and labor and consequently for frightened women's efforts to avoid conception and delivery.

The writer went on to encourage physicians to educate their patients, particularly young men, about physiology. After stating that she teaches young mothers how to talk to their children about sexuality, she insisted that men needed similar lessons: "Men should be taught moderation and to conserve their vital energies instead of wasting them as they do now. I remember seeing it stated in a medical work some years ago, that one ounce of semen was equivalent in vital force to forty ounces of blood. When you can fully impress men with this fact you will do a little toward stemming the tide of sexual dissipation that is well nigh appalling" (376). In addition to shifting the terms of the debate away from women's lack of interest in child-bearing and toward men's dissipation, this writer made rhetorical moves that few nineteenth-century women would have. She cited a medical text to support her argument that men's premarital sexual activity was the true cause of the falling birthrate among the middle and upper classes, and she used vocabulary related to male sexual functions in print. Without the interactions with a range of women and the access to medical terminology afforded by her profession, the writer of this letter would have had a very difficult time making the argument she did, defending women and frankly advising men about their sexual behavior. The writer's professional education and status clearly opened rhetorical opportunities to her that were not available to most nineteenth-century women. Even with the advantages of her professional status, however, such an argument made by a woman would have drawn strong resistance. Perhaps the writer's forcefulness in accusing men and in indicting male physicians for their role in the declining fertility rates explains her decision to withhold her name when she submitted the letter.

Late nineteenth-century women physicians' position as professional insiders gave them access not only to rhetorical forums such as the medical journal editorial and letter to the editor, but also to the information and experiences that were considered valid evidence in those forums. Countering centuries of medical misogyny, women physicians sought to improve physicians' attitudes toward women by presenting themselves as logical and fair-minded and positing alternative explanations for behaviors men characterized as negative. In concert with promoting a more balanced view of women, women physicians also confronted men physicians for their role in women's oppression, whether that took the form of limiting women's occupational opportunities, as in Pease's letter, or the form of neglecting their responsibilities to educate men and to take women's health care seriously, as in the letter by the anonymous respondent to "The Despised Office of Motherhood." Although women physicians were able to make these statements because they were members of the profession, their arguments had potential implications well beyond the profession, as physicians were persuaded by women physicians' letters to the editor to reconsider their attitudes toward their female patients.

Homeopathic medical journals published far fewer editorials and letters debating women's place in the field than did the regular medical journals at this time. Because women physicians' role as "provers" of the effects of homeopathic drugs on women had led to women's admission to the American Institute of Homeopathy in 1871, women's place in homeopathy in the 1880s and 1890s was more secure than their place in the regular profession. Consequently, women homeopaths wrote few letters to the editor defending their rights as physicians; instead, they demonstrated their membership in the profession by advocating actions that they believed would increase the numbers and respectability of homeopaths. Even though they wrote for different reasons than regular women physicians did, homeopathic women still adopted an assertive ethos that demonstrated their possession of "the courage which dares." For example, under the headline "From a Woman's Point of View" (1898), homeopath Sarah J. Millsop[12] of Bowling Green, Kentucky, directly confronted the editor of the *North American Journal of Homœopathy* (*NAJH*) in her letter contributing to an extensive epistolary conversation about the leadership and membership of the American Institute of Homeopathy. First, she drew attention to her rhetorical situation: "As you [the editor] have kindly opened the columns of the NORTH AMERICAN for discussion and criticism of the management of the American Institute of Homœopathy, and as women are proverbial fault finders, it is but fair that one should have a pen, if not a voice, in helping allay this little ruffling breeze which has been raised about our ears" (125). Although this introduction minimized both Millsop's own authority and the exigency she addressed, it nevertheless created a space in which Millsop could write a letter that occupied nearly four pages of the February 1898 issue of the *NAJH*. After offering material explanations for low attendance by young professionals at the American Institute of Homeopathy's meetings, including the expense of the journey and the effort and time involved in composing a paper for presentation, she speculated that homeopathic editors might also be to blame. Observing that "In the many allopathic [regular] journals which find their way to my table I note no criticism on the way in which offices are distributed in that organization as a cause for slim attendance on its meetings," Millsop asked, "Is it not possible that this continuous fault-finding and criticism on the part of all-wise [homeopathic] editors and others may be the 'wet blanket' which is thrown over lukewarm members and non-affiliating members of the Institute, and thus dampens their ardor and quenches their enthusiasm?" (127). She contended that a reader of homeopathic journals "may conclude, after a time, that the Institute is a badly managed body; that its younger members are unfairly treated; that its older members are grasping for empty honors and a 'grind' of work; that its sessions are too long and its memorial service too dry; that too much frolicking is indulged in and not enough attention paid to serious business; that, in short, its members, as a whole, are 'a bad lot,' and that it is a good Institute to keep away from." Then Millsop offered a rhetorical solution for the rhetorical problem she had identified: "Would it not be the better way to adopt the plan of the hypnotist, and make 'suggestions' that the 'dear old Institute' is all, or is becoming all, its most faithful adherents could wish it to be?" (127).

In publicly criticizing the editor of the *NAJH* in the pages of his own journal, Millsop needed to present a confident, assertive ethos that demonstrated her commitment to improving the status of homeopathy, despite finding fault with the editor of a major homeopathic journal. To do so, Millsop referred to her own experience with the institute as a conference attendee and as the chair of one of its sections (128, 125). She also expressed her loyalty to homeopathy, concluding her letter by asking, "And who of us can fail to wish and work for the prosperity of Homœopathy when it has done so much for us?" (128). Millsop tempered her criticism of one of homeopathy's leaders with a display of her devotion to the field. Like Millsop, other homeopathic and regular women physicians employed an ethos that conveyed their commitment to professional values, whether to homeopathy in particular or to more general principles such as science, logic, and confidence. Avoiding the "feminine" appeals common in women physicians' public rhetoric, the women physicians who wrote for medical journals in the 1880s and 1890s presented themselves as confident, assertive, logical, and witty: formidable contenders in editorial debates and professional life.

Women as Rhetorical Professionals

In composing editorials and letters to the editors of medical journals, nine-teenth-century American women physicians expanded the number of rhetorical forums in which women expressed their worldviews and argued for their social and professional rights. For the first time, significant numbers of women participated in professional discourse, shaping medicine's agenda and values. When women physicians demonstrated women's intelligence and confidence, proved their own commitment to professional values, and defended women from misogynist characterizations, they presented the medical profession with a positive view of women. Because physicians' descriptions of women's physical, intellectual, and temperamental tendencies were frequently used to justify restrictions on women's activities, women physicians' efforts within the profession to alter attitudes toward women had potential social consequences that reached far beyond intraprofessional debates. Because, as the editor of the *WMJ* complained in 1899, "The individuality as to error, as well as to praise, allowed men, [was] not . . . accorded to women" ("Dr. Mary Aiken" 246), women physicians' accomplishments within the profession had the potential to shape physicians' beliefs about nonprofessional women's abilities as well. Nineteenth-century medicine's misogyny was deeply ingrained, so any progress women physicians made in improving attitudes toward women was necessarily limited. Nevertheless, women physicians' frequent contributions to journals' editorial pages, particularly their arguments on behalf of women and women physicians, suggest that women physicians saw those pages as important sites for building positive representations for themselves and for articulating a professional identity for the field that would accommodate and respect women.

For rhetorical scholars, the editorial pages of the *WMJ* present an opportunity to learn about how discursive practices develop through intragroup discussions of proper rhetorical activity. This is particularly important in historical studies of women's rhetoric, because it helps to fill in our knowledge of women's perceptions of and beliefs about appropriate speech and writing, providing a counterpart to the long history of rhetorical theory and advice composed by men. In particular, the discussions of professional rhetorical activity published in the *WMJ* emphasized women physicians' frequent inability to control their own ethē because hostile audiences often attributed unprofessional characteristics to them. The *WMJ* advised women physicians to cope with this obstacle by building a collective ethos in which each woman had to guard her reputation as a woman and as a physician for the sake of all present and future women physicians.

Furthermore, the *WMJ*'s insistence that full professionalism required participation in medicine's rhetorical forums is evidence that the editors of that journal were aware of the increasing importance of contributing to the field's knowledge and its discourse. The editors were protective of the ideal of a medical journal and of women's access to it. In 1895, after an unnamed western medical journal published pictures of nude women that the *WMJ* deemed nonmedical, the editors criticized the offenders for blurring the boundaries of a professional journal: "When a medical journal begins to supply, or rather attempts to cater to all the wants of the profession, it will soon degenerate into a grocer's bulletin, and a trade journal, and the original idea of a scientific publication will be lost in the multiplicity of themes presented" ("Art for Art's Sake"). Although this editorial could be read as a defense against journals that published images hostile to women professionals, it was also an expression of the value women physicians placed on professional publication and their commitment to the scientific professional identity such publications made possible for women. Largely prohibited from teaching in men's or coeducational medical schools, working in public hospitals, or editing mainstream journals, nineteenth-century women's best chance to be acknowledged by the profession and to claim professional authority might have been in their contributions to national medical journals.

In many ways, constructing nineteenth-century women physicians as rhetorical professionals required women to perform roles conventionally gendered masculine but also associated with professionalism: women physicians addressed national audiences, they relied on their expertise and experience to authorize their arguments, and they directly and publicly refuted statements made by men physicians. Once they were accepted as legitimate physicians, being a professional excused, and in fact required, some rhetorical behaviors that were unacceptable for women in the public sphere. As the editors of the *WMJ* advised their readers in 1893, "it takes grit and backbone yet to stand up, each for herself," yet a woman physician must "simply assert [herself]" ("Sub Rosa"). Frank discussions of the medical aspects of sexuality, direct rebuttals of men physicians' opinions, and sharply pointed witticisms might all have seemed out of place in a respectable woman speaking in late nineteenth-century society, but such rhetorical acts were consistent with the conventions of medical editorial pages at the time.

The characteristics of the ideal woman physician that emerged from the *WMJ* editorials and women's letters to the editors of medical journals edited by men differed little from the ideal male physician constructed in similar rhetorical spaces. Unsurprisingly, professional journals, which depended on submissions and subscriptions, encouraged their readers and contributors to exhibit the traits best suited to the success of the national medical research journals that emerged near the end of the century. While the editorial pages of medical journals served as spaces in which women could demonstrate that they were capable of participating in professional discourse, the sections of journals devoted to research articles offered women the opportunity to enact the role they had constructed for themselves and to advocate rhetorical and epistemological agendas for the profession that would make medicine more "scientific" and increase the range and quality of physicians' expertise. These rhetorical acts are the focus of the next chapter.

6

Revising the Physician's Ethos: Women Physicians' Medical Research

> Women, being limited to the few small hospitals that they
> have themselves established, are in the position of emigrants
> in a new territory, or, as might have been said, of the advance-
> guard of an invading army, compelled to build their own roads
> and create their own facilities as they advance.
> —Frances Emily White, "The American
> Medical Woman" (1895)

One of the criticisms leveled against American women physicians in the nineteenth century was the argument that since women were responsible for no significant advancements in medical knowledge, they were either poorly educated or intellectually incapable of scientific research. For example, in 1870 a speaker at a meeting of the Pennsylvania Medical Society based his opposition to women in medicine partially on his perception that in the twenty years it had existed, the Woman's Medical College of Pennsylvania had "established no prestige or produced no great works in the way of scientific or literary contributions to medical progress" ("Medical Societies" 532). Women physicians interpreted the situation differently, as Frances Emily White, Professor of Physiology at the Woman's Medical College of Pennsylvania, did in her 1895 address to the graduating class of that institution, "The American Medical Woman." After recounting the history of American women in medicine, White discussed the current state of women in the field, including their contributions to medical research. She noted that "The chief disadvantages from which medical women in this country now suffer arise from their exclusion (during their professional career) from the work of the great public hospitals" (126–27). Citing an unpublished paper by Emily

Blackwell, White observed that "the hospital is no less important than the college in the training of doctors," yet "these public institutions, equipped and endowed at public expense, are monopolized by men" (127). According to White's paraphrase of Blackwell, women's exclusion from hospitals, where medical research might be performed, limited women's ability to contribute to medical research: "medical progress depends on the hospital and the laboratory, . . . the scientific writers and teachers, the great operators and other leaders in medicine are the hospital-men, and . . . the great journals are founded on hospital-records" (127). The pattern of exclusion nineteenth-century women physicians faced meant that, before women could perform medical research, they first had to, like "the advance-guard of an invading army, . . . create their own facilities as they advance" (127). White and Blackwell noted a crucial difference in the material and institutional resources available to women and to men; they suggested that this difference might explain any perceived deficiencies in women as medical researchers.

Critics of women in medicine, however, asserted that what they perceived to be the relatively small number of medical research papers by women demonstrated that women were incapable of contributing to medicine's scientific or therapeutic knowledge. Those who doubted women's ability to perform scientific scholarship drew on work such as Charles Darwin's *The Descent of Man* (1871), which characterized (white) women's intellect as different from and ultimately inferior to (white) men's: "It is generally admitted that with woman the powers of intuition, of rapid perception, and perhaps of imitation, are more strongly marked than in man; but some, at least, of these faculties are characteristic of the lower races, and therefore of a past and lower state of civilisation" (326–27). Women physicians, therefore, might become passable practitioners either through making intuitive assessments of patients or through applying existing medical knowledge in a rote manner, but they could never become *scientific* professionals who developed new treatments or surgical procedures, made physiological discoveries, and participated in the discourses through which physicians reported, tested, and confirmed therapeutic and scientific advances.

In the same year that Darwin published *The Descent of Man*, Alfred Stillé addressed the American Medical Association (AMA) as its president, explaining his belief that women's minds were not compatible with scientific thought: "We may admit that [woman] is in some sense a perfected man, and was created even a little less lower than the angels; we may admit that, guided by her affections, her judgments sometimes resemble inspirations; but in the business of life, and especially in the practice of a scientific art, it nevertheless may be true, and probably is so, that she usually displays a strange ignorance of the logic of reason, and a profound contempt for the logic of facts" (qtd. in Fishbein 83). Although some men believed women physicians might diagnose ailments more efficiently than men because they were caring, observant, and intuitive, women's supposed lack of reasoning skills was more often used to claim that they could not be true scientific professionals. Such doubt was expressed by L. Julien Picöt, who in 1885 advised his colleagues to "Praise [woman] (and you cannot praise her too much) for a tender and skillful nurse—for delicate assiduity and heroic endurance by beds of pain" (17). However, Picöt questioned women's ability to engage in the intellectual work of medicine: "We do not for a moment question woman's capacity to comprehend . . . the mysteries of anatomy, nor do we question the capacity of a gourd's holding water, only from long use and saturation it becomes rotten from watery contact" (15).

Although some critics questioned woman's intellectual abilities, others suggested that the limitations posed by her body made significant medical research impossible. An editorial published in the *Journal of the American Medical Association* (*JAMA*) in 1891, titled "The Province of Woman in Medicine," quoted the celebrated British gynecologist Lawson Tait, who characterized women as inescapably diseased: "From the cradle to puberty [women] seem to be on fairly equal terms with men, but from that moment, through the whole of the period of active life, their existence is one of prolonged suffering." The editor also quoted Tait's claim that "The great function of [women's] lives is led up to by troubles, and from it endless suffering springs." Referring to Tait's long and respected professional experience "with the subject of the sexual characteristics of the female," the editor asked whether or not women were physically capable of performing the work of the physician: "Can unfortunate, pain-afflicted woman ever occupy a sphere of unquestioned usefulness in medicine, where physical and mental vigor, fortitude, and endurance are eminently requisite, and where the strong must help the weak, help them by virtue of their strength, to healthier and stronger states?" The editor concluded that "woman has yet to achieve any greatness in the ranks of medicine," and asserted that if women could not be great physicians and researchers, they must "rest, in the unsought weakness of [their] nature, as . . . follower[s] of man" ("The Province"). Authoritative medical voices—among them Tait and the editor of *JAMA*—raised doubts about women's physical ability to succeed in the profession, even as late as the 1890s.

Despite misgivings about women's physical strength and their capacity for scientific thinking, many women physicians enthusiastically pursued medical research and writing in the nineteenth century, presenting papers at medical conferences and publishing articles in medical journals.

Historical women's scientific rhetoric, however, is an area that has received little scholarly attention. Gail Lippincott notes that "although a body of research exists on literary women or on suffrage or temperance proponents, the communication strategies of women engaged in scientific and technological activities have been largely overlooked." Yet what we do know of women's participation in scientific and technical communication demonstrates that these rhetorical activities "offer an important starting point for productive research on the intersection of technology, gender, and communication" (45). This intersection was particularly important for the women physicians who composed medical research articles, many of which focused on female biology and reproductive physiology in particular. Historian Nancy Theriot points to the significance of acknowledging women's roles in shaping medicine's rhetorical and epistemological uses of science: "Noticing women's voices in medical discourse, as patients and as physicians, forces us to reevaluate the unitary, male image of medical science and allows us to see gender and science as mutually constituting" (24–25). As Susan Wells describes in *Out of the Dead House*, nineteenth-century women physicians shaped the development of medicine's epistemology and its communicative forms. Wells identifies some of the effects women had on medical discourse, observing that "They invented central tropes and strategies for medical research and writing: the use of survey information, methods of taking patient histories, [and] conventions for telling case histories" (12). Most importantly, nineteenth-century women physicians "call into question any notion of scientific discourse as alien to women" (12). Despite opponents' doubts about women's intellectual and physical abilities, women physicians participated actively in medicine's rhetorical forums, not merely repeating others' research or adhering to established rhetorical conventions, but promoting their own models of professional values and medical discursive forms.

This chapter examines women physicians' research articles published in five national general-medicine professional journals from 1880 to 1900: the *Woman's Medical Journal* (*WMJ*), which was edited by women and published articles almost exclusively by women in its nineteenth-century volumes; the *Medical Record* and the *Journal of the American Medical Association* (*JAMA*), both regular medical journals edited by men; and the homeopathic journals the *Medical Century* and the *North American Journal of Homœopathy* (*NAJH*), which were also managed by men.[1] All five journals reached a national audience, took general medicine rather than one of the specialties as its focus, demonstrated an interest in the work and values of the profession, and included writing by women relatively frequently. The four periodicals edited by men published approximately one hundred pieces by women in their noneditorial sections in the twenty years studied here. Often under the heading "Original Articles," medical journals published reports of particular cases, collections of similar cases from a physician's private practice, compilations of records of hospital cases, the results of medical experiments, informative pieces describing a condition or anatomical feature, and advice for treating various ailments. Historian Charles E. Rosenberg characterizes medical journals around 1879 as not especially interested in biological science, and this feature of journals' content affected the genres of articles they published: "Even the most intellectually exacting of the clinical journals found little space in their pages for articles on the laboratory sciences, even in the sections devoted to abstracts. The great majority of the journal literature still consisted of case reports (albeit increasingly in the specialties), essays of clinical reflection and speculation, and transcriptions of clinical lectures at the nation's leading hospitals and medical schools" (29–30). Many of the articles published in medical journals were originally papers read at regional, national, or specialists' conferences. Women physicians wrote articles and conference papers representing the full range of nineteenth-century medical publications, adopting medical discourse and making it their own. Many of the features of medical discourse drew on the physician's professional standing, expertise, and experience; once women could claim these sources of professional authority, they found in medical research articles opportunities to engage in rhetorical activity previously inaccessible to women.

In their research papers, women physicians worked to improve their own ethē both directly, by displaying adherence to medicine's values, and indirectly, by working to change perceptions of two broad groups with which they closely identified: physicians and women. What I call "direct ethos work" is the crafting of one's own rhetorical character most often described in instructions for speakers and writers: the strategies by which an individual rhetor appeals to an audience through conveying the sense that he or she shares its values. I use "indirect ethos work" to refer to the effort a speaker or writer makes to improve an audience's attitude toward her by altering its perceptions of a broader group to which she belongs. Such an appeal is indirect because it is not focused on the character of the rhetor specifically or on a particular communicative act; instead, the speaker or writer seeks to change the audience's attitude toward a whole class of people, possibly realizing that such a change will occur only over a long period of time. The only effect such an appeal might have on the rhetor's ethos in the immediate rhetorical situation is reflective: if, for instance, a woman writer persuades her readers to think more highly of women in general, her status might be elevated in their eyes.

Indirect ethos might be said to have both a "simple form" and a "complex form." Using the simple form of indirect ethos, a woman physician might overtly argue that women are physically strong and intellectually capable, arguments that, if they were persuasive, would enhance the audience's perceptions of women and therefore of the particular woman physician speaker. The complex form of indirect ethos involves intervening in the epistemology or the worldview that supports a negative view of the group of which the rhetor is a part. As I will demonstrate, nineteenth-century women physicians promoted medical research methods and genre conventions that they believed would lead to more positive perceptions of women, perceptions that would strengthen the case for women in medicine. Further research may demonstrate that complex forms of indirect ethos are often an important part of the repertoire of rhetorical strategies employed by members of marginalized groups because their marginalization is frequently embedded in a worldview that supports their exclusion or oppression. Confronting only a group's marginalized status without also revising the broader systems surrounding it may have limited success as a rhetorical strategy for resisting domination. Women physicians enjoyed a unique opportunity to intervene in medical epistemology in late nineteenth-century America, because that period saw considerable changes in the profession's means of gathering and reporting information as well as in the characteristics attributed to the physician's professional identity. The relatively open nature of medical professionalism at the time presented women physicians with a chance to revise medicine's methods for performing and reporting on research; these methods carried with them particular sets of values that women believed would make a professional ethos more accessible to women.

The Professional Context

American women physicians who performed research on gynecological conditions and treatments, as many did in the 1880s and 1890s, entered into a complex conversation involving representations of women, the role of the physician, and competitive surgical innovation. Operations to remove female reproductive organs were controversial, with gynecologists asserting that the procedures they performed relieved women's suffering, while opponents argued that ovariotomy (the removal of ovaries known to be diseased), oöphorectomy (the removal of apparently healthy ovaries), and hysterectomy "unsexed" women and prevented them from conceiving children. Gynecologists countered that it was women's diseased organs, not surgery, that rendered them incapable of bearing children and that surgery alleviated women's pain, allowing them to perform their domestic duties and to care for the children that they had borne before becoming ill. Accompanying this therapeutic debate was a discourse constructing the female body and especially the female reproductive system as delicate and complex, a construction that reinforced women's confinement to the domestic sphere (Morantz-Sanchez, *Conduct* 107–12). Physicians and women also asked whether or not motherhood was the defining feature of femininity: if it was, then the reproductive organs must be maintained at all costs, no matter the patient's suffering. The possibility that women could be women without children or that mothers might willingly give up the chance for future children in order to find relief from their own pain posed a significant challenge to nineteenth-century models of femininity.

As gynecological surgery was being debated, physicians also disputed the source of women's mental and nervous conditions. Theriot's scholarship positions this conflict as part of the "professional turf battles" (4) between gynecologists, who believed women's insanity originated in dysfunctional reproductive organs, and alienists (specialists in mental illness) and neurologists (specialists in conditions affecting the nervous system), who attributed women's mental health problems to heredity and environmental causes. Whereas gynecologists believed that women's "nervousness" or insanity emanated from their reproductive organs, alienists and neurologists located those conditions in the central nervous system, which was invisibly but still inherently "feminine" (4–10). Physicians adopting the gynecological perspective believed that women's mental illness could be treated by gynecological surgery. According to Theriot, many nineteenth-century American women physicians, even those who specialized in gynecology, aligned themselves with the alienist/neurologist perspective because the delicacy of the female reproductive system had been used to justify women's exclusion from the medical profession and because attributing mental illness to environmental causes such as physical inactivity, monotony, and unceasing domestic labor reinforced women physicians' choice to pursue a professional career (12–14).

Questions about the validity of various medical research methods and epistemologies were woven into both of these interrelated debates. Morantz-Sanchez describes the mid-1800s as "a period of medical expansionism [that] represented a gradual shift from art to science, from general practice to specialization, from medical to surgical solutions" (*Conduct* 90). Throughout the second half of the century, medical conferences and journals occupied themselves with questions about the most effective methods of diagnosing and treating conditions as well as the most informative and most "scientific" methods of gathering information about conditions and drawing conclusions about etiology and treatment. Propelled by recent innovations in anesthesia and antisepsis, surgeons experimented with new surgical techniques, though surgical mortality rates were still high by today's standards. By the 1890s, medical science had been the site of substantial developments, including discoveries in bacteriology, the invention of new instruments, and therapeutic advances such as vaccines and aseptic surgical techniques. These developments were accompanied by institutional changes as well: some hospitals built laboratories and established affiliations with medical colleges (Tuchman, *Science* 13), increasing the scientific resources available to physicians and medical students.

The professional identity of the physician as a scientist, as a practitioner who intervened in bodily functions rather than primarily supporting the system on its way back to health, and as a specialist who focused on particular organs, tissues, and systems rather than taking a holistic approach to the body emerged at this time, and not without controversy. Because advances such as the discovery of disease-causing bacteria often did not immediately lead to more effective treatments, many physicians were skeptical of the value of science to medical practice. As some physicians were calling for greater reliance on "science," an older model of professional identity also existed, one in which knowledge and decisions were based on bedside observation rather than laboratory work and in which each patient was perceived to be unique rather than a case of a disease with a universal cause, such as *the* bacterium that causes tuberculosis. For members of this generation, the relationship between the doctor and his or her patient was crucial, as was the practitioner's professional judgment; science threatened to undermine both of these components of medical labor, as universal laws of health and disease seemed to automate the physician's work (Morantz-Sanchez, *Conduct* 97–98). For example, critics of bacteriology, one of the scientific fields that developed rapidly near the end of the 1800s, "warned that the scientific physicians who narrowed their microscopic focus to bacteria were at risk of losing sight of their patients" (Warner 464).

When women physicians entered these debates, they did so neither unanimously nor free of self-interest. Medicine's shift near the end of the nineteenth century toward laboratory science and hospitals and away from holism and home care presented a dilemma of representation for some women physicians. On one hand, these developments increased women physicians' persuasive authority along with the authority of the rest of the profession as they allowed physicians to draw on the prestige of science; however, scientific objectivity simultaneously undercut some of the most persuasive arguments for women physicians, especially the idea that women had unique insights and aptitudes that would allow them to practice a different kind of medicine, one particularly suited to treating women and children. As one might expect, women physicians did not unanimously or simultaneously choose to adopt the new or to retain the old model of professional identity. As Morantz-Sanchez has demonstrated, Elizabeth Blackwell and Mary Putnam Jacobi, both leaders in the woman-doctor movement, approached medical science from very different perspectives: Blackwell preferred holism, spoke of her medical work in religious and moral terms, and advocated a separate feminine medical sphere, while Putnam Jacobi was fascinated by laboratory science and resisted notions of female medical separatism (*Sympathy* 184–202). Even among women who adopted scientific approaches to medicine, the uses to which they put their scholarship varied. Historian Carla Bittel notes that "Some women in the nineteenth century used medical knowledge to construct the female body in ways that corresponded to their own views of womanhood," while "Other women physicians tried to dismiss sex differences" (120). For many of these women, science was a tool that they believed would produce more accurate representations of female health and temperament, representations that would alter the beliefs about women that underlay many of the restrictions on their behavior.

Although not all nineteenth-century women physicians supported the new scientific impulse in medicine, those who published research in medical journals constituted a subset of women physicians who were particularly committed to a scientific model of medicine. These women used their research papers to engage in indirect ethos work intended to align the characteristics attributed to women more closely with those expected of physicians. In order for the research that supported this indirect ethos work to be accepted, however, physicians had to recognize science as a component of their professional identity. One facet of women physicians' complex indirect ethos work, therefore, was convincing all physicians to adopt scientific values. Women physicians would benefit, alongside of men physicians, from a "scientific" discourse and methodology that tended to enhance the authority of the physician. Women physicians could potentially earn three rhetorical advantages from medicine's scientific professional identity. First, much of the expertise and many of the discursive practices associated with scientific medicine enhanced physicians' authority in conversations with patients; such authority was particularly valuable to women, who had historically enjoyed little rhetorical authority. Second, science offered women an "objective" stance with which to address the field, one ostensibly not feminine and one that authorized women's research-based claims. Third, if the profession learned from scientific studies that women were not inherently physically frail, then women's place in the field would be more secure.

Persuading All Physicians to
Adopt a Scientific Ethos

Advocating a scientific epistemology for medicine was not without risk for women physicians. Bittel explains that "As physicians debated the meaning and worth of 'science' in medicine, many of them saw it as a way to establish certain types of expertise and assign them to men" (6). Yet the women who published research in medical journals refused to abdicate the authority of science to men; instead, they positioned themselves as eager researchers and as advocates of a scientific mindset for all physicians. When late nineteenth-century American physicians advocated science as an epistemology for medicine, they generally meant the search for consistent causes of disease, such as a specific microbe; the development of reliable treatments that were effective across climates, families, and individual constitutions; the use of devices and methods for measuring the body and diagnosing conditions, such as the thermometer, X-ray, and microscope; and precision in recording observations and measurements that revealed the course of an illness and the effectiveness of its treatment. For some late nineteenth-century physicians, *science* referred both to a means of building knowledge and to an approach to daily practice. Even though it did not immediately improve the efficacy of medical treatment, physicians' adoption of the scientific practices described above did improve the public's perception of the profession and alter the characteristics of the physician's professional identity (Shortt 67; Starr 18).

One strategy used by several women physicians to suggest that the profession as a whole ought to cultivate a scientific ethos was praising the progress in medical and physiological knowledge made possible by science. For example, in "Microscopical and Chemical Examinations as Aids to Diagnosis," which was presented to the Tri-State Medical Society of Alabama, Georgia, and Tennessee before being published in the *WMJ* in 1896, Katharine R. Collins[2] attested to the value of recent advances in diagnosis. Her first paragraph extolled the virtues of these developments: "Some of the most valuable facts in the science of medicine have been obtained through the medium of the microscope and chemistry, and light has been thrown not [only] upon the causation of disease, but also the processes taking place during morbid conditions, thus with an accurate knowledge of etiology, treatment has been rendered more intelligent and great strides have been taken toward preventive medicine" (275). Collins went on to describe the physician as "a busy man" (275) who must decide between the convenience of a portable kit for testing bodily fluids and the accuracy of a thorough examination of the chemical and microbial makeup of those fluids. In doing so, Collins demonstrated her understanding of the constraints on a physician's daily decisions, building identification with her audience. The assumption that the physician would need some kind of testing equipment—that not scientifically testing bodily fluids was not an option—suggested that every physician should be a scientist. In making this assumption, Collins moved beyond sympathizing with physicians' busy lives to implying the kind of practitioners they ought to be. Collins also imagined the physician as a thorough researcher; she explained that the physician should not base his or her diagnoses on the observation of symptoms or on microbial and chemical analyses alone, but instead on all the information available: "We do not base our diagnosis upon any one symptom, but rather on a group of symptoms, and so the microscope and chemical tests cannot always give us definite evidence, but their results go to bear out the other symptoms. And they should be no more neglected than the consideration of any other one typical symptom of a disease which may sometimes be absent" (276). Finally, Collins acknowledged the need for scientific validity and reliability in her discussion of a case of diphtheria: "I will here give a few facts that came under my observation while a student[;] as I quote from memory and have but the one instance to offer, it cannot be of scientific value" (277). In constructing the recent history of medicine as significantly shaped by science, in describing the physician as engaged in scientific analysis daily, and in articulating scientific values in reference to her own study, Collins advocated an ethos for the general practitioner—not just the specialist or the academic physician—as a professional who regularly based his or her diagnoses and treatments on scientific analysis.

Whereas Collins encouraged physicians to rely on science in diagnosing and monitoring the progress of their patients, other women physicians, such as Margaret A. Cleaves, asked their audience to go one step further and systematically collect data that might be shared with the field in order to extend professional knowledge and guide practice. In her paper "The Expenditure of Electric Energy" (1898), Cleaves, the director of the New York Electro-Therapeutic Clinic, Laboratory, and Dispensary, concluded with a call for physicians to gather information about the processes of electro-therapy:

> I feel that this addition to our equipment [the volt and milli-ampere meters] marks a new era and one that can not fail to be fruitful in scientific results. . . . Instruments of precision have done much toward the establishment of scientific methods, and by carrying on the work in the lines indicated very much more will be accomplished. I would therefore most earnestly recommend the use of volt and milliampere meters and the watch or clock with both the directing and alternating currents, in daily

work. Data will thus be accumulated, which can not fail to be of
value to the profession and the cause of electro-therapeutics will
be advanced along scientific lines. (1226)

In this article, Cleaves advocated the use of volt and milliampere meters, two
instruments among the numerous devices that became available in the late
nineteenth century for the measurement of the body and of the effects of
medical treatment. Such instruments "added a highly persuasive rhetoric to
the authority of medicine" (Starr 137).[3] Because they gave physicians access
to information unavailable to patients themselves, because they fostered the
appearance of objectivity, and because they offered precise measurements,
devices for measuring and diagnosing the body contributed to the profession's ethos as a field based on scientific and interpretive expertise. Significantly, Cleaves did not recommend the meters to researchers exclusively
but rather to all physicians involved in the "daily work" of medical practice.
In encouraging practitioners to record the measurements made possible by
the volt and milliampere meters, Cleaves promoted a model of professional
identity in which every physician was a researcher.

Brooklyn physician Eliza J. C. Minard likewise imagined a scientific
model of professional identity, suggesting that physicians should be lifelong
students of their science. Minard's article, "Clinical Statistics.—A Word in
Favor of Free Dispensary and Hospital Work" (1890) called for all physicians
to extend their education by working in dispensaries and hospitals and studying the wide range of cases available there: "To the post-graduate physician,
and all physicians must be such for life, there is no place like one of these
institutions to perfect him in the practice of medicine" (680). Continuing
education was important, Minard argued, because "Scientific knowledge is
making such strides that there are no places for laggards" (681). The physician
who wished to emulate the leaders of the field should do as they did: "[The
masters] did not coquette with science, but courted in earnest, till death
wedded them to immortal fame" (681). In Minard's view, to make a name for
oneself in medicine—or even to keep up with recent advances—required the
physician to commit himself or herself to ongoing scientific study.

For homeopathic women physicians near the end of the nineteenth century, the necessity of demonstrating the scientific nature of their school of
medicine was even more urgent than for the regulars. Homeopaths sought to
contradict assertions that their techniques were nothing more than unscientific quackery, both to defend their right to practice medicine and to claim the
respect that accompanied scientific professionalism. Women homeopaths
participated in these efforts. For example, in "The Use of the Faradic Current

in Gynecology," an 1893 contribution to the *Medical Century*, Flora A. Brewster[4] of Baltimore insisted that the treatment of gynecological conditions with electrical current must proceed along scientific lines. Brewster informed her readers that "a battery will not give good results in medical practice unless constructed upon scientific principles" (298). Such an approach would, she suggested, prevent the problems many physicians had noted in this method of treatment: "The use of the Faradic current in gynecology has been attended with great disappointment to many gynecologists, and many of us might furnish an appalling list of accidents and cases which have unquestionably been aggravated instead of benefited by its use were it the fashion to chronicle our failures as well as our successes" (298). Mildly criticizing medicine's discursive conventions, Brewster argued that physicians' unscientific methods of treating women had produced unsatisfactory results.

She then set about rectifying this situation, first by reviewing scientific information: "You will pardon me if I remind you of some well known facts in anatomy and physiology before speaking of the effect of the interrupted current upon the pelvic organs" (299). After describing the blood vessels and the ligaments of the uterus and citing the research of physicians who had examined the muscular nature of the uterus, Brewster offered her readers advice on the proper use of the Faradic current. She concluded her article by again advocating a scientific basis for this method of treatment: "I know of no other means by which [the free flow of blood away from the uterus] can be accomplished so surely and so safely as by means of the scientific application of the interrupted current" (300). In Brewster's article, science offered a means by which electrical treatment might be rendered more effective and less harmful. In contrast to the physician who "expect[s] to get good results from an instrument which he does not understand, and with no definite idea of the results which he ought to expect" (299), Brewster suggested that the physician ought to be broadly informed about science, familiar not just with anatomy and physiology, but also with coils, tension, currents, and batteries (298).

In promoting "science" and related values such as expertise, reliance on instruments for accurately measuring the body, and the making of precise records of observations, nineteenth-century women physicians indirectly increased the authority of all physicians in their interactions with patients. Women physicians' identification as scientific physicians justified their claims to authority, countering centuries of the denial of authority to women. For example, in an 1881 paper titled "Case of Microcephalus," Putnam Jacobi asserted her place in the field through the use of medical vocabulary and by situating her work within a web of references to related research, character appeals that sanctioned her to insist on her own authority and to reject her patient's health care decision. Putnam Jacobi's paper, read before the New York Neurological Society and subsequently published in the *Medical Record*, recounted the case of a newborn who died as a result of her incompletely developed brain. Putnam Jacobi reported on the autopsy, employing medical vocabulary and putting her findings in the context of other researchers' comments on the same condition:

> This general appearance of the brain, constituted by the tapering of the frontal and occipital lobes, the uncovering of the cerebellum, the relative breadth and height of the parietal region, closely resembles a microcephalon described by Bischoff and another by Luschka, and the case of Sabin related by Wagner. On the other hand, in the two cases of microcephalus described by Marshall, although the cerebellum was largely uncovered, the general form of [the] brain was a short oval, rather than a long ovoid, as in this case. The tapering and flattening of the frontal lobes are seen in all the cases I have found described. (647)

Putnam Jacobi went on to compare her findings to those of nearly a dozen other scientists. In doing so, she situated her research in the context of previous work in the field, demonstrating that she was well educated on her topic and that she was participating in the cumulative nature of medical knowledge-building.

Because an important goal of medical research was improving treatment, most articles contained tentative explanations for the conditions described and suggested treatment plans based on those explanations. Putnam Jacobi included both features of medical discourse in her paper. Referring to the history of the case, she informed her audience that she had instructed the mother to remain in bed until the seventh month of her pregnancy in order to avoid miscarriage; however, the mother had exceeded Putnam Jacobi's advice and remained in bed for nearly the duration of her pregnancy. Citing a theory that the brain would grow only if the fetus's head were hanging upside down in the uterus, she suggested that the mother's decision to extend her bed rest beyond Putnam Jacobi's advice had led to the infant's underdeveloped brain: "Only in the seventh month does the [fetus's] head tend to assume a constantly dependent position during the upright position of the mother. But, in her recumbency, the head of the fœtus does not hang at all; and a maternal condition which would have no influence during the early months of utero-gestation, would certainly greatly change the condition of the child during the later months" (649). Putnam Jacobi's hypothesis suggested a cause for microcephalus as well as a means of preventing the condition. Although she did not overtly blame the mother for the infant's condition, Putnam Jacobi did imply that the infant would have been healthy had the mother followed her physician's advice exactly instead of taking her own initiative in extending the length of her bed rest. In doing so, Putnam Jacobi referred to her expert knowledge of anatomy and fetal development as evidence that the patient should have obeyed her instructions, establishing a rhetorical situation in which the physician was authorized to determine treatment plans and the patient was expected to follow those plans without exercising her own judgment.

In addition to enhancing women physicians' authority in interactions with patients, advocating a scientific approach to medicine opened rhetorical opportunities for women, because through medical-scientific rhetoric, women could speak and write in ways and about topics unavailable to them elsewhere. An example of the uses to which women physicians put the opportunities presented by their performance of scientific values can be found in Frances Rutherford's[5] article, "The Perineum and Its Care during Parturition," the lead article in the February 1894 issue of the *WMJ* and originally read before the Grand Rapids Academy of Medicine. In this article, Rutherford argued that physicians attending childbirth should do all they could to prevent damage to the perineum during delivery, and if necessary, repair should be immediate, though avoiding injury altogether was preferable. She faulted the profession for not attending more to the prevention of perineal tears: "Whole volumes are written on repair of the perineum, [but] only short paragraphs are occasionally published, suggesting a possible prevention of its mutilation, during a natural function [childbirth]. Fifty years ago, aye, twenty-five years ago, our best British authors asserted, it mattered but little if the sphincter-ani was not destroyed, although the laceration reached to it, and if the mother lived, crippled though she was ever after, it was considered a successful obstetrical case. . . . Our later generation of surgeons [has] been so assiduous in the laudable effort of repair that prevention is almost ignored" (30–31). To demonstrate the importance of the perineum, Rutherford provided her audience with a list of four functions it performs (30). She also presented a detailed description of external female genitalia and provided two plates from *Gray's Anatomy* to illustrate her anatomical discussion. The fact that she read this paper aloud to a mixed-gender audience challenges conventional perceptions of nineteenth-century women and their rhetorical activity. Adopting a scientific professional ethos allowed Rutherford to speak frankly to her mostly male audience, to circumvent conventional feminine modesty, and to argue quite forcefully for the value of protecting the perineum.

In addition to emphasizing the importance of the perineum by enumerating its functions early in the paper, Rutherford concluded her paper by making a strong case for protecting, and if necessary, repairing the perineum in the delivery room: "I would urge that when such an accident [a perineal injury] occurs it shall be a criminal offense, if repair is not attempted immediately. A fractured limb is not so serious in its after results as a perineum ruptured to the anus, unrepaired and the lesser tears are as injurious proportinateally [*sic*]" (33). Through medical discourse, which was becoming less holistic and more focused on discrete organs, tissues, and physiological functions, women professionals could respectably speak about specific body parts. Relying on her ethos as a physician, Rutherford could raise topics nonprofessional women might blush to discuss. A scientific approach to the human body, which involved naming and treating the body in parts rather than acknowledging the whole person and the (feminine and therefore modest) social position of the rhetor, allowed Rutherford to argue for a course of treatment—and even legal action—that would benefit parturient women. Because of the characteristics of medical discourse and the permission physicians had to discuss topics considered inappropriate in other venues, women physicians like Rutherford were able to assume rhetorical roles otherwise inaccessible to women in the nineteenth century. Incorporating scientific values, such as the usefulness of examining individual tissues and organs, into the medical ethos offered nineteenth-century women physicians important opportunities to speak on new subjects in order to improve medicine's treatment of women.

Shaping Medical Research Methods

Nineteenth-century women physicians confirmed their membership in the medical discourse community by crafting ethē that demonstrated their adherence to the field's emerging scientific values. Medicine's long history of misogyny, however, complicated women's efforts to show that they belonged: if they adopted prevailing medical attitudes toward women, women physicians would have undermined their own presence in the field. Furthermore, some women physicians were committed to goals and interests that were not well suited to the profession's existing priorities, research methodologies, and discursive practices. Consequently, women physicians worked to improve medical attitudes toward women's health, a change that would indirectly enhance women physicians' own ethē because they would less often be seen as unfit for medical practice due to their supposed frailty.

One approach to improving medical attitudes toward women involved encouraging physicians to study women's ailments scientifically rather than dismissing their suffering as inherent to femininity. This appeal is an example of the complex form of indirect ethos in that it sought to alter the epistemology that supported medicine's negative view of women. For example, physician Electa B. Whipple challenged those in her audience who would dismiss women's afflictions because such cases were not perceived to be interesting from a scientific standpoint. In a paper read before the section on Obstetrics and Gynecology at the Buffalo Academy of Medicine in 1893 and published in the August 1894 issue of the *WMJ*, Whipple introduced her subject, dysmenorrhea (painful or difficult menstruation), by insisting that the suffering caused by this condition justified her paper: "With some hesitancy would the topic under consideration be brought before this body of learned, representative gynecologists, were it not true that disease and suffering, however trivial they may appear in the light of science, demand reco[g]nition and must ever receive attention from the conscientious physician. Hence, no apology is required for presenting a subject trite as its literature is meager and broad as its pathology is obscure" (45). Although physicians might not believe that the study of dysmenorrhea would produce new scientific developments, Whipple contended that the affliction of the women who lived with the condition justified professional attention. She suggested alternative criteria for selecting topics for professional discussion: instead of choosing unusual conditions or innovative therapies, physicians might better serve patients by studying "trite" conditions that were widespread but still poorly understood. In promoting these reasons for studying conditions, Whipple resisted a professional ethos built primarily on the value science attached to novelty, privileging instead the "conscientious physician" who attended to even commonplace "disease and suffering." At the same time, Whipple constructed the dysmenorrheic patient as worthy of the physician's time and attention.

Furthermore, Whipple maintained that a condition like dysmenorrhea that did not appear to promise much in the way of scientific advancement might still require physicians' attention and scientific study because of inaccurate assumptions about the condition or those who suffered from it. After relating the details of six cases that she had attended, Whipple began to question common medical beliefs about the kinds of women prone to dysmenorrhea: "It is not surprising to find this condition in women clerks, standing all day upon their feet, laboring under more or less excitement, wearing their clothing unco[m]fortably tight, going to and from their work exposed to wet and cold, and evenings refraining from no plea[s]ures that may conflict with a proper care of their health. And we are not astonished that sewing women, stenographers, book-keepers, and those of sedentary habits, taking little or no exercise in the open air, and denying themselves of sufficient good nourishing food are generally sufferers from dysmenorrhea" (47). Whipple connected each of the classes of women she named with behaviors or situations that were believed to make women vulnerable to dysmenorrhea. Despite the facts that these women clearly engaged in activities that in the nineteenth century were believed to pose a risk to their health and that they therefore constituted a large number of the cases of dysmenorrhea, another group of patients, Whipple observed, received an undue amount of physicians' concern: "neither of these classes presenting themselves to the physician apparently receive[s] one-half the solicitude that does the school-girl. And when the mother consults the family physician regarding any irregularities that menace the health of her fond daughter, . . . it is quite popular to advise *immediate removal from school*" (47). Countering this common approach to treating dysmenorrhea, Whipple called for more research: "Much has been written upon this subject and some statistics have been gathered, and yet they are so few and incomplete that no logical conclusion can be deduced from them. No general, systematic research has been made to determine in what way physical growth and development, during the age of puberty, are influenced by the mental work imposed by our schools" (48). In calling for systematic statistical research on the effects of school on girls' reproductive health, Whipple challenged the profession's traditional representations of women and women's health, demanding more scientific evidence before she could support removing girls from school as a treatment for dysmenorrhea.

Such a shift in epistemology—from anecdotal to statistical evidence—had the potential to lead to more accurate representations of women and their liability to reproductive disorders. Whipple herself offered her audience "The health statistics of women college graduates, reported by a special committee of the Association of Collegiate Alumnæ, together with statistical tables collected by the Massachusetts Bureau of Statistics of Labor in 1885" (48). Although these statistics were not compiled for medical purposes, they allowed Whipple to begin to construct an alternative to the frail model of womanhood prominent in medical journals. Assessing the statistics, she concluded "that the female graduates of our colleges and universities do not seem to show, as the result of their college studies and duties, any marked difference in general health from the average health likely to be reported by an equal number of women engaged in other kinds of work, or, in fact, of women generally without regard to occupation followed" (48). Disproving the link between extended education and poor health was especially important for women physicians, because their careers depended on both a lengthy education and robust health. Statistical research methods would, Whipple suggested, produce more accurate information about the relationship between education and health for women; such information had the potential to alter physicians' attitudes toward women, indirectly enhancing women physicians' ethē as competent professionals.

Given the statistical evidence that extended education did not result in reproductive disorders or other health problems, Whipple asked, "Why, then, [do we have] the very diverse conclusions arrived at by those who have made but limited observations for special purposes?" (48). Whipple's reference to "limited observations for special purposes" may have been an allusion to texts such as Edward H. Clarke's 1873 book *Sex in Education; or, A Fair Chance for the Girls*, which relied on anecdotes from Clarke's career to support his assertion that extended education was harmful to young women. Whipple might also have been referring more broadly to the medical research genre of the case report. The discourse conventions for the case report favored extreme or unusual cases: a condition many physicians might not have encountered in their own practices or a rare presentation or progression of a common condition. A number of individual cases were sometimes accumulated and presented together in one paper, but even with the incorporation of additional cases, the genre lent itself to sensationalism and sometimes even to inaccurate representations of conditions and of the patients suffering from them, because physicians sought extreme cases to report in order to provide something interesting and memorable for their audiences. Such an approach to medical research could be particularly damaging to perceptions of women's health: a preponderance of unusual cases presented in medical conferences and journals might lead physicians to assume that all women were prone to such conditions. Resisting the conventions of the case report genre became one of the strategies some women physicians used to alter medical attitudes toward women and, indirectly, to improve their ethē as physicians.

An example of one nineteenth-century woman physician's efforts to improve medical representations of women through altering medical research methods and their attendant discourse conventions can be found in Grace Peckham's[6] 1888 *Medical Record* article "The Nervous Symptoms, Local and Reflex, Arising from the Displacements and Inflammations of the Uterus and Its Appendages." She opened her paper, which had originally been presented before the Section on Neurology of the New York Academy of Medicine, with the claim that gynecologists' methods of gathering information had skewed the profession's and the public's perceptions of women's health:

> In the scant literature which has been written upon the nervous
> affections dependent upon abnormal conditions of the uterus
> and its appendages, there has been presented, for the most part,
> an array of unusual and startling cases, until the profession, and
> the public, too, for that matter, have come to feel that a woman's
> organs of generation are seldom in a state of perfect health; rather
> more, that they are centres from which emanate the most terrible
> and awful nervous explosions. This is indeed, sometimes true,
> but not nearly as often as one is led to suppose from the articles
> which from time to time come from the pens of our most eminent
> gynecologists, illustrated with cases numbering from two or three
> to a dozen or more, setting forth weird reflex neuroses starting
> from the genital tract. (177)

To contest the medical discourse convention of presenting a few unusual cases and drawing conclusions about women's physiology from them, Peckham
chose to present statistics from roughly five hundred gynecological cases
out of the two thousand she had seen in the previous four years. "Nervous
Symptoms" participated in the extensive nineteenth-century debate about
the connection between female reproductive organs and mental illness; at
the same time, it contributed to the ongoing and intertwined negotiations
about the characteristic features of medicine, professionalism, science, and
femininity.

After describing her methodology and presenting her data both discur-
sively and in table form (figure 6.1), Peckham came to eight conclusions, including one that supported the hypothesis she presented in her introduction:

> Nervous disturbance outside of the pelvis is not nearly as fre-
> quent in disease of the uterus and its appendages as is generally
> believed. The impression that one severe case makes, effaces that
> of dozens of simpler ones. Moreover, gynecologists who are men
> are apt to meet only the severer cases, since women suffer long
> and in silence before undertaking a treatment which does such
> violence to their natural modesty. The eminent specialists who
> have done most of the writing on this subject encounter the most
> severe and difficult cases, and their object, often, in writing, is to
> present peculiar and extraordinary cases. (179)

In addition to criticizing the research methods and discourse conventions of
leading gynecologists, Peckham questioned the representativeness of their
samples, suggesting that women physicians had access to a more realistic
picture of the symptoms associated with reproductive ailments. She argued
that her evidence suggested that gynecological disease was only rarely associated with mental illness. Peckham offered an alternative model for gathering

TABLE OF 517 CASES SHOWING THE NERVOUS SYMPTOMS, LOCAL AND REFLEX, ARISING FROM DISPLACEMENTS AND INFLAMMATIONS OF THE UTERUS AND ITS APPENDAGES.

	Total number of cases	No pain present	Entire pelvic region	Extending down leg	Both sides	Right side	Left side	Hypogastrium	Sacral and lumbar	Flatulence	Dyspepsia	Nausea	Vomiting	General headache	Frontal headache	Vertex	Occipital	Dizziness	General nervousness	Hysteria	Other symptoms	Total number having symptoms extending beyond pelvis
Complete prolapsus	37	25	1			1	1	5	2		2								1			3
Prolapsus, second degree	25						4	1	5	4				2		1		1				5
Prolapsus, first degree	20		8				4		4	1	2								1			4
Anteflexion and prolapsus	6		2			2	1															0
Retroflexion and prolapsus	9				1		7		2					2	2							4
Total	97																					
Anteversion	8	1	4		1	2								2				1				3
Retroversion	34	6	16		1		4	1	2					4				2			Creeping sensations; cold perspiration.	6
Anteflexion	32		17		1	2	2		5	1	1			4						2		8
Retroflexion	39	5	20		1	2	4	1	7	3	4	3		11	1			3	2	3	1 Cold perspiration.	20
Total	113																					
Endometritis	45		27	3		1	9	2	8		2	3		8	1			3	3	3	1 General neuralgia; 1 eyes, and 1 paræsthesia.	15
Endometritis and anteflexion	29		19			3		1	5	6	2			8				1		3		16
Endometritis and retroflexion	37		21	2		2	4	2	3		8	5		6		1	1	1			1 Eyes; 1 melancholia; 1 chilly sensations.	13
Total	111																					

Broad ligaments.............	1	..	..	..	..	..	1	..	..												{ 1 Eyes ; 1 paræsthesia ;	12
Broad ligaments, left side ...	20	1	..	..	..	2	13	..	4	} 3	2	1	..	3	1	..	..	3		1	..	{ 1 faint ; 1 hiccough.	
Broad ligaments, right side .	5	..	..	..	..	1	2	..	2														
Broad ligaments and ante-flexion.................	6	..	..	..	..	2	4	..	..	..	..	..	..	..	..	..	..	1		..	..	....	1
Broad ligaments and retro-flexion.................	16	..	6	..	..	6	1	3	..	..	..	..	..	7	..	..	..	..		..	..	....	7
Total..	53																						
Ovaritis	16	..	8	..	2	3	3	..	..	..	..	..	..	2	..	..	2	..		2		1 Cold as ice on left side ; 1 faints.	5
Ovaritis and anteflexion	4	..	2	..	..	..	1	..	1	..	1	1	..	4	..	..	..	.		2		2 Pain in heart.	4
Ovaritis and retroflexion.....	4	..	2	..	..	..	2	..	..	..	..	..	..	4	..	..	..	..		4		....	4
Total.................	24																						
Metritis	26	..	16	1	..	2	2	1	4	..	..	..	..	5	1	1	..	..		..		3 Cold and chilly sensa-tions.	7
Metritis and anteflexion	4	..	..	..	1	..	..	1	3	..	..	..	..	..	..	..	..	..		..		....	0
Metritis and retroflexion	2	..	..	..	..	..	..	..	2	..	..	..	..	..	..	..	..	2		..		....	2
Total.................	32																						
Parametritis.......	26	..	16	1	3	..	1	..	5	..	4	1	..	8	1	..	..	..		..		1 Prickling sensation like needles.	9
Total................?	26																						
Lacerated cervix	14	..	5	..	2	1	1	2	4	..	2	..	..	1	1	..	..	..		..		1 Curious sensation about umbilicus.	2
Cervicitis and endocervicitis .	47	..	36	..	1	2	1	2	5	..	5	..	1	13	..	2	..	..		1		2 Sleepless and 1 drowsy.	20
Total.................	61																						
Grand total.............	517		226																				170

Figure 6.1. Table by Grace Peckham. *Medical Record*, 1888.

and presenting research, basing her conclusions on hundreds of cases rather than a few. Although she acknowledged that the categorization of symptoms that she had developed "may not be the most scientific way of regarding the symptoms" (177), Peckham ultimately challenged the science underlying the case report, one of the most common approaches to collecting data and drawing conclusions about the causes and treatments of disease. In doing so, she engaged in a form of argument and ethos building appropriate to her context. In this sense, Peckham has much in common with the women physicians Theriot studied, who "'out-scienced' their male gynecologist colleagues"; these women "argued their points from what they assumed to be a superior, more empirical, and therefore more scientific perspective" (11).

It is important to remember, however, that even as nineteenth-century women physicians provided a corrective to the long history of medical representations constructed primarily by men, women did not necessarily create objectively "better" constructions of femininity, medicine, professionalism, or science. As Theriot observes, women physicians researched and wrote from their positions in society: "Like their male colleagues, nineteenth-century women physicians' ideas about women's insanity and nervousness expressed their gender and class situation. The knowledge that women physicians created about the female body and female consciousness was not 'good science' as opposed to men physicians' 'bad science'; instead, both women and men physicians formulated concepts of women's mental illness from their different positions in the medical and gender power structures, positions that limited their vision even as their vision helped define their positions" (15). One significant aspect of women physicians' social position was their desire to be accepted by the medical profession and to attain the authority associated with professionalism. In this respect, they were much like many men new to the profession; however, women also sought to overcome doubts about their abilities as physicians and as medical researchers by altering medical attitudes toward women.

Far from being mere followers in the profession, nineteenth-century women physicians actively sought to shape the epistemological methods and discourse conventions of medical science. In questioning the representativeness of case reports, some women physicians advocated approaches to medical research and rhetoric that made the physician's curiosity and his or her fame secondary to developing accurate knowledge about conditions that affected large numbers of people. In doing so, women physicians sought to alter medicine's priorities and physicians' attitudes toward the patients they treated, indirectly suggesting that women physicians possessed the physical characteristics of respectable medical professionals.

The Implications of Women's Professional Discourse

Late nineteenth-century American medicine underwent a significant transformation, and its discourse evolved alongside changes to its epistemology, prestige, and authority. Despite doubts about women physicians' abilities as researchers and writers and their limited access to research venues, women physicians entered into this dynamic rhetorical and professional context, presenting patient cases, encouraging physicians to perform research, and proposing agendas and advocating values for the profession. As physician, lecturer, writer, women's club leader, and women's rights activist Ella M. S. Marble[7] explained in "Woman's Contribution to Medical Literature" (1896), an article recounting the history of women in American medicine and their accomplishments as researchers, "The wonder is not that woman has not written more, but that in the very few years in which they [*sic*] have had a chance to plant the seeds, they have been able to gather such an abundant harvest and give it so lavishly to those who hungered for the fruit" (63). The research articles by nineteenth-century women physicians were significant rhetorical acts not only because they involved women in new discursive venues and practices, but also because they marked the entrance of a previously excluded group into the discourse of a powerful faction in late nineteenth-century society. Altering professional attitudes toward women had the potential to affect not only the ethē of women physicians and medical researchers but also to increase the opportunities available to nonprofessional women, as the advice of family physicians evolved to reflect medical assessments of women's capabilities.

Alongside their efforts to improve the profession's perceptions of women, however, nineteenth-century women physicians also strove to increase medicine's status and authority, a commitment that would ultimately reduce the autonomy and agency of patients. As Francesca Sawaya observes, "professionalism . . . generally enforces the class divide—the divide between those authorized to speak and those enjoined to listen and obey" (144). Even as the alternative epistemological and discursive models nineteenth-century women physicians proposed potentially benefited women physicians and some female patients, it is also true that those women physicians who advocated a move away from case studies also cut off a venue in which patients could express their own perceptions of their conditions and the treatments they received. Case reports sometimes relied heavily on the patient's own representation of her history, symptoms, and recovery, occasionally even reporting the patient's own words. For instance, in "The Serpent Poisons in the Treatment of Ovarian Diseases" (1889), a case study reporting on the use of a particular class of homeopathic drugs, New York physician Louise Lannin relied on her patient's assessment of her recovery from ovarian pain to appraise the effectiveness of the drugs prescribed to treat the case. After a description of the three medications Lannin had tried, she gave an account of the results as they were reported to her by the patient and her family: "To my surprise [the patient] reported a decided improvement. Heat and tenderness were less, and there [were] less of the dragging sensations, and she had more inclination for her household duties. The improvement continued, and, at the end of four months from [the] time of her first visit, her husband called to say it was the first time in thirteen years that she was able to look after her household affairs and enjoy life. She has since gone to Europe, and while there sent word that she had not gone backward one step" (644–45). In this passage, the patient and her family assessed her improvement according to their measures of wellness: the ability to do housework and to travel. Although statistical studies might protect women from misrepresentations based on extreme cases, they also left little room for patients to participate in representing themselves.

Women physicians' promotion of the new scientific professional ethos might have enhanced their own social and rhetorical authority, and it might even have prodded male physicians into improved attitudes toward their female patients, but it also positioned a large number of people as unqualified to speak or to make decisions on medical subjects. The influence of nineteenth-century women physicians' research articles, then, was not limited to the profession itself; just as women physicians' ethē were enhanced indirectly through alterations of medical research methods, discourse conventions, and perceptions of women's health, the ethē of patients as autonomous determiners of their conditions and treatments was indirectly limited by the increasing authority of physicians' scientific professionalism. As they advocated a scientific professional identity for medicine, women physicians suggested changes in the field's beliefs, values, and priorities that would affect the larger society outside the profession in complex and important ways.

Conclusion:
Toward Feminist Ethos

It is simply impossible for me to name even the *Prominent*
women physicians who are practicing and writing to-day.
—Ella M. S. Marble, "Woman's Contribution
to Medical Literature" (1896)

The previous chapters have identified several strategies used by nineteenth-century American women physicians to respond to the ethos
problem posed by the mismatch between the characteristics associated with
woman and those associated with *physician*. Neither the challenges women
physicians faced in crafting persuasive ethē nor the practices of self-presentation women physicians developed in response to those challenges are
accounted for by most textbook or theoretical discussions of ethos. Arguing
that acknowledging women's place in rhetoric requires the revision of key
rhetorical concepts, Joy Ritchie and Kate Ronald explain that "The discovery of the available means was for Aristotle an act of invention that always
assumed the right to speak in the first place and, even prior to that, assumed
the right to personhood and self-representation, rights that have not long
been available to women" (xvii). Because women begin to speak and write
from a different starting point than most men do and because they confront fundamental obstacles to being accepted as rhetors, women's rhetoric
often entails the development of alternative communicative strategies. This
is especially true of ethos, since it is precisely the characteristics of a good
speaker that have historically been denied to women.

Despite the popular and professional resistance and even hostility toward
women as medical professionals, nineteenth-century women physicians produced a large and influential body of texts and speeches, not only creating

space for themselves in the profession but also translating their professional status into important contributions to late nineteenth-century social and medical thought. Indeed, women physicians imagined themselves to be part of a long history of women as medical writers. For instance, in "Woman's Contribution to Medical Literature," the lead article in the March 1896 issue of the *Woman's Medical Journal*, physician Ella M. S. Marble cited Trota, a tenth-century woman from Salerno, who "wrote a still existing treatise on 'Diseases of Women.'" According to Marble, this book "discussed all branches of pathology," and garnered international professional celebrity for its writer: "her fame in medicine extended beyond Italy and lasted until the 13th Century." Drawing attention to the value of this early woman's professional discourse, Marble asked, "What medical authority of to-day expects his most erudite productions to be quoted 300 years from now?" (61). Moving through history to her own day, Marble declared that so many women were engaged in professional rhetorical activity by the end of the nineteenth century that "It is simply impossible for me to name even the *Prominent* women physicians who are practicing and writing to-day" (62).

Although women physicians achieved considerable success in speaking and writing from professional positions in the nineteenth century, they still often faced obstacles in presenting their preferred ethē. One example of a situation in which assumptions about women physicians' ethos led to their silencing was reported in physician Marie Zakrzewska's autobiographical *A Woman's Quest* (1924), in which Zakrzewska recounted the ceremony marking the founding of the New York Infirmary. Established by women in 1857, the Infirmary was one of the few hospitals at that time in which women could work as physicians and so was an important early site for women's clinical education. Zakrzewska described the planning for the ceremony marking the hospital's opening, noting that prominent men including Henry Ward Beecher, Dr. William Elder of Philadelphia, and local supporter Dr. Richard Kissam spoke at the event. Zakrzewska expressed disappointment at one aspect of the ceremony, however; she wrote that "my proposition to have one of the Drs. Blackwell also speak and explain our intentions was refused by our patrons, because it was feared that she might speak 'like a Woman's Rights woman.' So we remained in the background, in the most elated spirits yet modest in appearance" (211–12).[1] Zakrzewska's account reveals the complex rhetorical situation of nineteenth-century American women physicians: Elizabeth and Emily Blackwell had both achieved a degree of fame in the United States—their graduations from medical school had been noted in the popular press—and both had traveled abroad as physicians. Their role in founding and running the New York Infirmary combined with their well-known efforts on behalf of women's medical education would have made them logical speakers at this event. However, to the sponsors of the New York Infirmary, the Blackwells were not just professionals with a stake in the institution; they were also potential women's rights activists who might taint the reputation of the hospital. Consequently, at the ceremony marking the opening of what Zakrzewska called the "first true 'Woman's Hospital' in the world" (211), no woman physician had the opportunity to explain the purposes of the infirmary or of the woman-doctor movement to which it contributed; instead, the three leaders stood modestly in the background.

The mismatch between what should have allowed the Blackwells to present good ethē and the assumptions about women professionals that kept them from the platform at this landmark in the history of American women physicians demonstrates the need for a model of ethos that reflects the obstacles to and strategies for successful ethos production by women. My analysis of the contexts in which early women physicians spoke and wrote and the multiple strategies they developed for presenting an acceptable rhetorical character in those contexts suggests five features of ethos that contribute to a feminist model of this crucial appeal. In contrast to conventional descriptions of ethos, which often assume an individual speaker who can identify and demonstrate the virtues most valued by his or her audience, this model assumes a culturally situated rhetor who may work in collaboration or contention with others, who may have to choose among competing sets of values held by a heterogeneous audience, and who may be believed incapable of some of the most prestigious virtues in her context. The features of feminist-inflected ethos outlined below are meant neither as an exhaustive list nor as an essentialist model of women's rhetorical activity. Just as the historical and social positions of the men who developed conventional notions of ethos brought some features of this appeal into focus while preventing them from seeing other features, the historical and social positions of nineteenth-century American women physicians bring only some features of feminist ethos into view.[2] With these limitations in mind, the features of ethos outlined here are best understood as overlapping strategic practices that the preceding study of historical women's speech and writing demonstrate are often selected and adapted by rhetors who must struggle to claim a persuasive ethos.

First, *a rhetor's ethos is shaped by the material resources available to her and the popular beliefs about those of her social position.* Throughout the nineteenth century, women's medical schools and hospitals often lacked the financial resources of the prominent medical colleges and hospitals in which many men studied medicine. This meant women generally had less access to patients and to the modern medical and laboratory equipment on which progressive medical researchers relied in pursuing their investigations. Although some women physicians worked diligently to secure access to patients and equipment for themselves and their students, other women physicians and students were hampered in their ability to present themselves as researchers and therefore as contributors to medicine's scientific progress because they could not pursue studies comparable to the work performed by the men who had access to large, well-established hospitals and laboratories.

On a more fundamental level, the assumptions about a rhetor's gender, race, and class also constrain the kind of ethos she can build. As Coretta Pittman asserts, "claims to ethos are . . . ascribed by the dominant and imposed on the marginalized." She suggests that the significant ethos challenge posed by dominant attitudes toward the marginalized can be mitigated by "reshaping reality" through personal narrative (48). In addition to the use of personal narrative, other rhetorical strategies might also function to destabilize the characteristics attributed to various social groups. For example, nineteenth-century women physicians selectively emphasized various aspects of their feminine-professional identity in order to circumvent negative assumptions about their abilities, such as their supposed lack of the intelligence and physical strength necessary to practice medicine or the belief that women who studied medicine "unsexed" themselves. To counter these negative attitudes, at different times women physicians emphasized their femininity, their middle-class backgrounds, and their scientific professionalism. In different contexts, claiming the social status associated with each of these characteristics benefited women physicians in their efforts to construct positive ethē.

Nineteenth-century women physicians' decisions to emphasize particular components of their identities demonstrate that, contrary to the common advice that rhetors should present the virtues most valued by their audiences, women physicians did not, indeed *could* not, simply reflect the rhetorical values and practices established by male physicians; instead, they developed ways of writing and speaking appropriate to their purposes for communicating and their social positions as women and as physicians. In fact, women physicians perceived their position outside the conventional masculine profession to be a means of contributing to medicine. In 1863, addressing the accusation that women's minds tended toward deductive rather than the inductive reasoning believed crucial to medical thought, Emeline H. Cleveland suggested that "feminine" ways of thinking might ultimately benefit the profession: "Many of our greatest modern discoveries attest the utility and power of deductive reasoning that the mind may [as] safely journey from ideas to facts as from facts to ideas, and possibly this very element of deduction in the female mind may become an element of progress in the medical profession" (qtd. in "Female Medical College" 143). As Cleveland indicated, women physicians intended to contribute to the field's knowledge, not merely to apply the knowledge male physicians had already developed. Although their social status as women was often an obstacle to the development of a persuasive ethos for women physicians, that social location sometimes allowed them to position themselves as contributors to and critics of the existing profession. In this way, women physicians' ethos location "between" femininity and medical professionalism allowed them to promise that they would add feminine elements, such as nurturance, tact, and Cleveland's deductive reasoning, believed to be missing from nineteenth-century medicine. Although being "between" could mean not being full members of the profession, it also allowed women physicians to make a persuasive case for the benefits they could offer the public and the profession. It is often the case that material and social constraints on a rhetor that limit her access to the virtues most valued by her audience are in fact part of the conditions she wishes to change. In such situations, an ethos that simply reflects existing values would produce neither a persuasive character appeal nor the social and material changes the rhetor desires.

Second, *ethos often is not crafted in response to a coherent and identifiable set of audience values but instead is composed in a dynamic context that includes multiple competing ideas about the "best" virtues; consequently, ethos formation frequently involves value negotiations as well as reciprocity between rhetor and audience identity constructs.* In some cases, the negotiations surrounding ethos create opportunities to reorder an audience's values. For example, women physicians asked audiences to consider whether sexual innocence was necessarily productively tied to ignorance about human sexuality. If audience members believed virtue in a woman was indicated by her utter lack of knowledge and her reticence about sex, then there was little chance women physicians could be accepted when they wrote about sex. If, on the other hand, audiences admitted it was desirable for women to be informed about sexuality, then the ethos of the women physicians who wrote sex-ed books was secure. To create a space in which women physicians and their sex-ed books would be accepted, women physicians had to persuade audiences to revise their ideas of feminine virtue, which they did by positing that women could better fulfill their roles as educators of children and as the moral guardians of their homes if they were educated about human sexuality.

The reciprocity between the ethos of the speaker and of the audience is evident in women physicians' reform rhetoric, in which the assertion of professional authority by women physicians suggested that audience members ought to adopt the complementary role of obedient patient. When women physicians positioned themselves as experts diagnosing social problems and prescribing cures, as Rebecca Cole did in 1896 when she identified lack of education and poor living conditions as the cause of crime and disease and called for a "treatment" (5) that would alleviate those problems, they simultaneously positioned the public as in need of the physicians' advice and bound to obey it. If audience members accepted the role women physicians constructed for them, then women physicians achieved a degree of rhetorical authority rarely accessible to historical women.

Rhetors are often advised to analyze their audience and the communica-tive situation in which they will be writing or speaking in order to formulate an appropriate ethos, yet audience members may disagree on priorities, creating a situation in which the ethos a rhetor conveys shapes audience values rather than simply demonstrating virtues the audience already admires. Furthermore, modern communicative contexts, including the nineteenth century's periodical press and today's audio, video, and electronic means of publication, make assessing audience values even more difficult because one's ultimate audience may be much more diverse than one's immediate audience. The unsettled nature of many rhetorical situations can make it difficult to select and represent the values most esteemed by the audience, because there is no widespread agreement on which virtues are the most important. On the other hand, the coexistence of several value structures can create space in which rhetors can promote the value structure most conducive to their social position and their purposes for speaking. For example, nineteenth-century American society respected both professionalism, which was understood to be inherently masculine, and ideal femininity. In this context, beliefs about women's morality and benevolence allowed women physicians to offer the public an altruistic approach to medicine that, they suggested, would correct the field's excesses, its greed, its lack of respect for the human body, and its immodest examinations of women. In privileging "feminine" virtues such as beneficence, altruism, and delicacy, women physicians overcame, at least partially, a competing set of values that cast medical professionalism as inherently masculine. In this way, women physicians capitalized on the unsettled nature of nineteenth-century medicine's professional identity as it developed from an art into a science in order to suggest the inclusion of "feminine" virtues in the physician's ethos.

The dynamic context to which ethos must respond is also evident in the multiple positions from which nineteenth-century professional rhetors spoke and wrote: sometimes they addressed colleagues as peers, sometimes they addressed the public as expert authorities, and sometimes they emphasized their similarities with the nonprofessional public. In other words, developing an effective professional ethos sometimes required reference not only to one's expertise and authority but also to one's status as a mother, an African American, a resident of a particular city, or perhaps all three at once. Models of professional ethos that emphasize the rhetor's efforts to convey objectivity and certainty do not account for the ways in which a speaker might be more persuasive when she builds commonality with her audience, even when such a position seems at odds with conventional performances of professionalism. In contrast to textbooks and handbooks that advise writers to strive to appear unbiased, well-informed, and credible, and to models of professional identity that emphasize objectivity and distance from one's subject, acknowledging that rhetors could position themselves differently while still speaking or writing as professionals opens up a greater range of persuasive devices to professionals, particularly identification and emotional appeals, depending on the audience and the purpose for communication. The persuasive nature of these appeals reflects the fact that various audience members prioritize values differently and not always consistently. Such a dynamic, unsettled rhetorical situation requires a great deal of flexibility in ethos construction rather than a narrow focus on identifying and demonstrating one set of ideal virtues.

Third, *ethos and genre are intertwined.* Risa Applegarth describes ethos as a "*location within and among genres*" (44); she explains that "genres shape audience expectations, including expectations for *ethos*" (52). Such interconnections between ethos and genre may be particularly important for women who lack a tradition of authoritative rhetorical activity, because genre conventions can prompt them to display characteristics that are different from those typically associated with "proper" femininity. For example, in editorials and letters to the editor of medical journals, the expectation that writers demonstrate assertiveness and wit—necessary for medicine's shared effort to develop and defend new knowledge and procedures—encouraged women physicians to present an ethos unlike that typically deployed by women in nonprofessional genres. Medicine's desire to avoid "feminization" might have made the readers of medical journals more willing to accept "masculine" rhetorical performances by women in professional journals than they would have been outside of professional venues.

Locating oneself within a prestigious or authoritative genre might also allow a speaker or writer to claim that she possesses characteristics that audiences might otherwise be unwilling to attribute to her. This aspect of the interconnections between ethos and genre is evident in women physicians' health information and advice books: the genre led readers to expect author-itative expertise. Claiming such authority was not simple or direct, however, because cultural assumptions about the writers' gender prohibited conven-tional performances of such an ethos. In response to persistent doubts about women's capacity to act as health advisers, the women who wrote health information and advice books had to convince readers that femininity did not preclude authoritative expertise and that authoritative expertise did not undermine femininity. Nineteenth-century women physicians accomplished this in part by adapting the conventions of the health information and advice genre in order to accommodate their ethos as feminine professionals.

The relationship between ethos and genre in women physicians' health information and advice books suggests that not only can "genres shape au-dience expectations . . . for *ethos*" (Applegarth 52), but also that the ethos a rhetor desires to present can shape her genre choices. She may even promote alternative genre conventions in order to change the collective ethos of an entire discourse community. For example, some women physicians sought to shift the virtues displayed by the medical researcher away from nov-elty and "interest" (represented by sensational cases) toward an ideal that emphasized the breadth of benefit offered to patients. Consequently, these women challenged the conventions of the medical case report, which favored unusual and extreme cases, proposing instead that medical research should also attend to "ordinary" cases which were less sensational but more likely to help a greater number of patients. Likewise, medical researcher and physician Grace Peckham preferred a medical ethos based in "science" and the rigor of numbers and so questioned the representativeness of the cases reported by male gynecologists, who saw only the most severe cases; therefore, she promoted changes to genre conventions regarding sources of information, from individual case reports to statistical analyses of hundreds of cases. The existence of multiple value sets (for instance, the value represented by the immediacy of first-hand reports or the value represented by the objectivity of numbers) is often interlinked with the presence of multiple genre options (case reports or tables reporting statistics, for example) and so constitute another means by which a rhetor can use ethos to negotiate competing values in order to sponsor social change.

Fourth, *the ethos choices an individual rhetor makes influence not only his or her immediate communicative situation but also the broader context and the persuasive options available to other potential speakers and writ-ers.* This aspect of ethos acknowledges the value many feminists place on interconnection rather than individuality; in particular, it asks those study-ing and engaging in rhetoric to look beyond individual persuasiveness to consider how one rhetor's choices influence the discursive options available to other writers and speakers. For example, in some cases, women physicians increased the range of options available to other rhetors, as they did when they modeled an ethos and other discursive features by which respectable women could talk about human sexuality. Women physicians believed that scientific health information would not only improve the well-being of women and their families but also that women would be able to use their new knowledge to participate in domestic and social decision making. In educating women about anatomy and physiology, women physicians offered nonprofessional women information and tools that they might use to build an effective ethos—vocabulary, knowledge, a moral rationale for addressing otherwise indelicate subjects—thus in a sense extending parts of their professional ethos to nonprofessional audience members. Likewise, the examples of an assertive and witty ethos as well as the encouragement to participate in medical conferences and to publish in medical journals provided in the *Woman's Medical Journal* showed women how to communicate effectively as professionals.

In other cases, however, women physicians limited others' rhetorical options in their efforts to secure their own right to speak authoritatively. Women physicians' medical journal articles asserting the authority of the physician and advocating research methods that eliminated patient voices from medical epistemology contributed to medical attitudes that have silenced patients. Recognizing that nineteenth-century women physicians participated in developing the features of professional rhetoric means recognizing that they promoted a discourse that has often dominated and silenced those excluded from its ranks. As historian Burton J. Bledstein explains of nineteenth-century professionalism, "regard for professional expertise compelled people to believe the voices of authority unquestioningly, thereby undermining self-confidence and discouraging independent evaluation" (xi). Histories of women's rhetorical activity should reflect the complexity inherent in some women's simultaneous status as victims of traditional rhetorical power structures and as exploiters of those same power structures. Ethos is fundamental to the rhetorical acts occurring in such conditions. Acknowledging the role of professional status in some nineteenth-century women's rhetorical activity is one way of "address[ing] the real fact that different women, due to their various positions in the social structure, have available to them different rhetorical possibilities and, similarly, are constrained by different rhetorical limits" (Biesecker 157). Future scholarship examining historical women rhetors ought to account for the complex combination of privileges and oppressions that constituted the rhetorical context for many women. Examining the ways in which some speakers and writers have opened up and closed off the rhetorical options available to others would be one means of accounting for such a context.

Fifth, *ethos can be collectively developed and deployed; consequently, a rhetor can develop her ethos indirectly, by shaping her audience's perception of the groups to which she belongs.* Laura Micciche explains the significance of acknowledging this feature of ethos for feminist rhetorical studies: "The rhetorical tradition places almost exclusive importance on definitions of ethos that privilege the individual speaking or writing well, while feminist constructs of ethos often emphasize collective identity and collaboration as significant to knowledge building and to the development of credibility" (175). Collaboration and collectivity can be strategies pursued by choice, or they can be imposed on a group of rhetors by those who doubt their abilities or their characters. Because rhetors from groups historically excluded from a powerful discourse are often seen as precedents or as representatives of their groups, marginalized speakers and writers frequently find themselves outlining an ethos for others like them, whether they want to or not. This was the position of the editors of the *Woman's Medical Journal*, who worked together with the journal's readers to determine the rhetorical practices appropriate for women professionals and necessary for their acceptance by the field. In their writing, women physicians expressed a keen awareness that they were being judged as precedents and that their successes and failures would determine the options available to the next generation of women professionals. The processes of collective ethos formation, which occur when similarly situated rhetors collaborate on or compete over the characteristics members of that group will demonstrate, are at work almost continuously within most groups. More research into how ethos is formed collectively and how it functions collectively would greatly extend our knowledge of this crucial appeal.

Rhetors can also engage in indirect ethos work, the effort to improve audience members' attitudes toward a speaker or writer by improving their perceptions of a group to which she belongs. Indirect ethos strategies are especially important for members of marginalized groups, who must often convince audiences of the worthiness and capability of their group in order to develop a persuasive individual ethos. Nineteenth-century women physicians engaged in indirect ethos-work regularly: their health information and advice texts blamed corsets and physical inactivity for women's poor health, insisting that women were "naturally" robust; African American women physicians sought to alter perceptions of African Americans as physically inferior and innately criminal, characterizations that affected the persuasiveness of individual women physicians; and women physicians used their research articles to change medicine's attitude toward women, a change that would solidify women's place in the profession. In complex forms of indirect ethos, a rhetor strives to change the perceptions of a group to which she belongs by altering the epistemology or worldview that supports its marginalization. For example, the revisions nineteenth-century women physicians proposed to medicine's methods of performing and reporting research would, they believed, prompt the field to pursue more "objective" research into women's biological abilities, producing more accurate information that would prove women were not inherently physically frail, thereby validating women's pursuit of higher education and professional careers and increasing the chances that women physicians would be accepted as competent researchers.

The Problem and Potential of Ethos

As the five features of feminist ethos described above suggest, ethos sometimes serves as a space in which otherwise incompatible social positions or worldviews can coexist, creating opportunities for the rhetor to achieve agency and promote change. This characteristic of ethos is particularly relevant to rhetorical activity by women and other marginalized speakers and writers, who often find themselves in incompatible social positions as beliefs about their lack of intelligence, authority, or moral character interfere with their desired positions as communicators whose ideas are taken seriously. Because the status quo and the values supporting it do not serve marginalized rhetors well, they often desire social change. Without minimizing the obstacles to overcoming ethos problems and to initiating social change, we might begin to explore how the very appeal that has often been the biggest obstacle for marginalized writers and speakers might also be the appeal that promises the most potential for substantial social change.

Because the professions are heavily reliant on ethos (acting like a professional is as crucial to professional status as education and skill sets), professionalism provides an especially illuminating view of ethos as a space that can contain apparently incompatible social positions, particularly in the context of historical women's professional rhetorical activity. First, contrary to notions of professionalism that cast it as requiring exclusively masculine rhetorical performances, nineteenth-century women physicians demonstrated that femininity could be a beneficial component of professional ethos. If women's goals as physicians were understood as gynecologist Ely Van De Warker explained them in writing for *Popular Science Monthly* in 1875, femininity would necessarily hinder women's professional and rhetorical success: "It must be the intent of every woman who essays a professional life to do man's work as well as man can do it, and to secure man's reward for such well-doing" (470). Most nineteenth-century women physicians, however, did not envision their work in this way; instead, they sought to combine professionalism and femininity, an early feminist effort to make powerful institutions more reflective of all people. Consequently, women physicians composed speeches and written texts in which professional discourse complemented discourses associated with femininity. In fact, the features common to both forms of discourse in the nineteenth century made professionalism and femininity quite compatible: both contained a strong moral thread, both asserted authority over domestic matters, and both often relied on experiential evidence. In the context of nineteenth-century medicine, the virtues associated with femininity, such as nurturance, selflessness, and delicacy, often worked to counter the negative characteristics attributed to physicians: their callousness, self-interest, and insensitivity. Moreover, for some, women physicians represented a newer, less-brutal form of therapeutics; because they came into the field as anesthetics and analgesics were becoming more widely available and because many chose homeopathy and hydrotherapy rather than "regular" medicine, with its history of "heroic" treatments, women physicians were often associated with gentler, less painful therapies. For those in the public who doubted the goodwill and efficacy of traditional physicians, the combination of femininity and professionalism could be quite persuasive. As this example illustrates, because ethos is a space in which potentially incompatible social positions, such as femininity and professionalism, can coexist, ethos can be used to increase a rhetor's opportunities for agency, as a less influential position is combined with a more powerful one to create greater opportunities to speak and be heard.

As long as women's historical involvement in professional discourse is ignored, it is easy to pit professional rhetoric against "women's" or "feminist" rhetorical practices. Because professionalism has historically entailed monopolistic authority, it has often excluded, dominated, and silenced nonprofessionals, and often those nonprofessionals have been women, ethnic and racial minorities, and members of the working class. Without denying or minimizing the tendency of professional discourses to silence, we can look for ways in which feminist rhetorical practices are promoted through professional discourse. For example, nineteenth-century women's sex-ed books offered nonprofessional women strategies by which to speak about sex, a subject of crucial importance for wives and mothers. Women physicians would not have been able to offer rhetorical resources to women for those conversations without the protection afforded by their professional ethos, which allowed women to speak "scientifically" on subjects that would otherwise have been inappropriate for women to address.

In fact, contradictions like those evident in women physicians' simultaneous sharing and monopolizing of rhetorical resources across genres may be a common feature of historical women's rhetoric. For example, Nicole Tonkovich writes of Sarah Hale, the influential editor of *Godey's Lady's Book*, that "Hale's protestations of domestic retirement and insignificance . . . masked both Hale's power and the contradictions by which she maintained that power. Her means of accomplishing this was simultaneously to expose and hide behind the enablements of writing, promoting it as a means of women's empowerment but always aware of its necessary inseparability from issues of power, propriety, and class" (180). Tonkovich maintains that such contradictions were widespread among nineteenth-century women: "[These paradoxes] attend the study of nineteenth-century writing and rhetorical practices generally and demand that such study confront the issues of class, gender, and genre" (180). In part, the contradictions we see in nineteenth-century women's rhetoric result from the tension produced by our ways of defining "feminine rhetorical practices." Because public rhetorical activity has historically been gendered masculine, women who spoke automatically found themselves in paradoxical positions as women engaging in a "masculine" activity. Scholars of women's rhetoric tend to identify as "feminine" the rhetorical practices that look very different from traditional (masculine) rhetoric, and recovering those practices is vital historiographic work. However, the boundary between "masculine" and "feminine" rhetorical practices, always fuzzy and permeable, becomes even less clear when women engage in what we might be tempted to call "masculine" communicative acts, as women physicians, Hale, and many other women who spoke from positions of authority did. If we accept that women contributed to developing the features of some influential discourses, such as those associated with medical professionalism, identifying "feminine" rhetorical practices in such contexts becomes impossible and even counterproductive, to the extent that calling out some features of professional rhetoric as "feminine" erases women's involvement in developing entire discourses, as they did when they advocated and modeled particular rhetorical practices for medicine.

Under these circumstances, understanding ethos as an appeal that can draw together apparently incompatible social positions and worldviews becomes particularly important. If we are accurately to account for the complexity inherent in the gendered performances of women engaged in supposedly-but-not-really "masculine" rhetorical acts such as those of professional women, we must explore the ways that ethos has functioned for those women to bridge their multiple social positions and investments in ideals of femininity and power. Acknowledging that historical women contributed to powerful discourses and recognizing the complex and contradictory ways in which women shaped, used, and resisted the practices of those discourses might help identify opportunities to promote more inclusive communicative situations despite our increasing reliance on expertise since 1900. Such work would make clearer to many of us—professionals ourselves—the feminist resources inherent in the rhetorical tradition of women as professional communicators that continues today.

Feminists should, however, proceed critically and conscientiously in this scholarship, always alert to the silencing and monopolizing potential of professional discourse. Even if we keep in mind Francesca Sawaya's advice that "The ambivalence most feminists . . . feel about professionalism should be encouraged" (145), we might also take a cue from nineteenth-century American women physicians, who perceived that professionalism was necessary to women's advancement. In 1894, Mary A. Spink, an associate editor of the *Woman's Medical Journal*, suggested that women had learned to be wary of pronouncements by men about their "nature" and so sought to study nature and identify "natural" behaviors for themselves:

> If women had not been physicians, lawyers, artists, rulers, and, in fact, had not made a success in not only all the professions, arts and sciences, but in every industry or business, men have appropriated as especially their own, they might believe men when they say that "it is not natural," and "it is out of their sphere," to wish to interpret the laws of nature for themselves, but with such brilliant examples before her how can she help but feel that there is no inhumanity so revolting as the spirit which says to her: "You shall develop so far as we choose, and your mental and moral life shall be subject to our pleasure?" [*sic*] (15)

Spink recognized the rhetorical and social power inherent in defining what is *natural* and claimed for women the right to study nature and to discover for themselves their aptitudes and limitations. In the same spirit, we need to continue the work begun here, of turning to women's rhetorical practices to discover the features of, influences on, effects of, and strategies for ethos development so that we can achieve a fuller understanding of the role of this appeal as it works in the speech and writing of a wide range of rhetors.

Notes
Works Cited
Index

Notes

Introduction:
The Ethos of the Feminine Professional

1. Readers interested in the history of women in medicine in the nineteenth-century United States should consult Ruth J. Abram's *"Send Us a Lady Physician": Women Doctors in America, 1835–1920*; Thomas Neville Bonner's *To the Ends of the Earth: Women's Search for Education in Medicine*; Anne Taylor Kirschmann's *A Vital Force: Women in American Homeopathy*; Gloria Moldow's *Women Doctors in Gilded-Age Washington: Race, Gender, and Professionalization*; Regina Morantz-Sanchez's *Sympathy and Science: Women Physicians in American Medicine* and *Conduct Unbecoming a Woman: Medicine on Trial in Turn-of-the-Century Brooklyn*; Ellen Singer More's *Restoring the Balance: Women Physicians and the Profession of Medicine, 1850–1995*; Mary Roth Walsh's *"Doctors Wanted: No Women Need Apply": Sexual Barriers in the Medical Profession, 1835–1975*; and biographies of early women physicians such as Elizabeth Blackwell (written by Julia Boyd), Mary Gove Nichols (by Jean L. Silver-Isenstadt), Mary Putnam Jacobi (by Carla Bittel), and Marie Zakrzewska (by Arleen Tuchman).

1. Debating the Character of
the Woman Physician

1. Hunt began practicing medicine in 1835, after an apprenticeship with the Motts, practitioners of botanical medicine. Although she never earned a formal medical degree, she was eventually awarded an honorary doctorate from the Woman's Medical College of Pennsylvania ("Harriet [*sic*] Kizia Hunt" 203).

2. In his study of the men who founded and taught at the Woman's Medical College of Pennsylvania, Steven J. Peitzman reminds readers that "male hostility to women's entry into the medical profession was . . . only *nearly* universal" (578). Indeed, women depended on men for medical instruction and professional sponsorship, especially in the early days before women had established their own medical institutions.

3. Women seeking to practice homeopathy faced less opposition in this field than in regular medicine; in fact, several of the leading male homeopathic physicians argued that women were necessary to the school's success. For example, in 1870 Carroll Dunham advocated women's admission to the profession as a means of improving the efficacy of homeopathy's treatments: "My studies have, for years past, shown me the weakness of the Homœopathic Materia Medica in respect of the physiological effects of drugs upon the peculiar organism of women. This is due to the fact that but few of the provers to whose observations we owe our Materia Medica were *women*" (159). Knowledge about what drugs to prescribe in what doses was developed through provings, the administering of drugs to healthy individuals to determine their effects. Typically, these tests were performed on medical students or on patients the physician could rely on to follow directions and report results accurately. Including women physicians in this research would extend homeopathy's knowledge of the effects of medications because women could recruit other women to participate in provings or perform provings on themselves, thereby identifying drugs' effects on women. Because it was believed that women were well positioned to further the scientific agenda of homeopathy, as early as 1869 prominent male homeopaths advocated women's full admission to the American Institute of Homeopathy, a recommendation that was adopted in 1871 (Kirschmann 76). In contrast, the "regular" American Medical Association did not formally admit women to its membership until 1915, although it had permitted women to be seated as delegates representing their local organizations starting with Sarah Hackett Stevenson in 1876 (Morantz-Sanchez, *Sympathy* 179).

4. Putnam Jacobi was extraordinarily prolific, composing over one hundred publications; although many of these were professional articles, she also contributed to public discussions of women's rights, vivisection, and the education of children. One of Putnam Jacobi's most important publications was *The Question of Rest for Women during Menstruation*, which refuted Edward H. Clarke's *Sex in Education; or, A Fair Chance for the Girls* (1873) and won the Boyleston Prize from Harvard University in 1876. She taught materia medica at the Women's Medical College of the New York Infirmary for Women and Children and worked as an attending physician at the New York Infirmary, opening a pediatric ward there in 1886. See Reed 97–111 for a bibliography of Putnam Jacobi's work.

5. See Tuchman ("'Only in a Republic'") for a discussion of physician Marie Zakrzewska's resistance to the idea that science was a masculine activity.

6. Ann Preston became the first woman dean of the Woman's Medical College of Pennsylvania in 1866. Rachel Bodley assumed that administrative position in 1874, followed by Clara Marshall, who served as dean from 1886 to 1917.

7. See chapter 3 in Susan Wells's *Out of the Dead House* for further discussion of Ann Preston's rhetorical strategies, particularly what Wells calls her "cross-dressed" gender performance.

8. Pope, Call, and Pope warned readers, however, that not all women (or men) were healthy enough to be physicians, but they differentiated between two sources of poor health: "Where there is any decided organic disease, the cases are rare which would be justified in undertaking [the study of medicine]; but where the impaired

physical condition is the result of the unhealthy mental state that an aimless life brings, or the in-door life to which the occupations of women to a great extent condemn them, we have known it to prove of great benefit" (8).

9. Julia Grice (later Kennelly) graduated from the Woman's Medical College of Pennsylvania in 1900 and then practiced in Cambridge, Massachusetts.

10. Fullerton graduated from the Woman's Medical College of Pennsylvania in 1882 and practiced as a medical missionary in India.

11. *Doctor Zay* (1882), a woman-doctor novel by Elizabeth Stuart Phelps, depicts the woman physician's social power in terms similar to, if not stronger than, those described in narratives by women physicians.

12. In 1890, Dixon Jones and her physician-son Charles were tried for murder and manslaughter after two of their surgical patients died. They were acquitted of criminal charges but held liable in a civil suit. In *Conduct Unbecoming a Woman* (1999), Morantz-Sanchez positions their trial in the context of public attitudes toward gynecology and women physicians.

2. Prescribing for Society: Women Physicians' Reform Rhetoric

1. Mary Edwards Walker earned a medical degree from Syracuse Medical College in 1855. She served as a Union surgeon in the Civil War, earning a Congressional Medal of Honor for her work, the first woman so recognized (the medal was revoked in 1917 and then reawarded in 1977). Walker was also famous for wearing men's clothing. See chapter 4 of Carol Mattingly's *Appropriate[ing] Dress* for more information about Walker's dress and her other rhetorical activities.

2. As historian Gloria Moldow notes, however, the "pioneer" women physicians (those who began practice shortly after the Civil War) were more likely to have been women's rights activists than the postpioneers (those born after the war), who were less interested in such activism because they believed that the natural course of history would lead to equal opportunities for women (2).

3. Some early women physicians, however, worked actively against votes for women. For example, in 1905, physician Emma Elizabeth Walker spoke before a committee of the New York Senate on behalf of the New York State Association Opposed to the Extension of the Suffrage to Women. See "Protest against Bill" and "Women Oppose Suffrage."

4. Despite Putnam Jacobi's statement linking Blackwell's medical work to the work for women's votes, in 1850 Blackwell herself wrote in a letter to her sister, "I cannot sympathise fully with an anti-man movement. I have had too much kindness, aid, and just recognition from men to make such attitude of women otherwise than painful; and I think the true end of freedom may be gained better in another way" (*Pioneer* 208).

5. Although many of the women who worked for the United States Sanitary Commission were nonprofessionals, some women physicians, including Elizabeth Blackwell, also contributed to providing supplies and taking care of soldiers during the Civil War. For Blackwell's complicated relationship with the USSC, see Geisberg, chapter 1.

6. Although a tradition of women providing health care among American Indians existed long before La Flesche attended medical school, only one other American Indian woman earned a medical degree in the nineteenth century. Lillie Rosa Minoka-Hill graduated from the Woman's Medical College of Pennsylvania in 1899.

7. In "Down by the River, or How Susan La Flesche Picotte Can Teach Us about Alliance as a Practice of Survivance," Malea D. Powell also notes La Flesche's desire to present the Omahas as "redeemable," and argues that this rhetorical strategy need not be viewed only as "negative and assimilationist," reminding readers that "La Flesche used the means available to her in order to keep the Omaha community intact *as a community*" (55).

8. In 1891, the *New York Times* reported that Halle Tanner Dillon (later Johnson) became "not only the first colored female physician, but the first woman of any race to pass the Alabama State medical examination." The test was "an unusually severe one, occupying ten days" ("A Colored Female Doctor").

9. After graduating from the Woman's Medical College of Pennsylvania, Cole worked as a "sanitary visitor" associated with Elizabeth Blackwell's New York dispensary, attending to poor patients in their homes. She later practiced in South Carolina and Philadelphia, opening a center providing medical and legal assistance to poor women in Philadelphia in 1873. In 1899, Cole was chosen to direct a home in Washington, D.C., affiliated with the Association for the Relief of Destitute Colored Women and Children ("Dr. Rebecca J. Cole").

10. After being denied admission to nursing school because of her race, Emma Reynolds convinced her brother, a prominent pastor, to help her seek reforms to improve African Americans' access to health care. Reynolds's brother sought assistance from Daniel Hale Williams, a well-known African American surgeon, who in 1890 founded Provident Hospital, the first interracial hospital, and a school of nursing in Chicago. Reynolds completed nurses' training in 1892 and then earned a medical degree from the Northwestern University School of Medicine. See Royster, *Profiles* 95, for more information about Reynolds's life. Reynolds was also active in the temperance movement, serving as superintendent of Purity Work in Louisiana's African American division of the WCTU ("The Temperance Cause").

11. Remember that Hunt herself had been denied access to formal medical education.

3. Educating the Public:
Women Physicians' Popular Health Advice

1. Mary Gove, later Mary Gove Nichols, was the first woman to lecture on anatomy and physiology in the United States in 1838. In her lectures, she promoted the vegetarianism and self-control of Grahamism and the benefits of water-cure. In addition to lecturing and practicing medicine, Gove Nichols founded the Hygeio-Therapeutic Institute, a medical school in New York. Later in her career, she and her husband gained notoriety as part of the Free Love movement, the work for which she is best known today. See Wendy Hayden's *Evolutionary Rhetoric: Sex, Science, and Free Love in Nineteenth-Century Feminism* for a discussion of Gove Nichols's free-love feminist rhetoric.

2. Eclectic physicians "freely borrowed any form of therapy that they felt was practical or effective" (Duffy 84). Although they relied on botanicals like the Thomsonians, unlike adherents of that sect, eclectics did not favor a do-it-yourself approach to medicine. They founded medical schools in the 1830s and 1840s, producing graduates who offered patients professional, rather than domestic, health care (Duffy 84, 87).

3. In keeping with their expressed intentions of treating only women and children, women physicians rarely addressed men in their popular medical writing. Mary Edwards Walker, however, did publish *Unmasked, or The Science of Immorality. To Gentlemen.* The title page credits only "A woman physician and surgeon," leaving Walker herself unnamed.

4. Lydia Folger Fowler graduated from Central Medical College, an Eclectic school in New York, in 1850, making her the second American woman to earn a medical degree. In addition to practicing medicine, Fowler published educational books and offered lectures on anatomy and hygiene to women in the United States and England, where she lived after 1863.

5. In fact, according to Regina Markell Morantz and Sue Zschoche's study of obstetrical case records in Boston from 1873–1899, women's medical practice did not differ greatly from men's, despite the perceptions of the public and of women physicians themselves to the contrary. Furthermore, Morantz and Zschoche observe, women's and men's attitudes toward medicine were not entirely distinct: "Women internalized many 'male' values, and men were sometimes advocates of 'female' positions" (571). Nevertheless, the widespread perception of difference was a fundamental part of nineteenth-century American women physicians' rhetorical situation.

6. Greene's gender-masking led several librarians to supply a masculine name for the author of *Build Well*: in the copy I used for my research, the name "Charles" has been penciled in, and the library database WorldCat lists "Craig E. Greene" as the author of several copies.

7. Identifying these rhetorical acts as "conversations" is in keeping with Jane Donawerth's argument that historical women tended to use conversation, rather than public speech, as a model for theorizing rhetoric (xxxviii–xl).

8. Little is known about Maxwell, except that she operated a private hospital in New York City, which her book promoted. It seems likely that she did not receive a formal medical education, yet like others at the time who practiced without a diploma, both women and men, she claimed the title of "M.D." In fact, women like Maxwell, who performed abortions under the title "doctor," motivated Elizabeth Blackwell to pursue a medical education. In her autobiography, Blackwell wrote, "That the honourable term 'female physician' should be exclusively applied to those women who carried on this shocking trade [abortion] seemed to me a horror. It was an utter degradation of what might and should become a noble position for women" (*Pioneer* 77).

9. Rebecca Lee (later Crumpler) became the first formally educated African American woman physician when she graduated from the New England Female Medical College in 1864. Her *Book of Medical Discourses* was one of the first medical books published by an African American. For more on Crumpler and her book, see Wells 51–54.

10. Crumpler might also have been criticizing white physicians' inattention to African American women and children, though she did not make that criticism explicit.

11. In referring to *Hygiene and Physical Culture for Women* as a "little book," Galbraith downplayed the extent of her work: the text runs nearly 300 pages.

4. Teaching Women to Talk about Sex

1. This quotation can be found in the front matter of both Wood-Allen's *What a Young Woman Ought to Know* (1892) and Drake's *What a Woman of Forty-five Ought to Know* (1902).

2. See Hayden's "'Audacia Dangyereyes'" for more about Anthony Comstock's crusade against late-nineteenth-century women who spoke publicly about sex and for a discussion of nonprofessional women's advocacy of education about human sexuality.

3. Sylvanus Stall, a Lutheran minister, sold over a million copies of his Self and Sex books, which were translated into at least twelve languages (Haller and Haller 105).

4. Although most women physicians emphasized the maternal role when writing about human reproduction, Walker took a different approach in her 1878 book *Unmasked, or The Science of Immorality*. The title page of this book indicated the intended audience: "To Gentlemen," whom she believed needed to be educated about the consequences of sexual immorality from a professional woman's standpoint. Walker herself remained anonymous; the title page identified the author as "A Woman Physician and Surgeon." In her introduction, Walker made it clear that she was speaking as a physician to men, reversing the genders of the typical nineteenth-century advice exchange: "If women generally can be benefited by ['private treatises' written by men physicians], it is but fair to suppose that men generally may be benefited by women physicians writing 'private treatises' to men, embodying advice, facts, observations, discoveries, etc., that are all important for men to learn in a pure way as matters of science, instead of acquiring [this information] with the most degraded ideas of life, and only such parts as are demoralizing and filled with the grossest errors" (1). Although any book that included frank discussions of sexuality could be said to involve women writers in topics that risked their respectability, Walker, who was no stranger to controversy, wrote well beyond the bounds of respectable femininity, and she did so without many of the strategies other women used to "purify" their rhetoric. *Unmasked* included chapters on "Hermaphrodites," "Kissing," "Hymens," and "Seminal Weakness," and Walker relied on her ethos as a physician, not a wife or mother, to justify her attention to these topics.

5. Wood-Allen wrote *What a Young Girl Ought to Know* (1897) and *What a Young Woman Ought to Know* (1892) for the Self and Sex series, and *Almost a Man* (1895), *Almost a Woman* (1897), *Teaching Truth* (1892), *Child-Confidence Rewarded* (1903), and *Ideal Married Life* (1901) for the Teaching Truth series.

6. Hayden also discusses the rhetorical usefulness of nineteenth-century scientific theories of heredity to women rhetors in her study of free-love feminism (*Evolutionary Rhetoric*, chapter 6).

7. Drake earned her medical degree from the Boston University Medical College. She practiced in Denver, where she was professor of Obstetrics at the Denver Homœopathic Medical School and Hospital. Drake published several popular women's health and sex-ed texts.

8. A notice published with *Marvels* informed readers that they could order a supplemental chapter on the "Birth-Chamber" from the publisher.

9. Writing of sex education in the 1920s and 1930s, Julian B. Carter observes that comparisons of human and plant reproductive strategies regularly disregarded plants' actual means of reproduction, which are often asexual, in order to teach children normative gendered behaviors and expectations for sexual relationships (140–44).

5. Developing Collective Ethos in Medical Editorial Writing

1. After 1900, the *WMJ* began publishing more articles by men and more abstracts of articles published by men in other journals. It seems that the *WMJ* was a site for publishing work almost exclusively by women for not much more than six or seven years just before the turn of the century.

2. After Roys-Gavitt's death in 1898, the *WMJ* listed several women as editors, but none had the designation "editor-in-chief" until Eliza H. Root took on that role in 1900; she served as editor for about a decade. Nearly all of the *WMJ* editorials examined in this chapter are unsigned. The *WMJ* ran from January 1893 until December 1919, after which point it was continued by the *Medical Woman's Journal*, which ran until 1951. It then existed briefly as the *Pan American Medical Woman's Journal* before it was incorporated as a section of the *International Record of Medicine and General Practice Clinics*.

3. As Harrison notes, even diaries were not always private discursive spaces; she cites the research of several scholars who "have asserted the value of women's diaries by arguing that the diaries were intended for an outside audience—that they were public and not private documents" (245).

4. These quotations were drawn from a section titled "To Contributors and Subscribers" in the July 1899 issue (9.7), but this section was repeated with similar content for several years.

5. This call, which was also repeated in several issues, appeared in "To Contributors and Subscribers" in December 1893 (1.12).

6. Frye earned her medical degree from the University of Buffalo in 1892. Over the course of her career, Frye held several positions in the Buffalo area, including clinical instructor on the subject of diseases of children at the University of Buffalo, visiting physician to the children's ward of the Erie County Hospital, and staff member at the Buffalo Woman's Hospital. She also served as one of the associate editors of the *Buffalo Medical Journal*.

7. Interestingly, the editor of the *Medical Record* was George Shrady, the author of "The Man's View," an article critical of women's pursuit of medical careers published in the *Ladies' Home Journal* in May 1891, just six months after "The Temptation of Johns Hopkins" was published in the *Medical Record*. "The Man's View" is discussed in chapter 1.

8. The "managing editor" referred to in the quotation above was likely Claudia Q. Murphy, who served as the *WMJ*'s managing editor from its founding in 1893 until 1898.

9. Elsewhere in its analysis of the editorial, the *WMJ* misquotes the original, converting "we fail to see why a woman, whose mental faculties have been well developed and whose natural inclination is toward medicine as a study and certain departments of medicine as a work can not make an average, and occasionally more than an average, success" ("Our Quondam Friends" 97) into "The conclusion of the first paragraph says we [women physicians] can not, mind you, *can not* make an average success" (98). In this case, the *WMJ* editors overreached in their effort to identify logical inconsistencies.

10. Sara A. Kime graduated from the University of Iowa in 1882. She spent the first two years of her career as assistant physician to the Hospital for the Insane in Independence, Iowa, making her one of the first women to hold such a position.

11. Pease spent part of her career as resident physician at the State Hospital for the Insane in Poughkeepsie, New York. Before taking that position, she worked for a short time with Mary Dixon Jones. When Dixon Jones accused the *Brooklyn Daily Eagle* of libel after it accused her of mishandling a number of surgical cases, Pease was called by the newspaper to testify to Dixon Jones's unprofessional behavior; Pease offered what Regina Morantz-Sanchez characterizes as "the most incriminating" statement against Dixon Jones (*Conduct* 176–77).

12. When the Homeopathic College in Louisville, Kentucky, was founded in 1893, Millsop was named its professor of hygiene ("Louisville"). Millsop graduated from the Hahnemann Medical College of Chicago in 1886 and established a practice in Bowling Green, Kentucky; she served as the vice president of the American Institute of Homeopathy in 1899 (Kirschmann 101).

6. Revising the Physician's Ethos: Women Physicians' Medical Research

1. Three of the five journals did not begin publication until after 1880. *JAMA* was first published in 1883; the *Medical Century* and *WMJ* began in 1893.

2. Collins was practicing medicine in Atlanta when she published the article cited here. She would go on to hold a fellowship at the Rockefeller Institute, to serve as assistant director of the bacteriological laboratories at the New York City Department of Health, to work as assistant director of the Georgia Board of Health, and to teach bacteriology and pathology in Buffalo, New York, while directing the laboratories at Buffalo City Hospital (Ogilvie and Harvey 282).

3. Paul Starr notes a shift beginning in the mid-1800s away from diagnostic techniques based on patients' reports of their symptoms and toward techniques relying on instruments such as stethoscopes, ophthalmoscopes, laryngoscopes, microscopes, X-rays, chemical and bacteriological tests, spirometers, and electrocardiograms. These devices not only increased physicians' ability to examine the body, but also increased their authority in patients' eyes and empowered them to determine the "normal" conditions of the body (136–37).

4. In Frances Willard and Mary Livermore's *A Woman of the Century*, Flora Brewster and her sister Cora Belle Brewster are credited with "open[ing] the medical field to the women of the South" (119) as well as with founding the *Family Health Journal*, later retitled the *Homeopathic Advocate and Health Journal* (118).

5. The *WMJ* misspelled Rutherford's name as "Ruthford." In the December 1895 issue, the *WMJ* reported that "The Perineum and Its Care during Parturition" had been translated and published in the Berlin *Medical Journal* ("Francis Armstrong Rutherford, M.D."). Rutherford was the first woman to have been named a city physician; she served in that capacity in Grand Rapids, Michigan, beginning in 1870.

6. Grace Peckham (later Murray) served on the editorial staffs of both the *WMJ* and the *Medical Record*. Her obituary in the *Bulletin of the New York Academy of Medicine* states that she invented the anesthesimeter, "an instrument for regulating the administration of anesthesia" ("Grace Peckham-Murray, M.D.").

7. Marble turned to medicine rather late in life; the *WMJ* reported that she "graduated in medicine after raising a family and *becoming a grandmother.*" Before studying medicine, Marble served as president of several women's clubs, including multiple suffrage associations; she lectured on subjects related to philanthropy and education; and she worked on the editorial staff of a newspaper in Washington, D.C. ("Dr. Ella M. S. Marble").

Conclusion:
Toward Feminist Ethos

1. Although Zakrzewska reported that the Blackwells were prohibited from speaking about the purpose of the Infirmary, according to Julia Boyd, Elizabeth Blackwell's biographer, Elizabeth briefly read a report on the infirmary's progress and reassured the public and the profession that women intended to prove their capabilities as physicians (164). Perhaps the difference in the two accounts reflects the difference between reading aloud and speaking and between reporting and offering a full rationale for the new institution and the woman-doctor movement it represented.

2. For example, other aspects of ethos have been explored by Karen A. Foss, Sonja K. Foss, and Cindy L. Griffin in their discussion of Gloria Anzaldúa's contributions to rhetorical theory, particularly what her work with the concept of "Borderlands" demonstrates about the constraints on and options for ethos in the rhetoric of culturally marginalized speakers and writers (122–23). The preponderance of women physicians with middle-class backgrounds also shaped the ethos strategies they employed; scholarship examining the rhetoric of speakers and writers from the working, rather than the professional, classes will doubtlessly uncover additional features of feminist ethos.

Works Cited

"Abolishing Women." *New York Times* 15 Feb. 1858: 4. *New York Times Archives.* Web. 11 Mar. 2011.

Abram, Ruth J., ed. *"Send Us a Lady Physician": Women Doctors in America, 1835–1920.* New York: Norton, 1985. Print.

"Another Account." *Philadelphia Press* 13 Nov. 1869. Scrapbook of Newspaper Clippings, Ledger, and Math Exercises. Legacy Center Archives and Special Collections, Drexel University College of Medicine. Web. 25 Jan. 2012.

Applegarth, Risa. "Genre, Location, and Mary Austin's *Ethos*." *Rhetoric Society Quarterly* 41.1 (2011): 41–63. Print.

Aristotle. *Rhetorica.* Ed. W. R. Roberts, E. S. Forster, and Ingram Bywater. Oxford: Clarendon, 1924. Print.

Aristotle's Master-piece, Completed. in Two Parts. New York: Flying Stationer, 1817. Early American Imprints, Series II, Shaw-Shoemaker (1801–1819). Web. 21 Sept. 2012.

"Art for Art's Sake." *Woman's Medical Journal* 4.4 (Apr. 1895): 91. Microform. National Library of Medicine. Bethesda: Remac Information, 1990.

"Barbaric Rowdyism." *Philadelphia Press*, n.d. Scrapbook of Newspaper Clippings, Ledger, and Math Exercises. The Legacy Center Archives and Special Collections, Drexel University College of Medicine. Web. 25 Jan. 2012.

Baym, Nina. *American Women of Letters and the Nineteenth-Century Sciences: Styles of Affiliation.* New Brunswick: Rutgers UP, 2002. Print.

Biesecker, Barbara. "Coming to Terms with Recent Attempts to Write Women into the History of Rhetoric." *Philosophy and Rhetoric* 25.2 (1992): 140–61. Print.

Bissell, Mary Taylor. *Household Hygiene.* New York: N. D. C. Hodges, 1890. Print.

———. *Physical Development and Exercise for Women.* New York: Dodd, Mead, 1891. Microform. *History of Women,* reel 507, no. 3847. New Haven: Research Publications, 1976.

Bittel, Carla. *Mary Putnam Jacobi and the Politics of Medicine in Nineteenth-Century America.* Chapel Hill: U of North Carolina P, 2009. Print.

Blackwell, Elizabeth. *The Laws of Life, with Special Reference to the Physical Education of Girls.* New York: George P. Putnam, 1852. Microform. *History of Women,* reel 245, no. 1627. New Haven: Research Publications, 1975.

———. *Pioneer Work in Opening the Medical Profession to Women.* 1895. Amherst: Humanity Books, 2005. Print.

Blackwell, Elizabeth, and Emily Blackwell. *Medicine as a Profession for Women.* New York: W. H. Tinson, 1860. Microform. *History of Women,* reel 943, no. 8545. Woodbridge: Research Publications, 1977.

Blackwell, Emily. "The Temptation of Johns Hopkins." *Medical Record* 38,23 (6 Dec. 1890): 650. Print.

Bledstein, Burton J. *The Culture of Professionalism: The Middle Class and the Development of Higher Education in America.* New York: Norton, 1976. Print.

Bodley, Rachel L. *Valedictory Address to the Twenty-Ninth Graduating Class of the Woman's Medical College of Pennsylvania.* Philadelphia: Grant, Faires, and Rodgers, 1881. Harvard University Library Page Delivery Service. Web. 6 Dec. 2009.

Bonner, Thomas Neville. *To the Ends of the Earth: Women's Search for Education in Medicine.* Cambridge: Harvard UP, 1992. Print.

"Book Reviews." Rev. of *Almost a Man,* by Mary Wood-Allen. *The Woman's Tribune* 14.6 (20 Mar. 1897): 23. Microform. *History of Women,* reels 230–32. New Haven: Research Publications, n.d.

Boyd, Julia. *The Excellent Doctor Blackwell: The Life of the First Woman Physician.* Phoenix Mill: Sutton, 2005. Print.

Brewster, Flora A. "The Use of the Faradic Current in Gynecology." *Medical Century* 1.9 (Sept. 1893): 298–300. *Google Books.* Web. 27 Dec. 2009.

Brodie, Janet Ferrell. *Contraception and Abortion in Nineteenth-Century America.* Ithaca: Cornell UP, 1994. Print.

Buchanan, Lindal. *Regendering Delivery: The Fifth Canon and Antebellum Women Rhetors.* Carbondale: Southern Illinois UP, 2005. Print.

Campbell, Karlyn Kohrs. *Man Cannot Speak for Her.* Vol. 1. New York: Greenwood, 1989. Print.

Carter, Julian B. *The Heart of Whiteness: Normative Sexuality and Race in America, 1880–1940.* Durham: Duke UP, 2007. Print.

Cheney, Ednah Dow. *Reminiscences.* Boston: Lee & Shepard, 1902. Print.

Christoph, Julie Nelson. "Reconceiving *Ethos* in Relation to the Personal: Strategies of Placement in Pioneer Women's Writing." *College English* 64.6 (2002): 660–79. Print.

Clark, Gregory, and S. Michael Halloran, eds. *Oratorical Culture in Nineteenth-Century America: Transformations in the Theory and Practice of Rhetoric.* Carbondale: Southern Illinois UP, 1993. Print.

Clarke, Edward H. *Sex in Education, or, A Fair Chance for the Girls.* Boston: James R. Osgood, 1873. Microform. *History of Women,* reel 374, no. 2596. New Haven: Research Publications, 1977.

Cleaves, Margaret A. "The Expenditure of Electric Energy." *Journal of the American Medical Association* 30.21 (21 May 1898): 1219–26. Print.

Cole, Rebecca J. "First Meeting of the Women's Missionary Society of Philadelphia." *Woman's Era* 3.4 (Oct./Nov. 1896): 4–5. Print.

Collins, Katharine R. "Microscopical and Chemical Examinations as Aids to Diagnosis." *Woman's Medical Journal* 5.11 (Nov. 1896): 275–79. Microform. National Library of Medicine. Bethesda: Remac Information, 1990.

Collins, Vicki Tolar. "The Speaker Respoken: Material Rhetoric as Feminist Methodology." *College English* 61.5 (1999): 545–73. Print.

"A Colored Female Doctor." *New York Times* 22 Sept. 1891, 1. *New York Times Archives*. Web. 26 Oct. 2010.

Cowan, John. *The Science of a New Life*. New York: Fowler and Wells, 1869. *Open Library*. Web. 21 Sept. 2012.

Crumpler, Rebecca. *A Book of Medical Discourses in Two Parts*. Boston: Cashman, Keating, 1883. Microform. Cambridge: Harvard College Library Imaging Services, 2004.

Dall, Caroline H. *"Woman's Right to Labor"; or, Low Wages and Hard Work*. Boston: Walker, Wise, 1860. *Google Books*. Web. 30 Mar. 2011.

Darwin, Charles. *The Descent of Man, and Selection in Relation to Sex*. Vol. 2. London: John Murray, 1871. *Google Books*. Web. 6 Sept. 2012.

Davis, Orin. "Women as Practitioners of Medicine." *Physicians and Surgeons' Investigator* 2.9 (15 Sept. 1881): 262–67. American Periodicals Series. Web. 14 Feb. 2010.

"The Despised Office of Motherhood." Editorial. *Journal of the American Medical Association* 26.17 (25 Apr. 1896): 835–36. Print.

"The Despised Office of Motherhood." Letter. *Journal of the American Medical Association* 28.8 (20 Feb. 1897): 375–76. Print.

Dillon, Halle T. "Practical Physiology." *African Methodist Episcopal Church Review* 9.2 (1892): 183–88. *Ohio Historical Society: The African-American Experience in Ohio*. Web. 29 Sept. 2012.

Dixon Jones, Mary. Rev. of *Woman's Medical College of Pennsylvania. An Historical Outline*, by Clara Marshall. *Medical and Surgical Reporter* 78.4 (30 Apr. 1898): 170–72. American Periodicals Series. Web. 6 Dec. 2009.

D. K. "The Late Medical Degree to a Female." Letter. *Boston Medical and Surgical Journal* 40.3 (21 Feb. 1849): 58–59. American Periodicals Series. Web. 14 Feb. 2010.

Donawerth, Jane. *Rhetorical Theory by Women before 1900: An Anthology*. Lanham: Rowman & Littlefield, 2002. Print.

Drake, Emma F. Angell. *What a Woman of Forty-Five Ought to Know*. Self and Sex Series. Philadelphia: Vir, 1902. Print.

———. *What a Young Wife Ought to Know*. 1901. Self and Sex Series. Philadelphia: Vir, 1908. Print.

"Dr. Clara Marshall." *Woman's Medical Journal* 1.12 (Dec. 1893): 238. Microform. National Library of Medicine. Bethesda: Remac Information, 1990.

"Dr. Eliza H. Root." *Woman's Medical Journal* 9.7 (July 1899): 245. Microform. National Library of Medicine. Bethesda: Remac Information, 1990.

"Dr. Ella M. S. Marble." *Woman's Medical Journal* 5.3 (Mar. 1896): 69. Microform. National Library of Medicine. Bethesda: Remac Information, 1990.

"Dr. Marian K. Bowles." *Woman's Medical Journal* 9.11 (Nov. 1899): 427. Microform. National Library of Medicine. Bethesda: Remac Information, 1990.

"Dr. Mary Aiken." *Woman's Medical Journal* 9.7 (July 1899): 245–46. Microform. National Library of Medicine. Bethesda: Remac Information, 1990.

"Dr. Rebecca J. Cole." *Changing the Face of Medicine*. National Library of Medicine, 19 May 2008. Web. 26 Oct. 2010.

Duffy, John. *From Humors to Medical Science: A History of American Medicine*. 2nd ed. Urbana: U of Illinois P, 1993. Print.

Dunham, Carroll. "Lilium-tigrinum—A Summary of a Few Provings upon Women." *North American Journal of Homœopathy* 19.11 (Nov. 1870): 159–71. *Google Books*. Web. 8 Feb. 2010.

Ellington, George [pseud.]. *The Women of New York; or, The Underworld of the Great City*. New York: New York Book, 1869. Microform. *History of Women*, reel 325, no. 2216. New Haven: Research Publications, 1975.

"An Epidemic of Aphasia." *Woman's Medical Journal* 6.9 (Sept. 1897): 279–80. Microform. National Library of Medicine. Bethesda: Remac Information, 1990.

"The Esculapian Caldron." *Philadelphia Press*, n.d. Scrapbook of Newspaper Clippings, Ledger, and Math Exercises. Legacy Center Archives and Special Collections, Drexel University College of Medicine. Web. 25 Jan. 2012.

Fellman, Anita Clair, and Michael Fellman. *Making Sense of Self: Medical Advice Literature in Late Nineteenth-Century America*. Philadelphia: U of Pennsylvania P, 1981. Print.

"Female Medical College." *Friends' Intelligencer* 20.9 (9 May 1863): 142–43. American Periodicals Series. Web. 6 Dec. 2009.

"Female Medical Practitioners." *Medical News* 25.293 (May 1867): 73–74. American Periodicals Series. Web. 6 Dec. 2009.

Fishbein, Morris. *A History of the American Medical Association 1847 to 1947*. Philadelphia: W. B. Saunders, 1947. Print.

Folsom, Charles F. Letter. *Century Illustrated Magazine* 41.4 (Feb. 1891): 636. American Periodicals Series. Web. 14 Feb. 2010.

"Forward! Forward!" *Woman's Medical Journal* 3.1 (July 1894): 11–12. Microform. National Library of Medicine. Bethesda: Remac Information, 1990.

Foss, Karen A., Sonja K. Foss, and Cindy L. Griffin. *Feminist Rhetorical Theories*. Long Grove: Waveland, 1999. Print.

Fowler, Mrs. L. N. [Lydia Folger Fowler]. *Familiar Lessons on Physiology and Phrenology, for Children and Youth*. 2 vols. New York: Fowlers and Wells, 1847. Print.

"Francis Armstrong Rutherford, M.D." *Woman's Medical Journal* 4.12 (Dec. 1895): 338–39. Microform. National Library of Medicine. Bethesda: Remac Information, 1990.

Frye, Maud J. "Some Sensible Remarks." *Woman's Medical Journal* 6.9 (Sept. 1897): 283–85. Microform. National Library of Medicine. Bethesda: Remac Information, 1990.

Fullerton, Anna M. "*Mater Dolorsa—Mater Felix*: A Sketch from Hospital Life." *Daughters of Æsculapius*. Philadelphia: George W. Jacobs, 1897. 53–65. Microform. *History of Women*, reel 623, no. 4203. New Haven: Research Publications, 1975.

Galbraith, Anna M. *Hygiene and Physical Culture for Women.* New York: Dodd, Mead, 1895. Microform. *History of Women,* reel 545, no. 4972. New Haven: Research Publications, 1976.

Giesberg, Judith Ann. *Civil War Sisterhood: The U.S. Sanitary Commission and Women's Politics in Transition.* Boston: Northeastern UP, 2000. Print.

Gleason, Rachel B. *Talks to My Patients: Hints on Getting Well and Keeping Well.* New York: Wood and Holbrook, 1870. Print.

Glenn, Georgiana. "Are Women as Capable of Becoming Physicians as Men?" *Clinic* 9 (20 Nov. 1875): 243–45. Print.

Gove, Mary S. *Lectures to Ladies on Anatomy and Physiology.* Boston: Saxton and Peirce, 1842. Microform. Cambridge: Harvard University Photographic Services, 1997.

"Grace Peckham-Murray, M.D." *Bulletin of the New York Academy of Medicine* 9.5 (May 1933): 353. *PubMed.* Web. 6 Nov. 2010.

"A Grave Responsibility." *Woman's Medical Journal* 5.12 (Dec. 1896): 309–10. Microform. National Library of Medicine. Bethesda: Remac Information, 1990.

Greene, C. A. *Build Well: The Basis of Individual, Home, and National Elevation.* Boston: D. Lothrop 1885. Print.

Grice, Julia. "A Maiden Effort." *Daughters of Æsculapius.* Philadelphia: George W. Jacobs, 1897. 43–52. Microform. *History of Women,* reel 623, no. 4972. New Haven: Research Publications, 1975.

Haller, John S., Jr., and Robin M. Haller. *The Physician and Sexuality in Victorian America.* New York: W. W. Norton, 1974. Print.

Halloran, S. Michael. "Aristotle's Concept of Ethos; or, If Not His Somebody Else's." *Rhetoric Review* 1.1 (1982): 58–63. Print.

"The Happy Hunting Ground." *Philadelphia Press,* n.d. Scrapbook of Newspaper Clippings, Ledger, and Math Exercises. Legacy Center Archives and Special Collections, Drexel University College of Medicine. 25 Jan. 2012.

"Harriet [*sic*] Kizia Hunt." *Woman's Medical Journal* 10.5 (May 1900): 202–5. Microform. National Library of Medicine. Bethesda: Remac Information, 1990.

Harrison, Kimberly. "Rhetorical Rehearsals: The Construction of Ethos in Confederate Women's Civil War Diaries." *Rhetoric Review* 22.3 (2003): 243–63. Print.

Hayden, Wendy. "'Audacia Dangyereyes': Appropriate Speech and the 'Immodest' Woman Speaker of the Comstock Era." *Rhetoric Society Quarterly* 42.5 (2012): 450–71. Print.

———. *Evolutionary Rhetoric: Sex, Science, and Free Love in Nineteenth-Century Feminism.* Carbondale: Southern Illinois UP, 2013. Print.

Heart, Aiken. [pseud.] *The Doctor Woman.* Detroit: American Observer, 1880. *Harvard University Library Page Delivery Service.* Web. 6 Dec. 2009.

Hine, Darlene Clark, ed. *Facts on File Encyclopedia of Black Women in America: Science, Health, and Medicine.* New York: Facts on File, 1997. Print.

Hunt, Harriot K. "Address on the Medical Education of Women." *Proceedings of the Woman's Rights Convention, Held at Worchester, October 23d & 24th, 1850.* Boston: Prentiss and Sawyer, 1851. 45–49. Microform. *History of Women,* reel 942, no. 8499. Woodbridge: Research Publications, 1977.

———. *Glances and Glimpses; or Fifty Years Social, Including Twenty Years Professional Life.* Boston: John P. Jewett, 1856. Print.

Johnson, Nan. *Gender and Rhetorical Space in American Life, 1866–1910.* Carbondale: Southern Illinois UP, 2002. Print.

"Just among Ourselves." *Woman's Medical Journal* 2.6 (June 1894): 136–37. Microform. National Library of Medicine. Bethesda: Remac Information, 1990.

"Just Three Years Ago." *Woman's Medical Journal* 4.12 (Dec. 1895): 323–24. Microform. National Library of Medicine. Bethesda: Remac Information, 1990.

Kime, Sara A. "Female Physicians in Insane Asylums." Letter. *Medical Record* 42.12 (Sept. 1892): 350. Print.

Kirschmann, Anne Taylor. *A Vital Force: Women in American Homeopathy.* New Brunswick: Rutgers UP, 2004. Print.

Kraus, Natasha Kirsten. *A New Type of Womanhood: Discursive Politics and Social Change in Antebellum America.* Durham: Duke UP, 2008. Print.

La Flesche, Susan. "Another Appeal." *Indian's Friend* 12.7 (Mar. 1900): 8–9. Microform. New York: Clearwater Publishing, 1981.

———. "From Dr. Susan La Flesche." *Indian's Friend* 12.4 (Dec. 1889): 2. Microform. New York: Clearwater, 1981.

———. "The Home Life of the Indian." *Indian's Friend* 4.10 (June 1892): 39–40. Microform. New York: Clearwater, 1981.

———. "A Letter from Dr. LaFlesche [*sic*]." *Indian Bulletin* 4.13 (Dec. 1891): n.p. Print.

———. "My Work as Physician among My People." *Southern Workman* 21 (Aug. 1892): 133. Microform. New York: International Microfilm, 1968–69.

———. "The Omahas and Citizenship." *Southern Workman* 20 (April 1891): 177. Microform. New York: International Microfilm, 1968–69.

———. "Our Medical Mission." *Indian's Friend* 4.9 (May 1892): 37. Microform. New York: Clearwater, 1981.

Lannin, Louise. "The Serpent Poisons in the Treatment of Ovarian Diseases." *North American Journal of Homœopathy* 37.10 (Oct. 1889): 644–46. *Google Books.* Web. 2 Jan. 2010.

"Lectures." *Graham Journal of Health and Longevity* 2.18 (1 Sept. 1838): 288. American Periodicals Series. Web. 21 Oct. 2010.

Lippincott, Gail. "Rhetorical Chemistry: Negotiating Gendered Audiences in Nineteenth-Century Nutrition Studies." *Journal of Business and Technical Communication* 17.1 (2003): 10–49. Print.

Logan, Shirley Wilson. *"We Are Coming": The Persuasive Discourse of Nineteenth-Century Black Women.* Carbondale: Southern Illinois UP, 1999. Print.

Longshore-Potts, Anna M. *Discourses to Women on Medical Subjects.* London: The Author, 1887. Print.

"Louisville." *American Homeopathist.* 19.21 (1 Nov. 1893): 337. *Google Books.* Web. 24 Apr. 2011.

Lozier, Clemence Sophia. "Dr. Lozier." *North American Review* 137.324 (Nov. 1883): 513–19. American Periodicals Series. Web. 30 Dec. 2009.

MacKay, Emma S. "Diagnostic Points Determining Age of Embryo and Foetus." *Woman's Medical Journal* 9.4 (Apr. 1899): 119–23. Microform. National Library of Medicine. Bethesda: Remac Information, 1990.

Marble, Ella M. S. "Woman's Contribution to Medical Literature." *Woman's Medical Journal* 5.3 (Mar. 1896): 59–63. Microform. National Library of Medicine. Bethesda: Remac Information, 1990.

"Mary Wood-Allen." Obituary. *Journal of the American Medical Association* 50 (22 Feb. 1908): 636. Print.

Mattingly, Carol. *Appropriate[ing] Dress: Women's Rhetorical Style in Nineteenth-Century America*. Carbondale: Southern Illinois UP, 2002. Print.

Maxwell, Mrs. W. H. *A Female Physician to the Ladies of the United States: Being a Familiar and Practical Treatise on Matters of Utmost Importance Peculiar to Women*. New York: The Author, 1860. Microform. *History of Women*, reel 341, no. 2344. New Haven: Research Publications, 1975.

"Medical Rowdyism." *Philadelphia Sunday Transcript* 14 Nov. 1869. Scrapbook of Newspaper Clippings, Ledger, and Math Exercises. Legacy Center Archives and Special Collections, Drexel University College of Medicine. Web. 25 Jan. 2012.

"Medical Societies." *Medical and Surgical Reporter* 22.26 (25 June 1870): 528–35. American Periodicals Series. Web. 6 Dec. 2009.

Men and Women Medical Students, and the Woman Movement. Philadelphia, 1869. Print.

Men and Women Medical Students, the Hospital Clinics, and the Woman Movement. Philadelphia, 1870. Harvard University Library Page Delivery Service. Web. 30 Sept. 2012.

Micciche, Laura R. "Writing as Feminist Rhetorical Theory." *Rhetorica in Motion: Feminist Rhetorical Methods and Methodologies*. Ed. Eileen E. Schell and K. J. Rawson. Pittsburgh: U of Pittsburgh P, 2010. 173–88. Print.

Miller, Carolyn. "Genre as Social Action." *Quarterly Journal of Speech* 70 (1984): 151–67. Print.

Millsop, Sarah J. "From a Woman's Point of View." *North American Journal of Homœopathy* 46.2 (Feb. 1898): 125–28. *Google Books*. Web. 3 Jan. 2010.

Minard, Eliza J. C. "Clinical Statistics—A Word in Favor of Free Dispensary and Hospital Work." *Journal of the American Medical Association* 14.19 (10 May 1890): 678–81. Print.

"A Misconstruction." *Woman's Medical Journal* 2.1 (Jan. 1894): 6. Microform. National Library of Medicine. Bethesda: Remac Information, 1990.

"The Modest (?) Medical Students." *Philadelphia Sunday Transcript* 14 Nov. 1869. Scrapbook of Newspaper Clippings, Ledger, and Math Exercises. Legacy Center Archives and Special Collections, Drexel University College of Medicine. Web. 25 Jan. 2012.

Moldow, Gloria. *Women Doctors in Gilded-Age Washington: Race, Gender, and Professionalization*. Urbana: U of Illinois P, 1987. Print.

Morantz, Regina Markell, and Sue Zschoche. "Professionalism, Feminism, and Gender Roles: A Comparative Study of Nineteenth-Century Medical Therapeutics." *Journal of American History* 67.3 (1980): 568–88. Print.

Morantz-Sanchez, Regina. *Conduct Unbecoming a Woman: Medicine on Trial in Turn-of-the-Century Brooklyn*. New York: Oxford UP, 1999. Print.

———. *Sympathy and Science: Women Physicians in American Medicine*. 1985. Chapel Hill: U of North Carolina P, 2000. Print.

More, Ellen S. *Restoring the Balance: Women Physicians and the Profession of Medicine, 1850–1995*. Cambridge: Harvard UP, 1999. Print.

"A Most Learned Judge!" *Woman's Medical Journal* 4.8 (Aug. 1895): 206–8. Microform. National Library of Medicine. Bethesda: Remac Information, 1990.

Mott, Mrs. *The Ladies' Medical Oracle; or, Mrs. Mott's Advice to Young Females, Wives, and Mothers*. Boston· the Authoress, 1834. Microform. *History of Women*, reel 170, no. 1111. New Haven: Research Publications, 1975.

Numbers, Ronald L. "Do-It-Yourself the Sectarian Way." *"Send Us a Lady Physician": Women Doctors in America, 1835–1920*. Ed. Ruth J. Abram. New York: W. W. Norton, 1985. 43–54. Print.

Ogilvie, Marilyn, and Joy Harvey, eds. *The Biographical Dictionary of Women in Science: Pioneering Lives from Ancient Times to the Mid-20th Century*. New York: Routledge, 2000. Print.

"The Old Year." *Woman's Medical Journal* 1.12 (Dec. 1893): 232–33. Microform. National Library of Medicine. Bethesda: Remac Information, 1990.

O'Neill, William L. *Everyone Was Brave: A History of Feminism in America*. Chicago: Quadrangle Books, 1969. Print.

"Our Boston Letter." *Chicago Press and Tribune* 14.2 (3 July 1860): 2. *ProQuest Historical Newspapers*. Web. 26 Sept. 2010.

"Our Quondam Friends." *Woman's Medical Journal* 3.4 (Oct. 1894): 97–98. Microform. National Library of Medicine. Bethesda: Remac Information, 1990.

"The Outrage of the Male Medical Students." *Philadelphia Press* n.d. Scrapbook of Newspaper Clippings, Ledger, and Math Exercises. Legacy Center Archives and Special Collections, Drexel University College of Medicine. Web. 25 Jan. 2012.

Pease, Caroline S. "Female Medical Education from a Woman's Standpoint." Letter. *Medical Record* 24.10 (8 Sept. 1883): 270. Print.

Peckham, Grace. "The Nervous Symptoms, Local and Reflex, Arising from the Displacements and Inflammations of the Uterus and Its Appendages." *Medical Record* 33.7 (18 Feb. 1888): 177–80. Print.

Peitzman, Steven J. "Why Support a Women's Medical College? Philadelphia's Early Male Medical Pro-Feminists." *Bulletin of the History of Medicine* 77.3 (2003): 576–99. Print.

"Pertinent Phrases from Our Esteemed Contemporaries." *Woman's Medical Journal* 4.10 (Oct. 1895): 277–78. Microform. National Library of Medicine. Bethesda: Remac Information, 1990.

Phelps, Elizabeth Stuart. *Doctor Zay*. Boston: Houghton, Mifflin, 1882. Print.

Picöt, L. Julien. "Shall Woman Practice Medicine?" *North Carolina Medical Journal* 16 (1885): 10–21. Print.

Pittman, Coretta. "Black Women Writers and the Trouble with *Ethos*: Harriet Jacobs, Billie Holiday, and Sister Souljah." *Rhetoric Society Quarterly* 37.1 (2007): 43–70. Print.

Pope, Emily F., Emma L. Call, and C. Augusta Pope. *The Practice of Medicine by Women in the United States*. Boston: Wright and Potter, 1881. Microform. *History of Women*, reel 943, no. 8551. Woodbridge: Research Publications, 1977.

Powell, Malea D. "Down by the River; or, How Susan La Flesche Picotte Can Teach Us about Alliance as a Practice of Survivance." *College English* 67.1 (2004): 38–60. Print.

Preston, Ann. "The Status of Women-Physicians." *Medical and Surgical Reporter* 16.18 (4 May 1867): 391–94. American Periodicals Series. Web. 3 Mar. 2010.

———. "Valedictory Address to the Graduating Class of the Woman's Medical College of Pennsylvania, at the Eighteenth Annual Commencement, March 12th, 1870." Philadelphia: Loag, 1870. Legacy Center Archives and Special Collections, Drexel University College of Medicine. Web. 24 July 2013.

"Protest against Bill to Allow Women in Third Class Cities to Vote." *New-York Tribune* 15 March 1905: 7. *Library of Congress: Chronicling America*. Web. 6 Dec. 2009.

"The Province of Woman in Medicine." *Journal of the American Medical Association* 16.25 (20 June 1891): 893. Print.

Putnam Jacobi, Mary. "Case of Microcephalus." *Medical Record* 19.24 (11 June 1881): 645–50. Print.

———. *"Common Sense" Applied to Woman Suffrage: A Statement of the Reasons Which Justify the Demand to Extend the Suffrage to Women, with Consideration of the Arguments against Such Enfranchisement, and with Special Reference to the Issues Presented to the New York State Convention of 1894*. New York: G. P. Putnam's Sons, 1894. *Google Books*. Web. 6 Dec. 2009.

———. *The Question of Rest for Women during Menstruation*. New York: G. P. Putnam's Sons, 1877. Microform. *History of Women*, reel 390, no. 2771. New Haven: Research Publications, 1977.

———. "Shall Women Practice Medicine?" *North American Review* 134.302 (Jan. 1882): 52–75. American Periodicals Series. Web. 6 Dec. 2009.

———. "The 'Temptation of Johns Hopkins.'" *Medical Record* 38.21 (22 Nov. 1890): 588–89. Print.

Reed, Elizabeth Wagner. *American Women in Science before the Civil War*. Minneapolis: U of Minnesota P, 1992. Print.

Reynolds, Emma A. "Woman Physicians and Nurses." Letter. *Galveston Daily News* 28 Sept. 1895: 12. Microform. El Paso: Southwest Micropublishing, n.d.

Reynolds, Nedra. "*Ethos* as Location: New Sites for Understanding Discursive Authority." *Rhetoric Review* 11.2 (1993): 325–38. Print.

Ritchie, Joy, and Kate Ronald. "A Gathering of Rhetorics." Introduction. *Available Means: An Anthology of Women's Rhetoric(s)*. Ed. Ritchie and Ronald. Pittsburgh: U of Pittsburgh P, 2001. xv–xxxi. Print.

Rosenberg, Charles E. "American Medicine in 1879." *"Send Us a Lady Physician": Women Doctors in America, 1835–1920*. Ed. Ruth J. Abram. New York: Norton, 1985. 21–34. Print.

Royster, Jacqueline Jones. *Profiles of Ohio Women, 1803–2003*. Athens: Ohio UP, 2003. Print.

——. *Traces of a Stream: Literacy and Social Change among African American Women.* Pittsburgh: U of Pittsburgh P, 2000. Print.

Russell, Rose A. "Diagnostic Points for Determination of Age of Embryo and Foetus." *Woman's Medical Journal* 9.5 (May 1899): 167–70. Microform. National Library of Medicine. Bethesda: Remac Information, 1990.

Ruthford [Rutherford], Frances. "The Perineum and Its Care during Parturition." *Woman's Medical Journal* 2.2 (Feb. 1894): 29–33. Microform. National Library of Medicine. Bethesda: Remac Information, 1990.

Ryan, Mary P. *Mysteries of Sex: Tracing Women and Men through American History.* Chapel Hill: U of North Carolina P, 2006. Print.

——. *Women in Public: Between Banners and Ballots, 1825–1880.* Baltimore: Johns Hopkins UP, 1990. *ACLS Humanities E-Book.* Web. 3 Feb. 2012.

Safford Blake, Mary. "A Visit to Dr. Harriet [*sic*] K. Hunt." *Woman's Journal* 3.47 (23 Nov. 1872): 376. Print.

Saur, Prudence. *Maternity: A Book for Every Wife and Mother.* Chicago: L. P. Miller, 1891. Microform. *History of Women*, reel 599, no. 4748. New Haven: Research Publications, 1977.

Sawaya, Francesca. *Modern Women, Modern Work: Domesticity, Professionalism, and American Writing, 1890–1950.* Philadelphia: U of Pennsylvania P, 2004. Print.

Seneca Falls Convention. "Declaration of Sentiments and Resolutions." *Available Means: An Anthology of Women's Rhetoric(s).* Ed. Joy Ritchie and Kate Ronald. Pittsburgh: U of Pittsburgh P, 2001. 139–42. Print.

Severance, Juliet H. *A Lecture on Religious, Political and Social Freedom.* Milwaukee: Godfrey and Crandall, 1881. Print.

Shaughnessy, Mina P. *Errors and Expectations: A Guide for the Teacher of Basic Writing.* New York: Oxford UP, 1977. Print.

Sherry, J. W. "The Status of Women Physicians." Letter. *Medical and Surgical Reporter* 17.1 (6 July 1867): 19–21. American Periodicals Series. Web. 7 May 2011.

Shortt, S. E. D. "Physicians, Science, and Status: Issues in the Professionalization of Anglo-American Medicine in the Nineteenth Century." *Medical History* 27 (1983): 51–68. Print.

Shrady, George F. "The Man's View." *Ladies' Home Journal* 8.6 (May 1891): 4. American Periodicals Series. Web. 11 Dec. 2009.

Silver-Isenstadt, Jean L. *Shameless: The Visionary Life of Mary Gove Nichols.* Baltimore: Johns Hopkins UP, 2002. Print.

Smith, Craig R. "*Ethos* Dwells Pervasively: A Hermeneutic Reading of Aristotle on Credibility." *The Ethos of Rhetoric.* Ed. Michael J. Hyde. Columbia: U of South Carolina P, 2004. 1–19. Print.

Spink, Mary A. "Woman in Medicine." *Woman's Medical Journal* 3.1 (July 1894): 15–20. Microform. National Library of Medicine. Bethesda: Remac Information, 1990.

Starr, Paul. *The Social Transformation of American Medicine.* New York: Basic Books, 1982. Print.

Sterling, Dorothy, ed. *We Are Your Sisters: Black Women in the Nineteenth Century.* New York: Norton, 1984. Print.

Stockham, Alice B. *Karezza: Ethics of Marriage.* New York: R. F. Fenno, 1903. Microform. *History of Women,* reel 689, no. 5512. Woodbridge: Research Publications, 1976.

——. *Tokology: A Book for Every Woman.* 1883. Chicago: Alice B. Stockham, 1889. Microform. *History of Women,* reel 490, no. 3680. New Haven: Research Publications, 1977.

"Sub Rosa." *Woman's Medical Journal* 1.12 (December 1893): 233. Microform. National Library of Medicine. Bethesda: Remac Information, 1990.

Tannenbaum, Rebecca J. "Earnestness, Temperance, Industry: The Definition and Uses of Professional Character among Nineteenth-Century American Physicians." *Journal of the History of Medicine and Allied Sciences* 49 (1994): 251–283. Print.

"Teaching Truth." Advertisement. *Baby's Firsts* by Mary Wood-Allen. End matter. Washington: Library of Congress Photoduplication Service, n.d.

"The Temperance Cause." *Daily Picayune* 12 May 1899: 3. *America's Historical Newspapers.* Web. 26 Apr. 2009.

"The Temptation of Johns Hopkins." *Medical Record* 38.20 (15 Nov. 1890): 550. Print.

Theriot, Nancy M. "Women's Voices in Nineteenth-Century Medical Discourse: A Step toward Deconstructing Science." *Signs* 19.1 (1993): 1–31. Print.

"To Contributors and Subscribers." *Woman's Medical Journal* 1.12 (Dec. 1893): 232. Microform. National Library of Medicine. Bethesda: Remac Information, 1990.

"To Contributors and Subscribers." *Woman's Medical Journal* 9.7 (July 1899): 245. Microform. National Library of Medicine. Bethesda: Remac Information, 1990.

"Tokology Encircling the World." *The Woman's Tribune* 9.21 (6 Aug. 1892): 163. Microform. *History of Women,* reels 230–32. New Haven: Research Publications, n.d.

Tong, Benson. *Susan La Flesche Picotte, M.D.: Omaha Indian Leader and Reformer.* Norman: U of Oklahoma P, 1999. Print.

Tonkovich, Nicole. "Rhetorical Power in the Victorian Parlor: *Godey's Lady's Book* and the Gendering of Nineteenth-Century Rhetoric." *Oratorical Culture in Nineteenth-Century America: Transformations in the Theory and Practice of Rhetoric.* Ed. Gregory Clark and S. Michael Halloran, 158–83. Carbondale: Southern Illinois UP, 1993. Print.

Tuchman, Arleen Marcia. *Science Has No Sex: The Life of Marie Zakrzewska, M.D.* Chapel Hill: U of North Carolina P, 2006. Print.

——. "'Only in a Republic Can It Be Proved That Science Has No Sex': Marie Elizabeth Zakrzewska (1829–1902) and the Multiple Meanings of Science in the Nineteenth-Century United States." *Journal of Women's History* 11.1 (1999): 121–42. Print.

——. "Situating Gender: Marie E. Zakrzewska and the Place of Science in Women's Medical Education." *Isis* 95.1 (2004): 34–57. Print.

"Valedictory Address." *Godey's Lady's Book and Magazine* 57 (Nov. 1858): 465–66. American Periodicals Series. Web. 11 Dec. 2009.

Van De Warker, Ely. "The Relations of Women to the Professions and Skilled Labor." *Popular Science Monthly* (Feb. 1875): 454–70. *Google Books.* Web. 23 Sept. 2010.

Walker, Mary E. *Hit.* New York: American News, 1871. *Google Books.* Web. 16 Aug. 2012.

[Walker, Mary Edwards]. *Unmasked, or The Science of Immorality.* Philadelphia: Wm. H. Boyd, 1878. *New York State Digital Collections.* Web. 20 Jan. 2010.

Walsh, Mary Roth. *"Doctors Wanted: No Women Need Apply": Sexual Barriers in the Medical Profession, 1835–1975.* New Haven: Yale UP, 1977. Print.

Warner, John Harley. "Ideals of Science and Their Discontents in Late Nineteenth-Century American Medicine." *Isis* 82.3 (1991): 454–78. Print.

Wells, Susan. *Out of the Dead House: Nineteenth-Century Women Physicians and the Writing of Medicine.* Madison: U of Wisconsin P, 2001. Print.

Welsh, Lilian. *Reminiscences of Thirty Years in Baltimore.* Baltimore: Norman, Remington, 1925. Print.

Whipple, Electa B. "Dysmenorrhea." *Woman's Medical Journal* 3.2 (Aug. 1894): 45–50. Microform. National Library of Medicine. Bethesda: Remac Information, 1990.

White, Frances Emily. "The American Medical Woman." *Medical News* 67.5 (3 Aug. 1895): 123–28. *Google Books.* Web. 7 Feb. 2010.

Willard, Frances E., and Mary A. Livermore, eds. *A Woman of the Century: Fourteen Hundred Seventy Biographical Sketches Accompanied by Portraits of Leading American Women in All Walks of Life.* Buffalo: Charles Wells Moulton, 1893. *Google Books.* Web. 26 June 2011.

Williams, N. "A Dissertation on 'Female Physicians.'" *Boston Medical and Surgical Journal* 43.4 (28 Aug. 1850): 69–75. American Periodicals Series. Web. 11 Dec. 2009.

"Woman Doctors." *Medical and Surgical Reporter* 2.13 (25 June 1859): 275–76. American Periodicals Series. Web. 14 Feb. 2010.

Woman's Medical College of Pennsylvania. *Daughters of Æsculapius.* Philadelphia: George W. Jacobs, 1897. Microform. *History of Women*, reel 623, no. 4972. New Haven: Research Publications, 1975.

"Women as Physicians." *Medical and Surgical Reporter* 44.13 (26 Mar. 1881): 354–56. *Google Books.* Web. 27 Sept. 2012.

"Women Oppose Suffrage." *New York Times* 15 Mar. 1905: 6. *New York Times Archives.* Web. 11 Dec. 2009.

Wood-Allen, Mary. *Almost a Man.* Ann Arbor: Wood-Allen, 1895. Print.

———. *Almost a Woman.* 1897. Cooperstown: Arthur H. Crist, 1911. *History of Women*, reel 788, no. 6286. New Haven: Research Publications, 1977.

———. *Child-Confidence Rewarded.* 1903. Cooperstown: Arthur H. Crist, 1910. Print.

———. *Ideal Married Life: A Book for All Husbands and Wives.* New York: Fleming H. Revell, 1901. Print.

———. *The Marvels of Our Bodily Dwelling.* Ann Arbor: Wood-Allen, 1896. Print.

———. "Moral Education of the Young." *The National Purity Congress, Its Papers, Addresses, Portraits.* Ed. Aaron M. Powell. New York: American Purity Alliance, 1896. 224–38. Microform. *History of Women*, reel 583, no. 4579. New Haven: Research Publications, 1976.

———. *Teaching Truth.* Ann Arbor: Wood-Allen, 1892. *Google Books.* Web. 6 Mar. 2010.

———. *What a Young Girl Ought to Know.* Philadelphia: Vir, 1905. Print.

———. *What a Young Woman Ought to Know.* 1892. Self and Sex Series. Philadelphia: Vir, 1905. Microform. *History of Women,* reel 627, no. 5005. Woodbridge: Research Publications, 1977.

Zakrzewska, Marie E. *A Practical Illustration of "Woman's Right to Labor"; or, A Letter from Marie E. Zakrzewska, M.D.* Ed. Caroline H. Dall. Boston: Walker, Wise, 1860. Microform. *History of Women,* reel 359, no. 2479. Woodbridge: Research Publications, 1975.

———. *A Woman's Quest: The Life of Marie E. Zakrzewska, M.D.* 1924. Ed. Agnes C. Vietor. New York: Arno Press, 1972. Print.

Index

The letter *f* following a page number denotes a figure.

Carolyn Skinner is an associate professor of English at the Ohio State University. She has published essays in *Rhetoric Review, Rhetoric Society Quarterly,* and *Technical Communication Quarterly.*

Studies in Rhetorics and Feminisms

Studies in Rhetorics and Feminisms seeks to address the interdisciplinarity that rhetorics and feminisms represent. Rhetorical and feminist scholars want to connect rhetorical inquiry with contemporary academic and social concerns, exploring rhetoric's relevance to current issues of opportunity and diversity. This interdisciplinarity has already begun to transform the rhetorical tradition as we have known it (upper-class, agonistic, public, and male) into regendered, inclusionary rhetorics (democratic, dialogic, collaborative, cultural, and private). Our intellectual advancements depend on such ongoing transformation.

Rhetoric, whether ancient, contemporary, or futuristic, always inscribes the relation of language and power at a particular moment, indicating who may speak, who may listen, and what can be said. The only way we can displace the traditional rhetoric of masculine-only, public performance is to replace it with rhetorics that are recognized as being better suited to our present needs. We must understand more fully the rhetorics of the non-Western tradition, of women, of a variety of cultural and ethnic groups. Therefore, Studies in Rhetorics and Feminisms espouses a theoretical position of openness and expansion, a place for rhetorics to grow and thrive in a symbiotic relationship with all that feminisms have to offer, particularly when these two fields intersect with philosophical, sociological, religious, psychological, pedagogical, and literary issues.

The series seeks scholarly works that both examine and extend rhetoric, works that span the sexes, disciplines, cultures, ethnicities, and sociocultural practices as they intersect with the rhetorical tradition. After all, the recent resurgence of rhetorical studies has been not so much a discovery of new rhetorics as a recognition of existing rhetorical activities and practices, of our newfound ability and willingness to listen to previously untold stories.

The series editors seek both high-quality traditional and cutting-edge scholarly work that extends the significant relationship between rhetoric and feminism within various genres, cultural contexts, historical periods, methodologies, theoretical positions, and methods of delivery (e.g., film and hypertext to elocution and preaching).

Queries and submissions:
Professor Cheryl Glenn, Editor
   E-mail: cjg6@psu.edu
Professor Shirley Wilson Logan, Editor
   E-mail: slogan@umd.edu

Studies in Rhetorics and Feminisms
Department of English
142 South Burrowes Bldg.
Penn State University
University Park, PA 16802-6200

Other Books in the
Studies in Rhetorics and Feminisms Series